A NEW LOOK AT PAST LIVES

A New Look at Past Lives

DEJA WHO?

JUDY HALL

New Age Books

ISBN: 81-7822-015-6

First Indian Edition: 2001

First Published in 1998 under the title
"Deja Who? - A New Look at Past Lives"
by Findhorn Press, UK

Published by
NEW AGE BOOKS
A-44 Naraina Phase I
New Delhi-110 028 (INDIA)
Email: info@newagebooksindia.com
Website: www.newagebooksindia.com

Printed in India
at Shri Jainendra Press
A-45 Naraina Phase-I New Delhi-110 028

Contents

Acknowledgements

I would like to thank Dawn Robins, David Lawson, Celia Gunn, Simon Jacobs and Robert Christoforides for their invaluable contributions to this book (which remain their copyright) and Justin Carson for his enormous patience and good humour. I am grateful to all my clients who gave permission for their stories to be used and to everyone whose experiences taught me so much over the years. Danny Lee of *Reincarnation International* was gracious with his time in answering questions and providing resources, and Chris and Peter Seers of *Greensleeves* were most efficient in locating out-of-print books. My thanks to them. Also to Hans Muller-Ruprecht for his invaluable assistance with the German research. My thanks also to publishers who so kindly gave permission to use extracts from published works (see Notes).

Preface
A Personal Note by David Lawson

As we approach the end of one millennium and the beginning of another, an ever-increasing number of us are drawn to answer some fundamental questions about the nature of our lives. These questions are not new. Some of these questions are infinitely old and, indeed, it could be argued that they emanate from the questioning spirit that has always been key to the human consciousness and that they are an integral part of the human condition. Questions such as 'Who am I?', 'Where do I come from?', 'Where am I going?' and 'What does it all mean?' seem to pervade and motivate the actions of us all, whether or not we are consciously seeking the answers to them.

Perhaps what is different about the end of the twentieth century, as compared to any previous period of history, is that there are larger numbers of people able to consciously embark upon this journey of self-discovery. No longer is this exploration the luxury of a minority elite made up of priests, philosophers and noblemen. Many of us now have the education, awareness and freedom necessary to explore ourselves in great depth and, while the underlying questions may be similar for everybody, the focus of our exploration and the methods we employ are unique to each individual. We may be searching for our own spiritual truths rather than just accepting what we have always been taught by the ministers of organised religion or we may be simply and profoundly looking for wholeness, but while our paths may be similar to those chosen by other people, they are never exactly the same.

To those of us who are consciously exploring these questions, the idea that we are each much more than a physical organism is not a new one. Indeed most major religions, spiritual philosophies and ancient forms of medicine would concur with this concept. Rather than see ourselves as just a human body comprised of flesh, blood, bone, sinew and nerve endings and run by a sophisticated organic computer of a brain, many of us view this wonderful organism as part of a bigger structure. This structure has been defined as spiritual, energetic or even electrical in nature and many theories imagine the physical body to be housed within a series of subtle bodies, parts of which have long been referred to using terms such as astral, etheric and auric. What is more, many would argue that these subtle energetic bodies are in turn part of something greater that can perhaps be best described as consciousness itself. In short, rather than viewing the human consciousness as housed within the flesh and blood of the human body, many people, myself included, would see it as being the other way round. The human body may even be regarded as the most physical expression of consciousness itself.

As a spiritual healer, teacher, astrologer and counsellor, my work and my own journey of exploration has inevitably led me to investigate issues of reincarnation. During my childhood I had a number of experiences common to those of us who describe ourselves as naturally intuitive or psychic. I often 'knew' things about other people that I had not been told by anyone around me and I would lie in bed at night, wide awake, watching swirls of subtle energy move around my bedroom. I also had memories of things that had happened to me in locations and situations that were completely alien to me at that time and my instincts told me that they had occurred before I was born. I did not particularly talk about these memories, but my family was certainly aware of my fascination with ancient cultures, especially the religion and mythology of ancient Egypt.

In my early twenties, when I was engaged in a regular practice of individual consultations with private clients, the concept of reincarnation often occurred to me as the most logical explanation for many of the experiences that I and my clients shared. During sessions of guided relaxation and hands-on healing a number of clients spontaneously regressed into memories, some fleeting but many tangible, that could not easily be attributed to their present lives or childhood experiences. The clients in question were invariably the most mentally balanced people you could wish to meet and in all cases there was a firm foundation of trust between us that allowed them to attain the kind of relaxed state conducive to a deeper exploration of their thoughts and feelings.

Initially I did not suggest to my clients that they might regress into what are often described as 'past' lives, and what may more accurately be termed as 'other' lives or enhanced states of consciousness; instead I did my best to support them to interpret these experiences for themselves. However, my experience soon taught me to offer the concept of reincarnation as one possible explanation of these regressed states although I was also keen to balance this with other theories such as the concept of ancestral or genetic coding and the idea that these memories were simply mental symbols or metaphors for the healing that had occurred. The former concept being that we have subtle cellular memories of the lives, joys and traumas of the previous generations of our family and that, by addressing some of those traumas, we can both bring spiritual healing to ourselves and heal our genetic line, while the latter is the one most in tune with the theories of modern psychotherapy. In reality I believe that all of these explanations are true sometimes and that the explanations themselves are far less important than my clients' search for wholeness and the healing of mind, body and emotions that subsequently occurred.

If the human body is the physical expression of our higher consciousness, then perhaps the illnesses of our bodies and the mental or emotional challenges we face are also expressions of that consciousness. Perhaps they are symptoms of our spirit on a quest for learning; seeking wholeness and some answers to those fundamental questions of identity and meaning that I mentioned at the beginning of this Preface. Perhaps also they are symptoms of a temporarily fragmented soul attempting to liberate itself from the 'karma' of old vows, choices and decisions that no longer serve its highest spiritual goals. It was my fascination with the process of healing and not a voyeuristic interest in 'past' lives that led me to actively develop my skills of regression. In the main, I am only interested in the past as a means of enhancing our present and future lives. Regression, psychic counselling that focuses on other lives, and all forms of psychic rescue or psychic retrieval, when conducted with skill and sensitivity, are certainly effective in safely dispersing forms of energy that are inappropriately attached to our subtle bodies, as well as restoring areas of our spirits that have become lost, damaged or depleted. In the process, profound healing changes often occur at a more tangible mental, emotional or physical level.

Working within this field you soon learn who the good practitioners are and create the kind of relationship with them that allows for a regular sharing of experiences and, in some cases, an active cross-fertilisation of ideas. Judy Hall is a regression therapist, astrologer and karmic counsellor whose work I have always respected. Her long experience of working with these issues of the soul has enabled her to move beyond superficial explanations of regression and reincarnation to a deeper and ultimately more fascinating exploration of our spiritual nature. Her integrity and skill have allowed her to be the catalyst for the profound healing experienced by the many who seek her help. Indeed, her counselling, karmic astrology and regression work invariably help people to create positive and permanent changes of consciousness that enable them to continue their spiritual development unfettered by the bonds of other lives. In numerous cases Judy has helped her clients to release themselves from the destructive patterns that had adversely affected their relationships, their careers, their finances, their health and their overall peace of mind. In doing so she has helped many to come a little closer to answering those fundamental questions of the spirit that we all face. I am sure that the insights she shares with us through the pages of this book will bring us closer still.

David Lawson

Broadcaster and Author of *An Oracle of Ancient Egypt — The Eye of Horus* (Connections/St. Martin's Press) and *A Company of Angels* (Findhorn Press)

Introduction
Deja Who?

I have been here before, But when or how I cannot tell;
I know the grass beyond the door,
The sweet keen smell,
The sighing sound, the lights around the shore ...
... I knew it all of yore

Dante Gabriel Rossetti: Sudden Light[1]

As a karmic counsellor who has spent the last twenty-five years exploring other lives, I believe implicitly in reincarnation and karma. And yet, I question the validity of some recalled past lives and recognise that delusion is all too possible. I have taken hundreds of people into other lives and I am firmly convinced that the majority of these were indeed past lives. But by no means all. The experiences have, in most cases, had a therapeutic value, but not necessarily so. When in regression, people also experience lives that are symbolic and allegoric, rather than actual, factual truth, but this does not make them any less valuable — if they are understood rightly. We will look later at how this information can expand and heal the present life.

Many people believe that they have lived before; in other words, that they have previously inhabited a physical body or, more likely, bodies, which existed and died somewhere in the past and that their soul moved on to incarnate again at sometime in the future.

Most of these people believe that their previous lives have affected their present life, sometimes for the better but frequently in a way which is detrimental to their health or which blocks relationships or other areas of their life. They believe that they somehow deserve the situation in which they now find themselves.

This first opinion is a belief in reincarnation, the second in the law of karma. It is the belief in the law of karma that urges people to seek karmic counselling or ushers them into Past Life Therapy, something which is becoming increasingly popular. Past Life Therapy has developed (or, more properly, redeveloped) over the last hundred years or so.

Notwithstanding, spontaneous regression to other lives has always propelled people into a belief in reincarnation. There are accounts going way back into history of such memories. Pythagoras (582–507BC) believed that the god Thoth (Mercury) had given him the memory of his past lives as a gift — a gift he could share with others, reminding them not only of their former incarnations but also of the period between death and rebirth. Nowadays remembering previous lives is happening more and more frequently, sometimes in a therapeutic setting but quite often triggered spontaneously by a place or a person. As a result, thousands of people are now exploring their previous incarnations, and quite a few are telling the world through books, articles and television appearances.

'Past lives' can, however, perhaps be better expressed as 'other lives'. As we shall see, once we move out of our present time-frame, time does not appear as linear and chronological but rather as a spiral that is all around us with everything happening at once. From the centre of the spiral, anything can be accessed and drawn into the present life.

I have a very different perspective on karma and reincarnation from that of most other writers on this topic — who are usually trying to prove or disprove reincarnation. My viewpoint arises from long experience. My understanding of karma has broadened considerably as I have worked with my clients. I do not see karma as a restrictive or retributive factor but as a means by which we grow spiritually. Karma is not punishment, rather it is a learning opportunity. It is not static: we create our karma with all our actions, not just those in the past. And I do believe most strongly that we can change our karma by going back into our other lives. Not all karma is bad. It is a system of credits and deficits, with unlimited potential. We can reap the rewards of our good karma as well as face our bad karma.

My understanding of how and why we reincarnate has arisen out of the many hundreds of regressions I have conducted. It is something which changes and evolves as I explore it further. I no longer believe that every individual regression or spontaneous memory is of an actual, factual past life belonging to one person and one person only. Over the years, I have found that certain characters recur time and time again. People apparently regress to the same past life personality, or are told by a psychic that they were that person — Mary Magdalene and Mary the mother of Jesus being prime examples. Others remember belonging to a specific historical group or being a particular person from the past. But, remembering does not always mean it is true. And lack of veracity does not equal a lie. There are levels and layers of truth here. It is knowing how to respond that is the key. If we seek proof in order to *know*, then our knowledge will be a long time coming. If we look for evidence, then we may be disappointed. However, in my experience, if we look for meaning then we have an opportunity to become enlightened.

When I began my somewhat unwilling exploration into my own past lives, I went through what I now see as ubiquitous experiences, common to many people. I remembered being part of various groups, I re-experienced some great traumas and dramas, and I recognised certain people as having accompanied my journey over several lifetimes. I began a book on my past life memories and then found that I shared them with too many people for them to be totally mine. I saw myself, for instance, as part of an Arthurian Group — not the historical Arthur, this was a much earlier figure — and as a leading figure in the Renaissance. A Cathar life surfaced in great detail, and seemed to be true — indeed, some particulars of that life were among aspects I have been able to prove. This was a year or two before I came across Arthur Guirdham's books on the Cathars, and several years before it became fashionable for everyone in-the-know to have had a Cathar life. When something becomes fashionable, so far as I am concerned, it becomes extremely suspect; the memory and any associated evidence become so easily tainted. I put the book on hold — where it has remained.

For some people, proving the details of past life memories indicates proof of reincarnation. There is a fascinating and most informative magazine devoted to past life memories that reads rather like *Who Was Who*. Its aim is to prove reincarnation and to bring as many cases as possible to the public notice. To further this goal it includes a great many memories, both spontaneous and hypnotically attained, many of which can be verified either by historical fact or other evidence. This body of evidence is impressive — and I will refer to some of it later in this book — and supports my own belief in reincarnation. While pursuing the laudable aim of bringing reincarnation to a wider audience, however, the magazine does tend to present cases of spontaneous memory and of hypnotic regression as unique and personal to the person concerned. This is also the case with most books on reincarnation. Early writers on the subject rarely considered that there could be other alternatives· unless they were seeking to disprove reincarnation altogether — when they tried to explain everything away as 'hidden memory'. Therapists and others writing today are more aware of other explanations and try to eliminate them, but most personal accounts are still firmly of the opinion 'this is me'. As we shall see, a unique personal memory is something that is not quite so easily proved, no matter how much we believers in reincarnation would wish it to be so.

There is great public interest in reincarnation and past lives. This has spawned a proliferation of books and television programmes on past life memories. Many of these memories are quite stunning, with immense detail and a deep emotional charge that says 'This is me as I was'. They are totally believable and the people concerned are clearly sincere in their belief. However, some of these memories are of the same historical personages — and the claimants equally sincere.

This is not a new phenomenon and the same old faces appear again and again in reincarnation accounts that go way back into history: Jesus and his disciples and the women in his life, King Arthur and his knights, the Pharaoh Akenaton and his court, Mary Queen of Scots and her entourage, Hapshepshut and Tutmoses III, the Taj Mahal group, and many others recur time and again. Some rather surprising personages also recur, such as Judas and Emma Hamilton (Nelson's mistress), bringing up contemporary issues of betrayal and homelessness. Three or four years ago there were a lot of Mary Magdalenes about but this was not the first time they had surfaced — both the Magdalene and the Madonna make frequent appearances as past lives. Later we will look at some cases in detail and explore possible explanations, such as collective memory, cryptomnesia, soul groups, accessing the Akashic Records, and imprinting souls.

We can ask why people want to remember their past lives at all. Is that not all in the past? Well, no. A great many past lives actually intrude rather painfully into the present. Personally, I do not see much value in exploring other lives simply out of curiosity — I prefer a therapeutic setting. But some people spend a great deal of time 'day tripping to the past'. We will look at the dangers and delusions of this and at the value there may be.

Not all reincarnation memories come about through regression. Many are spontaneous, triggered by a place (a sense of *déjà vu*) or they arise through dreams. Dreams can well carry the memory of another life. Recurring nightmares are closely linked to traumatic past life experiences. I had a friend who had dreamed since early childhood of a suffocating rain of searing hot ash that sucked the breath out of her lungs. She would wake up gasping for breath. When we went to see the Pompeii exhibition in London, she said she felt a strange recognition. There were images out of her dreams. Then suddenly she started gasping for breath and said, 'I just know I died in the eruption'. She never had the dream again.

Such dreams can be personal, but they can also carry a universal memory, as can past life memories. The well-known composer Henry Mancini is said to have experienced under hypnosis a life as an engineer engaged on building the pyramids. He is not the only one! This is a common memory. Not only have many other people had the same 're-living' in regression, but people have also reported spontaneous flashbacks and vivid dreams. Someone who had no interest in such things slept the night in my regression room. In the morning he complained about a vivid dream he had had of building the pyramids — and of many other apparent past life memories. Because the room had been used so much for regression, it was difficult to tell whether he was picking up memories that had been left there, or whether he was actually going into his own memories or accessing a collective level of memory.

Other memories occur when people see an artefact, such as a picture or statue, or hear a piece of music. I can remember standing mesmerised before a crystal skull in the Museum of Mankind 'watching' a life in South America unfold, which was the last time I had seen one of these skulls. Eventually the attendant came to see if I was all right. Other people have reported similar experiences with these skulls. Later, in a meditation with a friend, I relived the time 'When the Sun went Out' and my friend was sacrificed and torn to pieces. When I came out of the meditation he appeared to be jerking around in sleep. I spoke quietly to him and put my hand out towards him. 'Don't touch me', he said, 'I'm in pieces'. We had to 're-member' him — bring the pieces back into integration. When we checked, we had had exactly the same memory seen through the different characters.

Certain objects have this kind of power, especially objects that belonged to the person in a past life. I have a ring which belonged to my mentor, Christine Hartley. It was her wedding ring and she and her husband-to-be had spent a whole day scouring the Edinburgh antique shops looking for 'her ring'. She would know it when she saw it. Eventually, there it was — a Scottish Cairngorm stone which she had last seen as a plaid brooch on the shoulder of her beloved, Alan MacDonald, in the '45 uprising to restore the Scottish King. As a Campbell then — as now — there was no way she could be with her lover. Sadly, she had waved him off in a small boat. The Cairngorm stone had been cut down to make a ring sometime between then and now but she recognised it nevertheless. What is interesting about this ring is that two psychics, when holding it, have had exactly the same picture of that past life belonging to the ring and the person who owned it, as Christine Hartley did.

One of the tests for identifying reincarnated Tibetan lamas in young children is that they should pick out their 'own' belongings from amongst similar items. If they unhesitatingly select the right objects, they are recognised as *tulku*, a reincarnated lama.

Such recognition of a past life can be instant, overwhelming — and incorrect. When I first saw the compelling wooden face-mask of Queen Tiye, Pharaoh Akenaton's mother, it felt so familiar, so known, that surely it must have been me? After all, I had been told many times that I had a strong connection with Akenaton. My mentor Christine Hartley had told me I was at that court and that she had known me when she was the Princess Merit-Aton, daughter of Akenaton, and also when she had been his aunt of the same name. (There is a statue of the latter Merit-Aton in the Cairo museum that looks exactly like Christine and several people identified her as this rather obscure historical figure.) But Christine had never spelled out our connection. More than one psychic had linked my name with that of Queen Tiye, so could I perhaps have been her?

Alas, no. It appeared that I, as with so many others, was not such an august figure on the stage of history. When I meditated to check it out, I stepped into a scene I knew so well. It was as a young priestess in the Temple of Mut at Karnak (ancient Thebes) in Upper Egypt. But this time I was lying stretched out on the ground, face down, full of awe. I was prostrate before Queen Tiye, High Priestess of the Temple in which I served in a most humble capacity. Here was a living embodiment of the gods before me. Words cannot convey this absolutely overwhelming sense of being in the divine presence of true majesty. It was the *feeling* of this experience which convinced me. The sense of being utterly humbled, of worshipping with my whole heart a divine being, of serving a living embodiment of the gods. It was like nothing I had ever experienced in my present life. (I am not someone who bends a knee, let alone prostrates myself full length in reverence.) The feeling was of being someone utterly other and yet most intimately myself.

And my connection with Akenaton? Well, I once stood in the British Museum on a beautiful tiled floor and said to my partner, 'I remember sweeping this floor at Amarna' (Akenaton's palace). When I checked, it was indeed a floor from that palace. In my meditation, I traced that young priestess as she grew older. When Akenaton brought in worship of the one god, she had to leave Temple Mut. But Queen Tiye took her to Tel al Amarna as one of her servants — which was how I came to be standing quietly, sweeping that beautiful tiled floor and watching the drama of Akenaton's court unfold before me. And my connection with Christine Hartley at that time? Well, someone had to keep an eye on the young princess. There was more to it, of course, but that is another story.

Many years later another pupil of Christine Hartley, Alan Richardson, wrote *The Inner Guide to Egypt,*[2] a series of meditations through the power centres of Egypt culminating in the Temple of Mut at Thebes — a journey which grounds the spiritual energies into matter and brings about self-initiation, a reconnection with the eternal self. But, as Alan points out, 'Often it is hard to tell whether things end up in Thebes or in fact have their truest origins there'.[3] It is rather like T.S. Eliot's comment about the end of our exploring being to reach the place from whence we started and know it for the first time.[4] Does our spiritual exploration culminate in knowing the self, or was it the point we started out from? This is something we will be discussing at the end of this book.

I devoured Alan's book, working through the whole thing on a timeless one-and-a-half-hour train journey. Since then it has always accompanied me to Egypt. When I did the final meditation, I was back with that young priestess in what Alan describes as an act of self-creation, the giving birth to our self. But, as he also points out, we are all united as one: 'It is only the separate and lonely gaze of the "unconnected" individual who insists upon the exclusive nature of that vision of the "narrow" path. The narrow, silver light of the moon upon water links us all like an umbilical cord. It is only the mind which makes us separate; only the heart which can unite us all.'[5]

Later, when I tried out Alan's meditation (which is non-specific as to the people involved, setting out only the sacred lake at Temple Mut) with a past life group I was leading, everyone went back to a similar experience to mine. Several identified the High Priestess as 'Queen Tiye' or 'the Mother of Akenaton'. For all of us, it was an extremely potent moment. The feeling quality of that united 'seeing' was the strongest I have ever encountered. The group energy had never before reached such intensity, time had never before loosed its hold so effectively. Ancient Egypt was certainly in the room that day. Or, to put it another way, we were in ancient Egypt. Most of the group had worked with me before and were skilled in determining 'what is ours' from a universal 'far memory'. All commented that the feelings and emotions attached to it were the most powerful they had ever encountered.

It could be argued that a group of priestesses had been reunited to remember their ritual origins. But, it could also be said that I was telepathically transmitting my own vision, or that we were all picking up on an event that had happened but which had nothing to do with us personally. Individually and collectively as a group, we had all felt the power of the experience. We all believed we had stood on the bank of the sacred lake ritually washing as an act of purification, made our way back to the temple precincts, and bowed low before Queen Tiye before moving on to be initiated into the deepest mysteries of that arcane land.

I was far from unique in reconnecting to that particular experience. However, from the effect that my original reconnection experience had on my creativity (I look back to that time as the moment I gave birth to my ability to write creatively) I know that something much deeper and more important was happening to me. A seed was implanted, a talent reawakened. My spirit and purpose became more *alive*. It was perhaps the most seminal moment in my spiritual evolution. But still I have to question: was it after all *my* experience, or was it a tuning into the collective memory of the place? It certainly served to remind me that at a spiritual level, we are all one, no matter how separate we may seem on our individual journeys. After all, Temple Mut existed as a living entity for well over two thousand years. Generation after generation of young priestesses had that experience of bowing low before their Queen and High Priestess, the living embodiment of the gods — an experience which was impregnated on the land. It is still, to my mind, one of the most powerful places in Egypt, a spot that holds very strong memories indeed in the stones that are slowly emerging under the skilled hands of archaeologists working on the site. Was that careful physical exposure paralleled by the spiritual disclosure available to all those who read Alan's book?

My 'Queen Tiye' experience is idiosyncratic *and* ubiquitous. It seems to be so much *mine*, and yet I am not the only one to experience it. The quality of the experience convinces me, although logic offers other explanations. Nonetheless, intuition says that there may be more to it than would at first appear. If I say it is mine, or even that I recognise a group happening, and leave it at that, the deeper layers of the experience may be passing me by.

Other people have been so utterly convinced by the strength of their memories that they believe they alone were a historical personage. I personally feel that if it is only taken at that level, an enormous opportunity for spiritual growth is being overlooked. Why and how this occurs is something this book will explore in greater depth. Perhaps in order to understand how any or all of this can be possible, we need to look at what exactly a soul is and how it moves from incarnation to incarnation.

The Story of the Soul

Many years ago, indeed it feels like several lifetimes ago, I was a small child in school learning about precipitation. I was told that rain falls to the ground from clouds, drains into rivers and streams, which eventually run into the sea. The water evaporates and forms vapour, which makes clouds. Clouds drop their rain... And so on throughout eternity. As I got older, I learned that it is not quite that simple. Out of a cloudless sky, in a place where it never rains, a few miles from the coast, 'invisible water' can distil and provide an ever-flowing spring of pure water: gallons of the stuff every day. In the middle of a desert, a rare shower brings the flowers into bloom, only to disappear as though it had never been. In the deep-freeze of a glacier, water is locked away for centuries. Sometimes the 'rain' is actually hail or snow. And in England, the land of the rains, we can run out of water all too frequently.

You may wonder what this has to do with the soul and past lives. Well, the drop of water analogy is the best I can come up with to describe the soul and its incarnations and associations. The soul, while seeming to be individual, can easily merge back into a larger 'soul group'. I prefer this term to that of 'group soul' as there is considerable evidence from the between life state that a soul can rejoin and break away from the soul group many times without losing individuality. There are times, however, when that soul goes back into the group 'oversoul', that is, moves up another level of vibration into a much closer sense of union. It is like the raindrop, having been in the puddle, going back to rejoin the cloud it emerged from. But this process is nowhere as simple as our first encounter with the idea would suggest.

You know how it is with rain. You cannot always rely on clouds to produce it. Even the most thunderous of clouds can dissipate into a clear blue sky. Sometimes only a few drops fall out of that clear blue sky. At other times the heavens open and there is a deluge. Such a deluge certainly makes an impact. It can change the face of the earth. But the gentle persistent rain too has its effects. It patiently wears away rock unobtrusively shaping the landscape.

Spirit is like this. Spirit is the stuff that underlies our incarnations, and our discarnations too. Our spiritual self is the eternal part of our being. Our ego self, on the other hand, is the personality we form during a particular lifetime. We may take some fragments of that personality with us when we die, especially attitudes and desires, but we are much more than that ego self. The ego self is rather like the pipes and conduits through which water has to run in order to hold its form. It subtly alters the shape and flow, but the basic beingness of water — and soul or spirit — is the same.

Raindrops Keep Falling

If we look at the 'drop of water' analogy, we can see spirit as a rain cloud. It is heterogeneous and yet homogeneous. Many and diverse, and yet one and the same. From the pool of spiritual essence that is our rain cloud, individual droplets can fall as gentle rain, a downpour, hail or snow. Droplets can be locked up as ice, or run free. The basic molecule is the same, but it takes different forms. It is exactly the same with the soul.

For rain to fall, change is needed in the conditions holding the cloud together. For spirit to incarnate, it requires a change in vibration. The light and high vibration of the spiritual realm falls into the denser and lower vibration of the earth plane. Each droplet of water is the equivalent of a soul incarnating on earth.

In practice it is rather more complex than that. From my research and long experience of taking people into the between life state, it seems certain that there are actually stages in which the soul metamorphoses before it reaches the earth. Each soul carries its individual spark of spirit out of the pool, but some souls are clustered together in groups (like large hail stones or those huge rain drops we sometimes see). As the group of souls come down through the different vibrations, they may fragment. But they may also remain in close contact.

So far so good, but in this case what happens to that individual soul? This process is much more complex than a soul coming into incarnation, occupying a body, dying and then moving onto another incarnation, and another and another. Many parts of the self are not in incarnation. They exist on other levels. The soul as we know it — a soul that is inhabiting a body — is only a fraction of the overall self. As we shall see throughout this book, souls can fragment too, both in and out of incarnation. (Bringing the pieces together again is called 'soul retrieval'.) Is this process of disintegration and reintegration purely personal, involving one individual soul, or are much larger groups of souls involved? Can the fragments of souls combine into a different soul? Can one soul — and one soul only — inhabit a physical body at any one time, or is it possible for a group of souls to actually combine to share the experiences of one body (rather like all the droplets of rain forming a puddle)? What about the souls who become 'stuck' in a particular cycle of incarnations, or at a certain place, just as the ice in a glacier remains static for hundreds of years? What happens to these souls? Are they doomed to remain that way, or is intervention possible? We will look at the options.

We will also need to be aware that the soul which incarnates is in touch with what I can best describe as 'the higher self'. It is higher because it is vibrating at a faster level and also because it has available all the other incarnations it has, or is in. The higher self acts as a kind of governing principle holding together the disparate parts of the soul and passing memories and wisdom to the incarnated soul as and when necessary. When I am working with reincarnation memories, whether in regression or by psychic 'far memory', I always try to access both my own higher self and my client's higher self as I find this is much more reliable and therapeutic than using the subconscious mind. The subconscious mind has access to the memories but also has its own agenda when dealing with them. The higher self, on the other hand, is concerned with the overall evolution of the complete entity.

As far as I can ascertain (and most of this information comes from souls who reach one or more levels of the between life state during regression), the ultimate purpose for all souls is to rejoin the whole — to evolve individually and then to take knowledge and learning back to benefit the overall awareness — to help the cosmos evolve — to go back into the cloud, as it were. From there, some souls may choose a new incarnation cycle; others may go on to some other evolutionary path. Some may choose to aid those on earth as guides and yet others will stay in the spiritual pool.

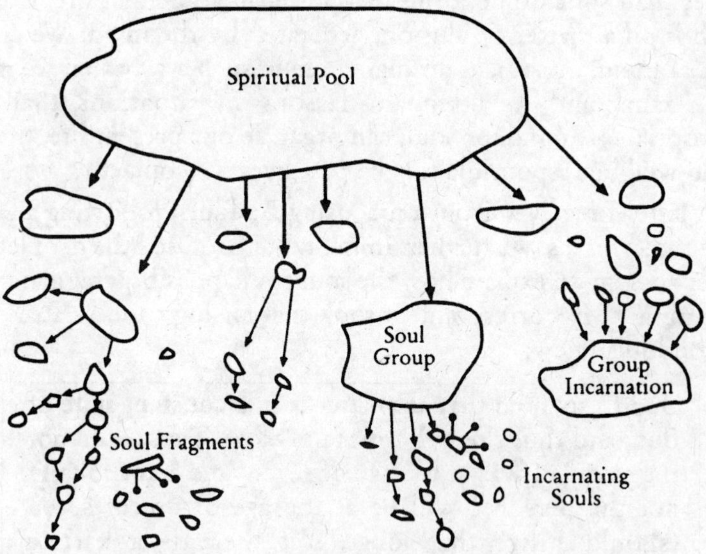

FIGURE 1: THE POOL OF SPIRIT AND ITS INCARNATIONS

If we look at this picture in terms of past life memories, we can see that it is possible to share memories at various stages. Souls coming down out of the cloud, or in close contact with a soul group certainly in the initial stages, may have memories in common because other souls returning to the pool of spiritual essence, or to the soul group, will have shared their experience. The further away the soul moves from the cloud or the soul group, the longer it stays close to the earth and experiences life in a very individual fashion, then the less it will share memories — unless, of course, it is tuning into another level, such as collective or genetic memory.

There are theories of reincarnation, or rebirth, which do not rely on an individual soul at all. When I was at college doing my religious studies degree, I was taught that Buddhists believe that at death the soul separates out into five aggregates. Each of those aggregates then goes its own way and combines and recombines with many other aggregates. So the incarnating soul is not uniquely individual and personal, it is made up of all these pieces of soul that have inhabited hundreds, if not thousands, of bodies. To Buddhists, of course, the overall organising principle is mind, rather than soul. Some forms of Buddhism argue that life here on earth is all a matter of illusion, generated by the mind. We could look at mind, or soul, as arranging life in such a way that we meet our karma and its attendant lessons in situations that are appropriate. If mind, or soul, can organise our present life, then it could well be responsible for the past lives we contact.

A letter I received from a practising Buddhist following a talk I gave took this a stage further. In my talk I had used the droplets of water analogy to explain how the soul could possibly fragment and recombine. My correspondent took that analogy and related it to the Buddhist view:

> Buddhists hold that all matter is in a constant state of flux, and thus the 'self' does not exist. Thus, I am not the person I was at the age of seven, and I am equally not the person I will be at the age of ninety-seven (should I live that long). Yet there is a karmic continuum linking *me* together from birth to death. Why not therefore extend that continuum before the cradle and after the grave? It therefore follows, from a Buddhist point of view, that there is no such thing as a soul which reincarnates... This, on the surface of things, may seem hostile to your ideas, but I don't think so, as I will explain.
>
> Eastern philosophy teaches that all matter is mind-conditioned. Western materialism, on the other hand maintains the opposite, that mind is generated by matter, namely the chemistry of the brain... [If Eastern philosophy is true and] matter is a vehicle for mind and not the generator of it, then a lot of your ideas, and mine, fall into place. Thus we may posit the conceptual model of a karmic flow, which conditions matter throughout time... [and] in which each 'soul' is but a drop ... it seems that great archetypal karmic
>
> *continued...*

forces, such as Cleopatra, Judas Iscariot, Napoleon, or whoever, may indeed be tapped into by several people contemporarily. The sceptics who doubt that several, or even a large number of people, can share the same reincarnation as contemporaries, would seem to be 'hung up' on the Western materialist model of the individual brain as the generator of the individual consciousness, the individual body being the generator of the individual soul.

Islands in the Collective Sea

The 'drops of water' theory is one view of why we can share memories that appear to be *our* past lives with other people. According to that theory, we all learn what we can and take the experience back to our soul group and then on into the pool of spiritual essence, where there is a united, shared consciousness. In the Buddhist view, it is all part of the overall continuum. There is another view, however, which is virtually the opposite. The 'islands in the collective sea' analogy, derived from Western psychotherapy, says that we all share a collective unconscious, a deeper layer into which all racial, ancestral and cultural memories fall. Our individual consciousness rises up out of that sea, but still has its roots deep within the 'psychic goo' of the sea bed. The collective unconscious sounds as though it has no awareness, and no consciousness, but this is not so. It actually contains all awareness, past, present and future, within it. It has no personal volition, but it certainly has action and effect, and is expressed through individuals, as well as the whole. In fact, it is rather like karma (the operating principle behind incarnation, see Chapter 3).

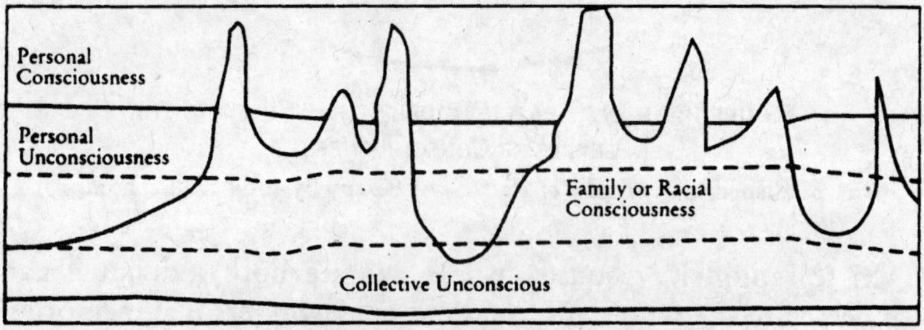

Figure 2: Islands in the Collective Sea

Integration

But are the two interpretations really so different? In one, the sharing occurs at a very deep level — the 'collective unconscious', in the other at a very high level — a kind of 'supraconsciousness'. In Figure 3, which needs to be imagined in at least three dimensions rather than flat on the page, the higher consciousness meets the collective unconscious, surrounding and interpenetrating personal awareness.

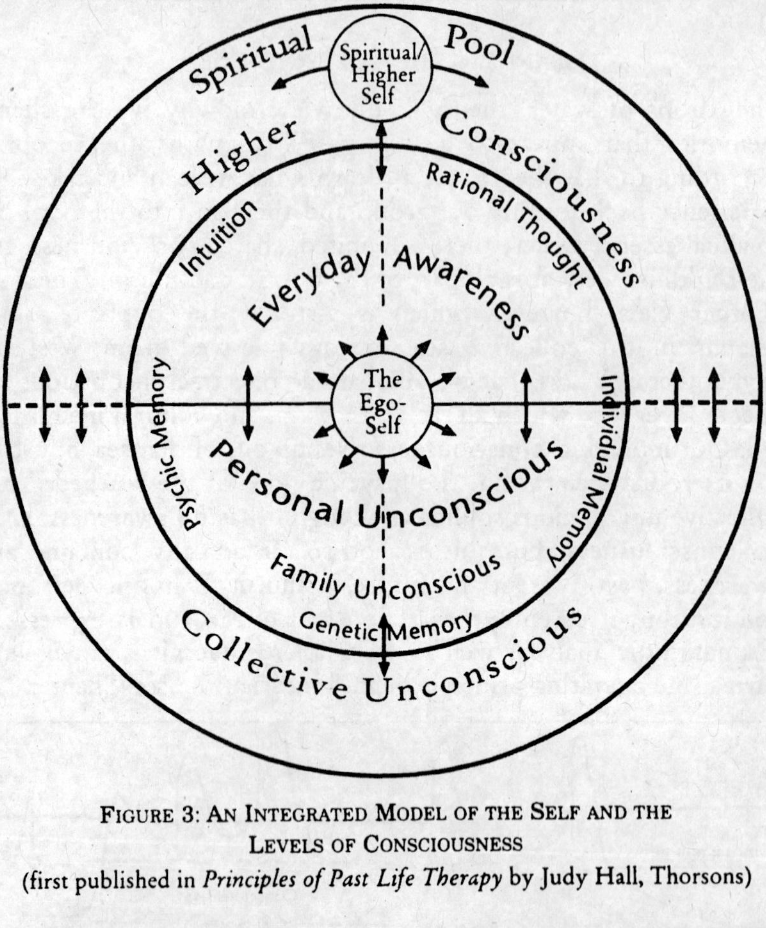

Figure 3: An Integrated Model of the Self and the Levels of Consciousness
(first published in *Principles of Past Life Therapy* by Judy Hall, Thorsons)

In this model of consciousness, we are both individual and connected to the whole. We can have our own personal memories, and we can share the greater memory. If we were telling our story, we could call on our memories — our own unique experiences — or we could plug into the record of our cultural or racial heritage, which is carried in history and archetypal tales. If we went far enough into the collective unconscious, we could draw out stories from the whole history of humanity, the 'legends of the past' that are recorded as fact or myth, religious and otherwise.

We could look at the biblical story of Adam and Eve, for instance, and believe that we were seeing the story of the first man and the first woman. We could believe that woman was made from the rib of man — in other words, somewhat inferior to man on whom she relied for her very life. With a little delving, however, we could learn that (in Hebrew myth) Lilith, not Eve, was the first woman created and that Lilith like Adam was fashioned from clay. Lilith was created free and equal, so free in fact that tiring of Adam and his attempts at mastery she flew off to the Red Sea and lived a very independent life.[6] After which God created the much more pliant and docile Eve to keep Adam happy.

There are people who believe that the Garden of Eden with its innocent inhabitants actually tells the story of the soul while it is still in a euphoric state of oneness with God. That is, the soul before it has left that pool of spiritual essence we have been talking about and begun its long journey down into matter. Many people accept the Adam and Eve story as myth — religious truth embodied in a story which may have little to do with factual truth but which is a truth, nonetheless. There are others who believe that the story of Adam and Eve is actual, literal truth: that these two were the first ancestors of man and from them stemmed all the peoples of the world. This belief is held despite the fossil evidence which points, it would seem, indisputably towards evolution and a multiplicity of ancestors. If we look at the Adam and Eve myth from the Christian point of view, it says that knowledge equals sin. From the Jewish perspective, however, it is a tale of choice.

The Planning Department

When a person dies, consciousness leaves the body. The soul gathers itself together, with its memories and experiences, and moves onto another level. (As we shall see, however, not all the soul necessarily leaves, some of it may remain 'stuck' at the moment of death or at some other point in that life.) Fairly soon after death there is — usually but not necessarily — a life review. So the important details of the life are imprinted onto the more ethereal bodies that exist after death. If the soul moves onto higher and higher levels, some of these bodies are shed and the memories of earth drop away but the essential points remain. If the soul stays in the realms close to earth, the memories and desires of that life stay strong. As there is no time in these realms, aeons may pass or merely a few months. Eventually there comes a time when the soul decides to return to earth. This return may be prodded by an unfulfilled desire or by the higher self's desire for the soul to evolve.

The reason why so many past lives do seem confused may well have to do with what I call the Planning Department. Therapist Dawn Robins calls it the Council; other therapists have called it the Assessors, the Judges and the Guides. Basically, it is a group of advisers who can help the incarnating soul to lay out objectives, purpose and lessons for the forthcoming life. However! It has become clear to me over the years that some people plan their incarnations very carefully and others do not plan at all. As we shall see in Chapter 3, strong desires can pull someone back into incarnation with only one motivation in mind: to obtain what is craved. The soul may not even realise the body it previously inhabited has died. It may appear to still be living in exactly the same way, or it can find itself in a kind of limbo. In these cases, the soul hangs around close to the earth vibration and hops into the first available body that seems to offer an opportunity of satisfying the desire: this is usually, but not necessarily, a gestating baby. There are cases where the soul 'shares' an adult body with its more usual occupier. Clearly what follows can be very haphazard. If it is a person that is craved, then the souls may well come together, but not always in the way that allows the desire to be satisfied. If it is a substance, then it may well quickly develop into a full-blown addiction. If it is a position or power, then the soul may find itself endlessly repeating an old pattern. Without purposeful planning, the life offers little opportunity to evolve and grow.

At the end of a life a desire is often expressed, 'I want to be with him or her forever' or a promise is made, 'Say you will love me forever'. People make promises to themselves. My favourite is the lady who said as she was dying, 'Next time he's going to marry me'. She now laughs and says, 'He did! He was the vicar who performed the ceremony!' Such things often manifest literally — or symbolically.

Without careful planning things can go badly awry. We arrange to meet up with someone for a specific task, but we somehow don't quite get round to the details. We go through life feeling that there is something we ought to be doing, but we don't know what. Or we want to have a relationship with someone else and merely say, 'See you soon' — a loose arrangement they could well forget, meeting and marrying before we find them again. We may also discover that they have incarnated in an inappropriate body or setting for such a relationship to develop. When this kind of inadequate planning occurs we miss out time after time. Too much is left to chance.

In more purposeful incarnations, a different sequence is followed. From the between life work that I and my clients have undertaken, it is clear that at some time after death — and this is not always immediately afterwards — there is usually a life review (of the kind so often reported on in near death experiences). The soul will look back, sometimes with the higher self, at other times with a guide or guides, at what was achieved or what was left unfinished in that life. At this stage connections may be made with other lives. If any learning or healing is needed, then the soul goes off to another part of the between life state to do the necessary work. Then when the soul is ready for incarnation again, the planners get together and review both past lives and the immediate present.

These meetings often have the souls with whom we intend to be in incarnation present. Decisions are taken which might well surprise us from our earthly perspective. For instance, if we need to learn a very hard lesson, then someone who loves us greatly may agree to incarnate with us and provide the difficult circumstances which will allow us to experience what we have decided we need.

Our way out of ingrained patterns may well be to experience them to such an extent that we simply have to find an exit. If we have taken on a belief, such as, 'I don't deserve love', then we may be given an experience where we lack love to such an extent that we have to find it within our self. The permutations are endless.

I have seen cases where a mother will say to her prospective child, 'I will give birth to you, but I don't promise to stay around to see you grow up.' In such cases, that child may have needed to detach from an over-dependence on the mother figure or may have needed to learn what it feels like to lose a mother at a young age. (In cases where adoption has taken place, agreements have also been made prior to incarnation.) Children may agree to come for a short time to allow a parent to learn about loss and grief. Two people may agree to be attracted to each other, perhaps for a purpose other than sex. Partners too may agree to be together, but may perhaps need to learn to separate and find their own space. Many of our problems arise from the fact that no matter how much we may plan and try to allow our karma to be balanced, everyone has free will and once in incarnation we do, of course, forget all those agreements we made back at the planning stage. So two people who agreed to learn how to separate might find that one desperately wants out, while the other one is equally desperate to hold on. Two people with a task to do might find that one is willing but the other one is not.

Surprisingly often the disasters we meet in life are actually our higher self helping us to get back onto our path. Illnesses too have a way of focussing us back onto what we are doing with our life. The higher self keeps our plan in mind and when we seem to be straying too far away from our purpose gives us a nudge or brings just the right person to our side. As we will see, apparently random acts can actually bring past lives to our notice, linking us up with people from the past. The question is, however, is what comes to us really *our* past or is it a past which we may share with other souls and, even more importantly, does it really matter? Do past life memories surface merely to fulfil our curiosity about who we were, or do they have a much deeper purpose?

The Nature of Time

My usual way of explaining the eternal now is to say that there is no time: it is just a convenient measurement that we need to make sense of our experience while we are in a physical body. We need past, present and future to organise our time. But the clock with its arbitrary division into hours, minutes and seconds is a cultural creation determined by how our particular society has decided to carve up the day. When we give ourselves up to the flow of life we experience something different. We all know that time is elastic. If we are caught up in something, time flies by, but if we are in danger, time goes into slow motion. In a few moments of sleep we can dream a whole lifetime. When we meditate, time is suspended. Then there are those times when we are transported back in time, to an earlier memory, be it present or past life. Everything is there just as it was; we can see and smell and taste the experience. We are in the past. And I have the strong sense that some things are actually evolving backwards. Egypt would be a prime example. Ancient Egyptian religion and building starts at a very high level. There is nothing leading up to it. It still has many secrets to reveal, particularly about its origins. So from the point of time in which I now stand, it is still evolving. Fortunately quantum science has now come up with little particles, called tachyons, that are apparently moving back into the past, so my explanations do not sound quite so outlandish as they did.

The picture — and it can only be a symbol — I find most useful in looking at time is to see myself in the centre of a spiral. The centre is the present moment. Time is all around me and by moving up or down the spiral I can access what seems to be past or future at any point and bring it into the present moment — the eternal now.

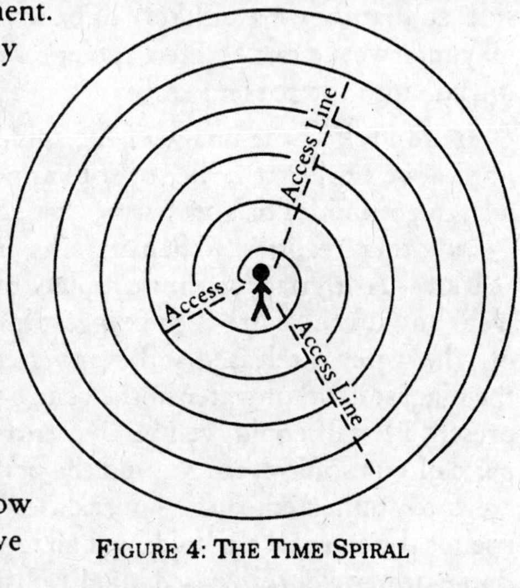

FIGURE 4: THE TIME SPIRAL

Another view (see next page) is to stand at the centre of a wheel with time all around you on the rim. The spokes split time up into segments. Follow a spoke and you move around in time.

Our view of time, whether linear or not, usually presupposes that there is only one time. But there is another idea which may well be more relevant, and which could explain why some people

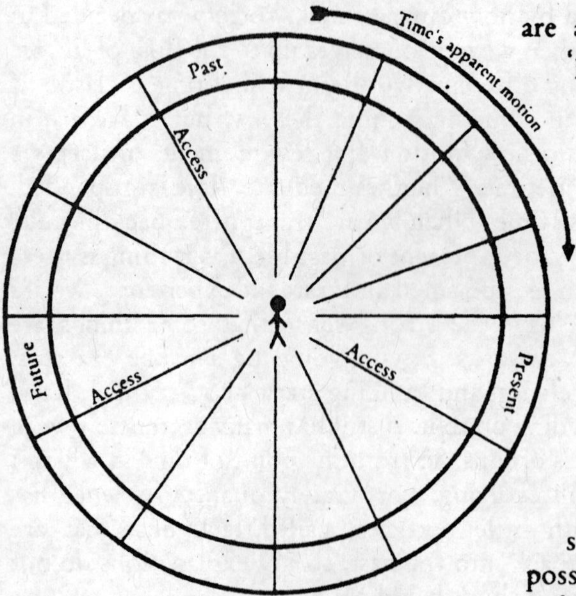

FIGURE 5: THE WHEEL OF TIME

are able to seemingly 'prove' evidence for their past lives while other people have the same detailed information and yet can find no trace of themselves 'back in the past'. The concept of parallel dimensions, or parallel realities, suggests that all possible consequences of any one action are lived out *in different time-frames.* These time-frames may run parallel, that is side by side, so that they are unlikely to be inadvertently accessed; or they may interweave rather like a spider's web, which means they could intrude into the present reality.

If we look at the image of the spider's web and go back to the notion we explored earlier of soul as a drop, or droplets, of water, we can get an idea of how parts of the soul can remain in other lives — or other realities. When it rains, a spider's web glistens and sparkles. A myriad of tiny droplets of water adhere all over the web, but at the centre is the biggest 'drop'. Then as the web dries off, the water is released and evaporates. If you look carefully, it is the biggest drop of water in the centre that disappears last. So, our present life self could well be the centre of the web with the other parts of our soul spread around the periphery. Because all the lines are interconnected, different realities can be accessed. The web itself is the eternal self, holding it all together, no matter what time-frame or parallel reality seemingly exists.

We will come back to experiences with the flowing nature of time shortly — or 'longly' depending on how quickly you are reading this book.

Notes:

1. Quoted in *Reincarnation: An East-West Anthology,* compiled and edited by Joseph Head and S.L. Cranston (New York, The Julian Press Inc., 1961), p.135.
2. Alan Richardson and B. Walker-John, *The Inner Guide to Egypt* (Bath, Arcania, 1991), now sadly out-of-print.
3. *Ibid.*, p.136.
4. T.S. Eliot *Four Quartets: Little Gidding* see *The Oxford Anthology of Great English Poetry, vol.2*, ed. John Wain (London, BCA, 1996), p.638.
5. Richardson and Walker-John, *The Inner Guide to Egypt,* p.142.
6. The story of Lilith appears in Middle Eastern myth from the start of recorded history. She is mentioned in the Jewish Talmud, the laws and legends of the Jewish people which incorporated Babylonian ideas and was set down in writing around AD200 but which drew on a much earlier oral tradition. The two stories of the creation of woman appear in the Old Testament, see Genesis 1:27–28 and Genesis 2:7 and 2:18.

Chapter 1
Who Do You Think You Were?

(Pythagoras) was accustomed to speak of himself in this manner: that he had formerly been Aethalides. At a subsequent period, he was reborn as Euphorbus, and was wounded by Menalaus at the siege of Troy, and so died. In that life he used to say that he had formerly been Aethalides.

Diogenses Laertius: Life of Pythagoras[1]

While there are dozens of spontaneous flashbacks to other lives recorded, and many children remember their past lives from birth, the majority of people who have past life memories have them under hypnosis or another method of 'going back into the past'. In other words, in regression.

People have many different reasons for undergoing regression to other lives. Sometimes they have a burning curiosity to 'see who I was' or an inexplicable pull to a certain period in history. At other times they have a sense of having been someone in particular and wanting to explore that. They may need to reconnect to old skills or abilities, or to know that there was a time when they could handle certain situations, emotions or relationships well. Sometimes knowing that things have not always been so bad can be a healing in itself. Then there are the people who are undergoing problems in their present life which they feel must stem from a another life. Many present life problems do have their roots in the past. There are people, however, who do not want to work on those roots; they simply want to find a life that makes them feel better about who they are now. If we want to boost our ego, to have a sense of importance, then we may compulsively explore other lives until we can say, '*I was someone special*'.

One woman who came to see me had a severe inferiority complex. She had been regressed by one hypnotist seventy-nine times. She was looking for the one incarnation that would make her feel good. In the end, the therapist told her to go away and work on herself as she was now. Instead, she came to see me. Having heard her story, I refused to do regression but offered instead to put her in touch with her higher self. At first she was reluctant because she felt her goal of being 'Someone' would elude her. Eventually she agreed to work with me. She went out of the door looking altogether different and with a much stronger sense of her own self. We will explore the value of past life therapy in a later chapter.

In my twenty-five years' experience as a past life therapist, most regressions have been quite prosaic and ordinary. Some have had masses of trauma and drama, plenty of raw emotion and not a little tragedy. There have been lives of great happiness and fulfilment, but there have also been years of boredom and drudgery. Some have been evidential, a few provable. Others have been set in a definite historical context but could not be verified. A handful have involved an historical personage.

On the whole, my clients' spontaneous memories and regression experiences with other therapists have followed the same pattern, as have the psychic readings I give on past lives. At times the karmic readings I have done — without meeting the person concerned, as I work from a photograph — actually fit in with a regression a client has done without my having details. It may also clarify what has happened during a regression. For instance, after sending a reading I received a postcard which said:

> Many thanks for the tape which I found both enjoyable and interesting. The Canadian Second World War pilot theme was very intriguing as during a regression I found myself also a pilot during the First World War and had some difficulty as the plane kept alternating between an old biplane and a larger World War II type. I have also had a very vivid dream about sitting in a mess room with others and also blackness and flames.

I had seen him shot down in a plane after a most determined effort to become a pilot during the Second World War. He had volunteered because he so much wanted to fly. It was unfinished business from the past which had propelled him into a completion of his obsession with flying, but at the cost of his life.

With one or two rare exceptions, I have never set out to 'find evidence'. Indeed, it has been my experience that where my clients need to have the fact of reincarnation proved to them by a verifiable memory, it seldom happens. A young man came on a workshop. He was desperate for proof, but although he did some very important symbolic work, he had nothing that even seemed like a past life. Some time later he phoned me, very excited. He had been for hypnotic regression and had all the details of his past life, down to the church where he was buried and where his birth and death had been registered. He had stood and watched himself buried under an old tree, an unmistakable place. He had seen his name and the dates on his tombstone, so he was off to verify it.

He called later very crestfallen. He had been to the church which was exactly how he had seen it in the regression. Going to the specific place in the churchyard, he found someone else's grave. He looked at all the graves, but the name was not there. He obtained access to the church records, only to find no trace of himself under the name he had been given, and nothing that remotely fitted with the birth and death dates he had seen. He toured other churches in the area, just in case he had been mistaken about the name of the church. But to no avail. Of course, if we take the idea of parallel realities into account, he could well have been buried there in another dimension. But he wanted to know it was true in his present reality. Unfortunately, it was not to be.

In my own memories there have been verifiable incidents. A partial eclipse of the sun on a particular date was verified by the Royal Observatory — although it is extremely rare for me to get that kind of detail. From the same 'seeing' a suit of armour was identified by the College of Heralds as French armour of a similar period. It confirmed what I saw, but the deep recognition and gut feel of my memory had been what convinced me it was true. It was a memory that came early in my training for this work and it was more curiosity than anything that led me to check the details. It would not have shaken my belief in reincarnation and past life memories had it not been verified. I have applied the same principle to my clients. My work is concerned with the therapeutic use of soul memory not with proving incarnation. I accept that relivings can be symbolic or 'borrowed'. It is what that shows my client and what he or she can learn from that experience that is important. However, as we saw in the introduction, many people do desperately want to prove the truth of reincarnation memories.

REINCARNATION: THE EVIDENCE

Perhaps the best evidence for reincarnation comes from the memories of children who remember having lived before. As Roy Stemman, editor of *Reincarnation International*, says:

> One of the most striking aspects of cases suggestive of reincarnation [in children], quite apart from the weight of verifiable evidence, is the degree of conviction and emotion expressed by the young subjects in proclaiming their pre-existence...
>
> Put simply, the evidence suggests that some children bring into this life memories of a past life which are still vivid in their minds — often because their exit from that existence was either violent or traumatic...[2]

There are many well-documented cases. Memories vary from those of having been a child of the present family, who had died previously in an accident or other trauma, to having been a child in an earlier time, to having had a life as an adult in some other time and place. Some children are haunted by their memories; others take them for granted. In the Indian cases studied, several of the children remember being an adult who died just before the child was born. They were able to identify people with whom the dead person lived, to describe the places they spent time. Several of the children have even convinced the widows of the men they believe themselves to be that they are those men reincarnated.

Dr Satwant Pasricha has been working on cases like this for over twenty-three years. Her doctorate was the first to be obtained for work on reincarnation memories and she has worked in close collaboration with Professor Ian Stevenson, an American professor who has devoted his life to such work and who has published many books on the subject. Dr Pasricha has published a book of her work[3] which contains a statistical analysis of the information given by the children. Many of the children began speaking of their memories by the age of three — a finding which agreed with Professor Ian Stevenson's cross-cultural study, which showed an average age of between two and four. In addition she tabled significant personality traits and abilities. Interestingly, all the children she studied expressed a desire to return to their previous family. In her conclusion she suggests that if the root cause of a child's distress or disfunction cannot be found in childhood, then we can 'justifiably conjecture that it derives from events even earlier than those of childhood or infancy, namely those of a previous life'.[4]

The striking thing about children's memory is how matter of fact and direct it is. The children talk of their other life right from the beginning. Very young children will say, as happened to a friend of mine, 'Do you remember when I was your little girl before and I had that pink teddy bear. We went to fetch Lucy from school. Then the nasty car came and I wasn't with you any more. A nice lady helped me. And then I was in your tummy again and now I'm here with you.' The child gave many finely detailed scenes from her young life — which had been cut short when she was killed by a car outside a school. Both she and her parents were strongly convinced that she reincarnated as the child they conceived just after that traumatic event.

Other children have powerful past life memories of earlier lives. Another friend of mine had a teenage son who was obsessed with the idea of going into the Royal Air Force. Ever since he was a small boy he had had repeated nightmares in which 'my plane is going round and round and falling down into the sea'. (Many people share such memories, maybe because a whole generation of young men had their lives cut short, dying under traumatic, memorable circumstances, and then incarnating again soon afterwards.)

The young child would re-enact this with toy planes, one chasing the other. Then one plane would peel off, spin, and hit the water with a splash. What seemed to upset him most was not the circumstances of the crash but the fact that he had lost his beloved plane. By the time he was old enough to properly describe the dream, it became clear that he was in a plane that was shot down during a dog-fight and then spiralled down out of control into the sea. He did not have time to parachute out. He would talk quite matter-of-factly about his life in the Air Force during World War II, describing the airfield he was stationed at and the missions he flew. He was still at the stage of finding the war a very exciting place to be — after all, he died only weeks after qualifying as a pilot, having waited desperately since the start of the war to be old enough to fly.

One day he got very excited and called his mother to come quickly. He had seen 'his' airfield on television. His mother checked out the details he had given her and a young airman of the name he had used since early childhood did indeed die in the closing months of the war.

Many other children have similarly vivid stories to tell. Some of them forget their memories as they grow older; others became more and more certain. In people like Jenny Cockell[5] and Simon Jacobs (for Simon's story, see Chapter 4) their certainty compels them to investigate the circumstances of their remembered past life and to meet, as in Jenny's case, her 'children'.

Jenny had always had dreams and flashbacks to her 'other life' in Ireland. She drew pictures and maps and gathered together a great deal of material. She was convinced she had been a young mother who was separated from her children by an early death. Returning to Ireland, she verified much of the detail she had and was eventually reunited with her 'son' who was by now in his seventies. He confirmed her story and said that while he himself did not believe in reincarnation he did recognise that Jenny Cockell has memories that only his mother could have. Jenny Cockell has been convinced since childhood that she was that Irishwoman. It is a compelling case.

These childhood memories are very different to the past life memories that come much later in life to adults. With adults, the memory tends to arrive suddenly and 'all of a piece' — although flashbacks can be experienced which gradually build up the story. Children assume 'this is me before'; adults tend to say 'this was me in a former life'. Adult identity is separate from the other persona. While there may be other explanations (see Chapter 2), there is an increasing body of verifiable past life memories that seems to point to reincarnation as a fact of life.

In one issue of *Reincarnation International,*[6] for instance, there is an example from the work of Dr Bruce Goldberg, an American dentist who turned to past life therapy. In his book *The Search for Grace*[7] he chronicles the story of a young woman who remembered being a murder victim, and thereby unravelled a fifty-year mystery. As the *Reincarnation International's* reviewer says, cryptomnesia (remembering something previously read but not consciously recalled) could possibly account for the story and was not ruled out by Dr Goldberg, but the sheer volume of verifiable fact is striking. In the same issue, there is the story of a past life therapist who has written what seems to be a novel,[8] but which is based on transcripts of one of her client's regression sessions. The author, Linda Tarazi, spent a year in Spain researching the events in minute detail — much of the evidence coming from an obscure book written in Spanish, a language with which neither she nor her client were familiar. She was extremely careful to rule out alternative explanations for her client's experience. The book tells the story of a life lived under the Spanish Inquisition when the client was in an obsessive love affair which had carried over to her present life. (The regression was originally undertaken as part of her therapy for this obsession.) The regressee also had had powerful memories as a child and had experienced regressions prior to going to this particular therapist. But, try as she might, her therapist could not find any explanation for her story other than that it was a true memory.

Of course, there is another regression experience which can confound people. This is believing that you were one thing and then finding out you were something rather different. I had another client who had a recurring dream of being shot down in a plane over the sea. He was upside down, looking at the White Cliffs of Dover. He always assumed that he was an English pilot who was shot down just before he made it home. In an effort to identify the plane he saw, he went to the Museum of Army Flying — not the only one of my clients to start a reincarnation search there, as we shall see. To his great surprise the plane he identified was German, a Messerschmitt. When he came to me for regression he brought a Luftwaffe pilot's hat with him. He wanted to go into that life to sort out some anomalies. He had had many short glimpses but no coherent story. The regressions brought all the disparate parts together for him. As the story unfolded, we found that he had died on his first mission. He so much wanted to get to England that he had incarnated there shortly after his death!

Past Life Likenesses, Birthmarks and Scars

One of the arguments for past life memories being true is the presence of birthmarks and scars in a position in the present life where there was an injury in a past life. Although she was not born with the scar, one of the most striking examples I have seen was a woman who remembered being guillotined in the French Revolution. In her present life she had needed a thyroid operation and had a scar that went from ear to ear. I have seen scars from burns, sword wounds and other injuries. There are people who carry birthmarks where they had injuries in previous lives. Professor Ian Stevenson has carried out considerable research into this aspect of past life memories and believes it is the most important evidence for reincarnation.[9] He examined 250 cases looking both at the birthmarks and at the remembered cause of death. In each case, the sites were of significance. He concluded that a template — which he calls a psychophore — is the vehicle for carrying the imprint from the past life to influence the formation of the new body. (We will look more closely at how this occurs in Chapter 6.)

The evidence from birthmarks and scars is compelling. What I find much less compelling is the supposed likeness between past life personages and the people who claim to be their new incarnation. No doubt we all have our doubles somewhere in the world, but many people do claim that they must be someone because they resemble them. I find that doubtful. Having said that, I have seen some startling likenesses: the opera singer who found herself and two other members of her family in an obscure Russian book, which confirmed all the details of a life she had seen; Jill Mayner (whose story we will look at later) and her likeness to Catherine Parr; and a woman I knew whose photographic double hangs on the wall of St Michael's Mount, are all most convincing, although the latter case seems to conflict with fact, unless we take time out of the equation.

I wrote to the owner of St Michael's Mount asking him about this photograph and telling him the story of how whenever this woman left the Mount she had tears pouring down her face. I explained that she was sure she had lived on the Mount and had wondered whether this photograph was of her former incarnation. He was most tolerant and gave me the information that this photograph was of his mother, an American, if memory serves me correctly. As she had died comparatively recently, if chronological linear time is to be believed, she could not be the incarnation of the woman — who had no specific memories to back up her supposition. However, he said, so many pilgrims came to the Mount in times gone by and numerous people have lived on the island over the years, so he believed she could have been recalling her sorrow at having to leave sometime in the past. I had enclosed a photograph of the woman and he commented that, apart from the modern clothes, it was the image of his mother at that age.

In *Reincarnation International*[10] Scottish regressionist Tom Barlow looked at the facial similarities between the writer A. J. Stewart and James IV, whom she claims to have been and about whom she has written two books. Her memories started in childhood and as a young child she said that Stewart was her name — she later assumed it for the purpose of her writing. She has detailed knowledge of the life and times of James IV. Tom Barlow compared slides of the two faces. He used a portrait of James IV that A. J. Stewart 'remembered having had painted' before she saw the actual portrait, together with a black and white photograph in which she had recreated as closely as possible the portrait she remembered. The original of the portrait was discovered at Newbattle Abbey long afterwards and A. J. Stewart apparently has documentary evidence that she could not have seen it earlier. The pictures are strikingly similar in pose and costume. But the expression is different; there is a melancholy in the James IV portrait that does not exist in the A. J. Stewart and the eyes are much more hooded. Tom Barlow says that when one slide is superimposed upon the other, the eyes are perfectly aligned, the distance between the eyes is exactly the same and there is total symmetry between the skulls. He is convinced this is evidence for a past life match.

When people recognise other people from their present life in a past life, what they usually say is that the eyes are the same. From time to time they do say that there is a similarity in body and features, but more often than not this is not the case. It is only the eyes that are recognised. Eyes are said to be the windows of the soul and it seems that there is an essential *something* reflected in the eyes from life to life.

Of course it might be a passing resemblance to someone famous, of whom a portrait has been seen, that triggers a spurious 'past life memory'. One of those subtle and hidden things that can so easily become 'me'. In the next chapter we will examine other possibilities.

'Someone From History'

When we looked at Pythagoras' story at the beginning of this chapter, we immediately confronted one of the major problems about past life memories. Unfortunately, many people do tend to believe they were famous in the past, someone they identify closely with now. Spontaneous memories are all too often of being someone well-known. Every past life therapist meets people who insist they were someone from history and who are very disappointed indeed if they do not regress to that persona; also frequently met are those who secretly hope to find they had a glamorous or exciting life and go away dissatisfied if such a life does not surface during regression.

Twenty years ago I used to do workshops in a centre which threw a 'Come as You Were' party in the evening whenever they had a reincarnation weekend. There were usually at least one Boudicca and a Queen of England and probably a Cleopatra or two. There would certainly be an Egyptian pharaoh and a disciple and possibly a Roman emperor among the men. (What was interesting was that no one ever seemed to change sex.) This is something I have seen repeated time after time. Get a group talking about their past life memories and you can be sure there will be several people who claim they were these historical characters.

The same kind of thing happened with past life readings by psychics. At one time, almost everyone seemed to be someone famous — or wanted to be. I remember doing a reading for a 'Boudicca' from one of the past life parties. Strange as it may seem, the lives I saw were very ordinary! 'Oh Judy,' she said, 'No Boudicca, no Joan of Arc. So many people have told me that was who I was. Why didn't you see it?' I could only reply that I see what I see, not what my client wants me to see.

A few years on, I remember someone rushing up to me at a workshop and asking if I knew I had been Pope Joan. Intrigued, I went away to research this female pope of whom I had never heard. I must say it amused me to explore the possibility that I was a female who successfully masqueraded as a man but who had a lover and had the misfortune to give birth in the street during a procession, almost on the Vatican steps — and who had caused a special chair to be used thereafter at the ordination of popes so that the youngest cardinal could check that the new pope was really a man. I think I would have enjoyed such a life, but I did not take it that seriously. After all, it wasn't even clear that Pope Joan had been a real historical person; several commentators saw her as a figment of Protestant imagination trying to discredit the papacy.

However, strange to say as I write this book some ten years later, Pope Joan's story is splashed across every major newspaper and is being explored on quite serious radio programmes. No doubt a television programme is in the offing and a film is rumoured. With intriguing synchronicity, one of her biographers thinks she may have been born just down the road from here at Wimborne Minister, another that she may have studied there. An appealing thought, but I'm not sure that from one 'you were...' by a psychic who I had not even consulted, I should really see myself as this interesting lady. But maybe I should read the book to see if I recognise anything? Others will most certainly do so. No doubt, I will soon be reading the story (or stories) of people laying claim to her memories. As we will see, some so-called memories of past lives do come from books or films while others can be confirmed by historical research.

Although the situation is gradually changing, nowadays, when we read about past life memories quite a few will still be of someone of importance, someone who made a mark on history. Everyone sincerely believes that their own particular experience was unique and true — that they were that person in the past. To suggest to any one of these people that they could actually be sharing memories with someone else would cause an uproar. To intimate that it might not after all be their memory would probably cause a lynching. A response I had recently is typical. A prospective client, having written to ask me if I could look at his remembered past lives — as someone famous — and having had my response that I did not believe all such memories were necessarily true or personal but I would be very happy to look at his with an open mind, he responded that he knew all about souls fragmenting, collective memory, etc. — but he was still convinced that he was 'the real and only one'. As far as he was concerned, it was his memory. He had suffered quite badly in the past from ridicule and disbelief, but still maintained his view that his was the true memory. I do not yet know who the historical person is but if past experience is anything to go by, there will undoubtedly be other contenders for the title. All of whom utterly and most sincerely believe that they too are 'the real and only one'. This is not to denigrate his belief. He quite clearly feels, as do so many people, that this is his uniquely personal memory.

Something is clearly going on here — and it is not just an ego problem. I have lost count of the number of people who have told me that they were King Arthur. For a while, almost everyone having spontaneous or meditation-induced past life memories found a connection with King Arthur. This changes much as fashions change. For instance, a few years ago I had several clients who went back to being Judas. One arrived already certain that he was Judas and remained certain after the regression. Another went into the memory spontaneously in a workshop and believed it was genuine. Someone else had done it as a regression with another therapist and most adamantly did *not* believe it was her own life. Her therapist wisely said, 'Well, play it out anyway and let's hope it heals something for the real Judas and anything in your past lives which is to do with betrayal.'

Betrayal is after all a ubiquitous experience. One can work on forgiveness both in a personal and universal sense. Therapists in Holland, the States and Germany have all told me of similar incidents. What fascinated me was that the story these people lived out was the same — and it was not the biblical story. Shortly afterwards, a television programme investigated Judas and there on screen were several of the ideas that featured so strongly in these 'relivings'. It was clearly bubbling up out of the collective cauldron of memory. I had already done a great deal of research into Judas when I was doing my religious studies degree some years previously, so when the regressions came up with material which I had covered, I knew it could be true. It was in an effort to check out that I was not in any way influencing what had happened that I contacted the other therapists.

There are several explanations (see Chapter 2). One could be that a soul — Judas — was trying to communicate his experience as widely as possible and 'popped in' whenever and wherever the opportunity occurred. Another is that, with all of us having a betrayal experience somewhere in our past, the subconscious mind was using a well-known story to work that betrayal out — a kind of psycho-drama for the soul (although this would more probably be the biblical story). It also could be that a soul who was Judas fragmented and went into several other souls — although it seems to be stretching coincidence too far that they all then went to past life therapists at the same time. Of course, if we move away from the idea that one individual soul moves from life to life in a linear, chronological sequence of time, it becomes more possible to accept that several people could carry these soul memories. But why would those souls suddenly remember at the same time? Other possible explanations are that a soul group shares its memories and the Sufi idea that souls who are leaving the earth pass on their memories to the souls who are coming into incarnation. American Reincarnation Therapist Dolores Cannon puts forward the theory that if you happen to need a particular experience in the past for the incarnation you are about to embark on, but you have not actually had that experience yourself, then you can go off to the Akashic Record and get yourself imprinted with it — the Akashic Record holding the memory of everything and anything that has happened or may happen.

I personally believe we can tune into the Akashic Record at any time, whether to read our own past incarnations or those of other people. If we need to 'borrow' knowledge or skill from a past life experience, it is rather like going to the library to find a suitable reference book. There may be half a dozen that will give us the information we seek, but we select the one that we can read the most easily. If we are technically minded, we may chose a technical manual. If we are not, then we go for the 'idiot's guide'. All could give us what we need, but we choose what is most appropriate for us and our present level of knowledge. It may be one of our own past lives, but it could equally well be that of someone else. We can benefit from all experience everywhere.

Experiences of Reincarnation

I have always had a deep affinity with Egypt and many of my reincarnation experiences have featured Egypt. People do query why quite so many Egyptian lives come up in regression and spontaneous memory. As the ancient Egyptian civilisation lasted for longer than the Christian has, and as Egypt had such an interest in the continuing life of the soul, I don't think this is anything to be surprised at. The Egyptian temple was a great training ground for spiritual work, and life for the ancient Egyptians was a spiritual experience. The deities were very much a part of life. Priests and priestesses took on the role of the gods in ritual work. In doing so, they became that deity. Such experiences make a deep imprint in the soul.

In a very powerful experience I had long before I stepped on Egyptian soil this time around, I went back to being a high priestess who was enacting a ritual in which she became the goddess Sekhmet and then Hathor, the milder face of the goddess. Sekhmet was sent on the rampage by her father Ra to kill humankind. She could not be stopped and so was tricked into drinking gallons of beer to drug her. The god Thoth took her home for healing and reconciliation. There was much more to this 'reliving' including a very graphic vision of a sandstorm at Temple Mut at Karnak. I was able to visit the places I 'saw' in that vision some ten years ago and returned yet again earlier this year. Despite its fantasy overtones, the core of the experience still resonates with me, especially my connection with the goddess Sekhmet. The spontaneous regression began very suddenly and seemed to last a lifetime but only took fifteen minutes or so in present-day time. It was very hard to come back. As my notes from the time say, 'And I awoke in Essex feeling totally bereft and torn from my roots. It took me some time to acclimatise myself to the 1970s and a completely different reality.'

Strangely enough, the first time I went to Karnak in my present life a violent sandstorm blew up out of a clear blue sky. We were over at the back, at Sekhmet's small temple paying our respects. (A temple I had seen in several regressions and which was exactly where I knew it would be.) This is one of the few temples which is still intact with its goddess in place. Walking into the dim room with its seven-foot high statute of the goddess made me shiver with remembrance. By the time we made our way back to the temple entrance we had sand everywhere. It had a most familiar feel. Sometime later when in Morocco, I watched a news report of a severe sandstorm in Cairo. The colours and the eye-witness reports were so similar to my vision. Many people recounted thinking that the end of the world had come or that the old gods had returned. I knew exactly how they felt.

Aware that he had had reincarnation memories almost from birth, which also included 'becoming' one of the gods, I asked David Lawson, the author of *The Eye of Horus — An Oracle of Ancient Egypt* to share these memories. David is a leading international healer, teacher and natural intuitive and, as we shall see, his past life experiences are what enable him to do such excellent work in his chosen field:

I have always believed in reincarnation. It was easy for me to believe because, even as a small child, I knew I had lived before. At the age of four I had conscious recollections of other lives. My memories were hazy and a challenge for my four-year-old mind to quantify, but it was the feeling that came with them that had the most profound effect upon my development. I could feel that I was more than the child body I was inhabiting and I knew that I was 'older' than most of the people around me, including my elder siblings and my parents. Indeed, the state of being a child was often frustrating for me because I also knew that my personal autonomy would be restricted until I reached adulthood. I spent my formative years with the feeling that my spirit, and my ego, had come down to earth with a bump.

When asked, I simply tell people that I know about other lives from personal experience. Indeed, I continue to have emotional, mental, visual and sensual memories of being in other bodies and experiencing other times. My earliest memories were of being female and I think it may have been a shock for me to realise that I was male this time around, but more recently, I seem to find it easier to access memories of

continued ...

male incarnations. I believe the reason for this is that we tap into memories and feelings that can best serve our development in the present moment. My earlier feminine memories helped me to access and establish the powerful intuitive abilities that are now at the core of my work as a healer, psychic counsellor and astrologer. Also, they challenged all the assumptions about gender that were present in the beliefs and attitudes of the small, village community that was my home until I left for drama college at the age of seventeen. Indeed, a theatre review of one of my student performances described my character as 'a go-between for the sexes' and while I would now consider myself to be predominantly male, I am able to develop a deep intuitive understanding of my female clients.

In addition to my memories of other lives, I also have a sense of what it is like to be liberated from a human body with its extraordinary physical strengths and limitations. I love my body, give or take the odd lump and bump, but I know that I am much bigger and lighter than it can ever be. Our spiritual bodies exist without the solidity and firm structure required for us to walk upon the earth. My recollections of between life states and non-physical incarnations feel freer, more fluid and more natural for me than my memories of being anchored in physical form. I imagine us all putting on our human bodies as if we are donning spacesuits or diving gear. It is the appropriate attire for the environment. This physical form acts as a kind of encounter suit that enables us to interact with each other in a very special way. It is by being spirits on a human path and learning to relate to each other with the illusion of being separate that we gain much of our experience so we can evolve and grow. In our natural form we are not really separate from each other and we are larger, finer and brighter than we appear to be while on earth. When we choose to wear a human body, I believe we wear it on the inside.

continued ...

I have been drawn to the mythology and culture of ancient Egypt for as long as I can remember. As a child, I was fascinated by books about the ancient Egyptians, even those in language that was too adult for me to fully comprehend. Yet I had a strong sense of the truth behind the words. I still do. Numerous psychics have linked me to the Egyptian world and it does not surprise me that other people also feel linked to the mythology, culture and beliefs of the ancient Egyptians. Many souls, alive today, experienced multiple incarnations during the vast period of history that encompassed the rise and fall of the pharaohs. Although I believe civilisation to be much older than even the Egyptian world, Egypt was the first great nation state in recorded history. Numerous souls who contributed to that period of human evolution have now incarnated in the western world and the strong economies of the East so that they may continue to be a part of the leading edge of civilisation, philosophy, science, art, commerce and exploration. In short, we are now continuing the work of social and spiritual evolution we began in ancient Egyptian times.

My two most powerful memories of ancient Egyptian lives relate to deities from the Egyptian pantheon. The first is Anubis, guardian god of the dead and embalming. The second is Imhotep, a god of civilisation. Imhotep was an unusual figure within Egyptian mythology because he was a living man whose powerful influence upon the development of this ancient culture caused him to be deified. This is not dissimilar to the canonisation of the saints of Roman Catholicism; real people whose lives embodied some of the spiritual principles upon which the religion was based and who therefore became an object of worship at some time after their death. In Egyptian mythology, Imhotep and Anubis were very different figures whose origins, lineage and symbology were quite dissimilar, but they did have some similarities of purpose that are significant for my

continued ...

current life. Chiefly, they were both gods associated with healing.

I first experienced my link with the Egyptian god Anubis during a regression conducted by a friend. I was guided into a relaxed, trance-like state where I felt liberated from my physical form. When asked about my identity, I simply replied that I was Anubis. Within the symbology of Egyptian temples and tombs, Anubis was usually depicted as a man with the head of a jackal or, more simply, as a crouching jackal, but I felt much too big to have a body in the physical sense. In addition, I felt infinitely powerful and assured of my own strength, wisdom and eternal existence. I did not have the need for guile or arrogance because I was unquestionably a being of extraordinary influence and divine magic. A god has no need to question himself or to prove himself by over-inflating his importance. What is curious about this is that I would not normally consider myself to be the kind of person whose ego would motivate them to 'discover' that they were some great being or famous figure from history. I am perfectly happy to find that I was a serving wench in a historically unremarkable household or the third archer on the right in a forgotten army, so it has taken me some time to come to terms with this experience and theorise about its validity.

Subsequent memories of Egypt have included visions of being a priest of Anubis working with others to conduct funerary ceremonies of embalming, preservation and preparation for the life beyond. I have seen myself as part of a group, dressed in sacred robes and jackal masks, and invoking Anubis to look favourably on the souls of departed noblemen as they begin their journey into the afterlife. These memories frequently visited my mind at home in England, as well as during my trips to Egypt, but it was not until a recent conversation with Judy Hall that I finally made the full connection between them and my regressed

continued ...

god-like state. Judy reminded me that priests of Anubis sought to embody their god during sacred ceremonies. While there was certainly a degree of theatricality involved in these rituals, the embodiment of Anubis was not mere play acting but a real merging between human beings and the deity they worshipped. Simply put, there were times when the priests actually became Anubis in a way that is similar to a medium channelling a spirit guide. As someone who had experienced this phenomenon on numerous occasions in a former life, it would have been natural to regress into this all powerful, god-like state. Indeed, the trance I assumed during regression was probably similar to the trance states that were induced for the purpose of embodying the deity during those sacred ceremonies. This extraordinary regression helped me to enhance my psychic awareness, strengthen my belief in eternal life and, at a time when I needed confirmation of my abilities and purpose, boost my confidence.

My connection to Imhotep first presented itself through memories and dreams and only later as snatched glimpses during regressions. For many years I have had a sense that I was a high-ranking official in ancient Egyptian times. I knew that I was a man of great wealth and power who had acquired his position through his creative brilliance and unbridled ambition. I also knew that in this life I had been highly educated and was proficient in a number of skills including architecture, medicine, writing, administration and a magical form of mathematics that is currently lost knowledge. Once again, these memories have been challenging for me to come to terms with. While I do have creative ambitions in this present life, I would not consider myself to be particularly important or to have a great need for worldly status, power and recognition. Indeed, I did not talk about these memories for a long time because I did not want to be considered arrogant or to have delusions of grandeur. When I first read about Imhotep, I realised that, when

continued ...

he was alive, he was the kind of man I remembered being in this former existence and I immediately felt a strong link between him and myself. Imhotep had been a high-ranking official for King Djoser. He is attributed with being the architect who created the step pyramid at Saqqara and he was indeed a scribe, a man of medicine and, probably, a skilled mathematician. My considered opinion is that rather than being Imhotep himself, I was one of a number of high-ranking officials of a similar nature who came after him. As a god, he would have been the patron of other successful, educated men and the skills he excelled in were skills that others would have emulated. Scribes, architects, doctors, administrators and mathematicians would have learnt and practised their sacred professions in his name.

In my present incarnation, I am again a scribe, although I work with word processors and manuscripts rather than clay tablets, and I am a healer whose knowledge of spiritual healing has undoubtedly come to me from previous lives. I have also had dreams about sacred mathematics and magical geometry, but I cannot profess to be a great mathematician or an architect. I can always hope that some of these skills will develop later in life, but I am aware that it is not my purpose to simply repeat any of my previous incarnations. Indeed, I believe that my memories of this particular Egyptian lifetime serve to help me create a present one where worldly ambition is tempered by compassion, humility and spiritual evolution.

During one holiday in modern-day Egypt, my dear friend and travelling companion, Kitty Campion and I visited the Isis temple of Philae at Aswan. Kitty, who is a highly respected medical herbalist and complementary health practitioner, had spent most of the preceding week letting her hair down and enjoying the social opportunities of the holiday. She had not been particularly impressed with the other temples we had

continued ...

visited, despite my enthusiasm for them, so it came as a surprise to me that both Kitty and I experienced a powerful change of consciousness at Philae. Instinctively, we were drawn to a small side temple and without great discussion both decided to meditate in this spot.

The meditation was short but powerful; I felt as if I had been lifted from my body and transported to a higher plane of consciousness. There was a great sense of peace and healing which Kitty and I shared. Afterwards, we discovered that while Philae was dedicated to the goddess Isis, this small side temple was dedicated to both Isis and Imhotep and that it was a centre for healing. We were two modern-day healers paying tribute to the healing powers of the ancient world and receiving the blessing of the gods in return. My memories of Egyptian lives inspired me to write my book *The Eye of Horus — An Oracle of Ancient Egypt* which is a positive system of divination based upon the gods and goddesses of the Egyptians. Both Imhotep and Anubis continue to inspire my life and work.

David's experience epitomises many of the topics and scenarios that we will meet throughout this book. As with so many people, it is his own memory that convinces him that reincarnation is a fact. David also believes that it is not the factual truth or otherwise of the incarnations that matters, it is what they offer to his life and how they expand his spiritual perception that is important.

Encounters with the Past

So, does it really matter whether past lives are true or false? Well, it matters to a surprising number of people. Some of them have a great deal invested in past lives. Writers, therapists and people who gain a sense of identity from their other lives all have a vested interest in believing — or in proving — that we have lived before. (It can be very empowering to see yourself differently in another life.) Other people seem to have an equally strong need to prove otherwise. In between are large numbers of people who have had personal experiences which lead them to believe that they could well have had other lives. Some have problems and blockages in their lives which they feel must come from a past life. They may have a theme running through their present life which is all too familiar, or they may have an urge to overcome difficulties surrounding an issue with which they seemingly have no cause to have become involved.

Jill Mayner, whose story we will now share, found herself in her present life drawn to changing how women give birth. She has devoted her life to something which, on the face of it, has little to do with her. According to her mother, she had had a perfectly ordinary birth. When it came time for her to give birth herself, she was a bit older than most mothers and absolutely terrified of pain and death, so she decided the best way for her was a gentle water birth. At that stage it did not occur to her that she might be bringing forward past life issues, but some years later spontaneous recall brought up several past lives in which she had died a painful death during or just after childbirth.

Past life memories often have a particular theme running through them, something which links them together rather like a string of coloured beads in various shades of one particular hue. Spontaneous memories of other lives can be very detailed and graphic. When they are followed up by regression, more detail emerges which *fits* the life in question. It must be true then, mustn't it? Well, it may well be, but it is not as simple as that.

The following story draws these two strands of our exploration together. One strand is a repeating lifescript which carries two themes. The themes are death in childbirth and great love. The other strand is the gradual bringing together of a group who believed they have lived together before. The story brings in two historical personages, however, and Jill Mayner, whose experiences these are, is by no means the first person to 'return' to these two particular characters. Jill herself is still very open-minded about these memories. At one level they were extremely real and true; at another she questions whether they were actually her past lives. She has no ego involvement in them. At the end of the day, while she found it extremely interesting and illuminating for her life now, it does not matter to her whether or not she was Mumtaz Mahal or Catherine Parr. She did not set out to seek either memory:

> One night in November 1994 my friend Nick offered to take me out for a meal. We tried several different restaurants but they were either too smoky or too expensive. Eventually Nick suggested we try an Indian restaurant, which was very local to my home. It was quite late when we arrived and we were the only customers. During the meal, I had a spontaneous past life regression which took me back to India. I was able to talk about the personalities of Shah Jehan and Mumtaz Mahal as if I knew them and was able to describe things about their palace and the Taj Mahal. (This was not the first time I felt a connection. I had previously been in a large group regression — which included Nick — at a workshop run by Denise Linn and at the end of the session, a very vivid picture of the Taj Mahal came to my mind and Nick was connected with this in some way.)

Many people are familiar with the story of how the Taj Mahal came to be built. When she was dying in childbirth, Mumtaz Mahal asked her husband, the Mogul Emperor Shah Jahan to build a fitting monument to their great love. Few people know Mumtaz's personal story, however. The mother of fourteen children, Mumtaz was much more than a mere wife. A lively and intelligent woman, she was his lifelong confidante and adviser. She took part in the government of the country and even accompanied her husband on his military campaigns. When I researched her for a piece I was writing, I was surprised just how much power she had had. Jill, however, knew little of this when she had her spontaneous regression:

> I, in this life, knew very little about the Taj Mahal or the palace where Mumtaz lived but the waiters were quite knowledgeable and asked me if I was clairvoyant when I asked them to verify the details I was recalling. Although I am clairvoyant, I knew that I was having a spontaneous past life regression and felt that I had actually been Mumtaz Mahal. I can remember one of the waiters saying to me, 'Mumtaz Mahal was beautiful inside and outside, just like you.' (What a schmoozer!)

When Jill rang me to tell me about this spontaneous regression, it certainly sounded very real and genuine. The depth of feeling it had aroused in her was unmistakable. Her rather cool and collected account above was written some three or four years afterwards and lacks the immediacy of the story she sobbed out over the phone to me. (The sobs were more of joy than sorrow and she was clearly very deeply moved by the whole experience.) At the time she said: 'I have never in my present life known what it is to be totally loved by someone, and yet through this experience I know exactly how it feels. It will help me to recognise it when I find it again.'

As it happened, I had just seen an article in *Reincarnation International*[11] about a highly experienced and much respected American past life therapist, Winafred Blake Lucas who believed that she, physician Gladys McGarey who works with the Edgar Cayce Foundation, and an Indian writer Mantosh Devji-Singh, had been connected with Mumtaz Mahal. In a multiple regression carried out by Chet Snow, Winafred had seen herself as one of the daughters of Mumtaz, and Gladys McGarey was the midwife who delivered the child. In the article, Winafred stated they were convinced that their reliving was a true one. I was aware however that at least one other group of people had also 'regressed' to this same incarnation and also believed that they were personally involved (but client confidentiality means that I cannot give the details here. It will have to suffice to say that it was a very similar story). It seemed as though one of the complex multi-group interactions with which I had become increasingly familiar as my work progressed was underway. I sent the article to Jill:

> When I saw the photo [of Winafred], I burst out crying and knew this soul. She had been a blood relative in the Taj Mahal lifetime and, although I had never been to America, I knew I had to go to meet her.
>
> While in America she suggested I underwent a past life regression with a leading therapist to obtain 'proof' of who I had been. I was very reluctant to do this as I knew it would prove difficult. However I agreed. At first I saw myself as a young girl. I was very isolated and there were not many other children around. I was
>
> *continued ...*

kept within the walls of a very big house and rarely saw my mother but had a kindly lady to look after me. I was more like a young adult and did not go out to play much.

The next thing I knew, I was about sixteen and outside and there was this handsome man with a beard and the most beautiful eyes I have ever seen. I was asked his name, it was Jahan. As I looked into his eyes, I knew I was falling deeply in love with this man. The experience was so powerful and intense that I had to ask the therapist to take me out of the experience for awhile. This was because I had never experienced such a deep love in this lifetime and it was too much for me to cope with. I could not have drawn this experience from anything I had experienced during this lifetime.

I saw myself seated on a small throne at right angles to Shah Jahan who was seated on a much larger throne. People were filing past me being presented to Shah Jahan. I had to keep very still and look straight ahead and was not allowed to look at anyone in the eye. I was very much in love with my husband but I rarely saw him. I was in a room with other women and the sisterhood between a few of us kept me going. I was not particularly happy. I was always worried about my children (of whom Nick was possibly one; this could be why I have been overprotective of him in this life, although I am sure there are other lifetimes when he has been my son). I loved my eldest daughter Jahanara (Winafred) dearly but she was certainly a law unto herself. I could not go to my husband, he always had to come to me. Many women were jealous of me. I could trust no one apart from the 'sisters', the closest of whom was Gladys, who also delivered all my babies. I could confide in no one else. I remember lattice work around me.

A very vivid memory was of being transported in a closed carriage, like a sedan chair. It was being carried by men. It was very dusty. I was heavily pregnant and

continued ...

it was extremely hot. I passed out. At this point I asked the therapist to take me out of the experience as, again, it was frightening and like nothing I had ever experienced in this lifetime. The therapist took me to my death. I was very reluctant to do this. I was frightened. There was blood everywhere and screams. One woman ran out screaming. They brought my husband back. I know I felt very guilty because it was a time of battle and I had helped my husband make a decision that led to people's deaths and I felt that battle was going on around us at the time of my death, but it was the lesser of two evils — a different decision would have been worse for us. I had only wanted to bring peace to the earth and I was so very unhappy that this was not working out and I really had no desire left to live. I felt this *very* strongly. I told my husband that when I died he was to build a mausoleum that would symbolise peace on earth, so that at least I could leave something to bring hope to people; this was not out of ego but out of my love for mankind. I did care about the ordinary people and loved them but could not reach them during my lifetime, as I felt so distant from them due to protocol. I especially felt for the women. I made my eldest daughter Jahanara (Winafred) promise me she would look after Jahan. She was someone who always liked to do her own thing and I knew this would be difficult for her but I knew he would need her. Also I thought she needed the responsibility to keep her out of harm's way; she was always getting into trouble. [In the event, Jahanara actually looked after her father during the seven years he was imprisoned by his son who had deposed him as Emperor. (This was a very troubled family.) During that time, she managed to have a scandalous affair with a young poet who as a result was skinned alive, something Winafred saw in her regression.]

In the spirit world, I knew there were plans to build the Taj Mahal and special energy was directed and

continued ...

interpenetrated the marble of the Taj Mahal. Spirit definitely helped with the building of it. Shah Jahan wanted to make a black Taj Mahal opposite, so he could be buried in it. That was absolutely typical of him! I knew this was not meant to be, because the 'darkness' would have detracted from the 'light' of the Taj Mahal — giving a yin-yang balancing effect rather than the Taj becoming a symbol for peace, hope, love and beauty. The Taj was also a symbol of the 'sisterhood' that was so special to me in that life. A hope for downtrodden women — just like the work I am doing in this present life!

I had asked Jill to pinpoint the significance for her of that life intruding into her present life. She said:

The most important things I learnt from this experience were that I would like to fall in love in this lifetime the way I did in that lifetime (and I've got just the person in mind now!) and that I have come back to heal childbirth in this lifetime together with Shah Jahan. When my kinesiologist tested before I went to America if I had been Mumtaz, it came out positive and also that Shah Jahan was also present in this lifetime. Of course, this does not necessarily mean that we will be lovers in this lifetime and it could well be a man I am working with professionally. (He certainly walks around as if he's Yul Brynner in *The King and I!*)

This was not the only past life Jill recalled where she was an influential wife:

I went for healing at my local Spiritualist Church one morning in the summer of 1996 and the healer suggested I take my son Michael to a park I had never visited before. When I did, we wandered off the beaten track to look at some ducks. There was no one else around and then this lady came by to feed the ducks.

continued ...

She offered Michael some bread and asked me if he was born in February. I replied, saying, 'Yes, you're right and no, you're wrong! He is an Aquarian but he was born in January!' Obviously we were on the same wavelength. We then got talking and decided to meet up for lunch one day. When we did, we started to talk about reincarnation and I told her I felt I had known her in Tudor times. She knew of a past life she had spent in Tudor England and I started to talk about people we had both known. She asked me how I knew so much and 'something' told me that it was because I had been Catherine Parr [last wife of Henry VIII]. Although this surprised me, it made sense of the knowledge and people we had mutually known at this time. I had always had a fear of being beheaded and, of course, Catherine Parr was nearly beheaded for her strong religious ideas. She had to keep a balance between having her own strong and progressive ideas but also respecting and bowing down to the King's authority. She married him out of duty but was a kind and loving person always trying to do the right thing. She had a timid personality and was not very beautiful, but she was calm and collected and reserved.

The interesting thing was that when I read up about her life, she died in childbirth — or just after childbirth. She actually died of a broken heart because the only man she truly loved, Thomas Seymour, betrayed her. She had been married twice before Henry VIII, to older men whom she did not really have any passion for. She had married them out of duty. Of course, she did not want to marry the King really and did this out of duty too and, in a way, to please Thomas — to get the power so that he would really respect her. She had passion for Thomas but he was power-obsessed and he did not really love her, although she thought he did, but she was mistaken.

Interestingly enough, only yesterday I was in a stately home associated with Henry VIII when a very familiar face looked at me from a painting. At first glance it was Jill! But no, it was actually

Catherine Parr. While I do not believe that past life likenesses necessarily indicate the same soul inhabiting both bodies, there was certainly an uncanny resemblance in both facial features and body shape between these two women separated by 450 years.

When Jill visited Syon Park, she was able to point out the spot where Henry's body had lain overnight on its way to Windsor for burial. She remembered that the body had been placed in a ruined chapel of the former priory and that the lead coffin had burst its seams and leaked 'blood' (actually other bodily fluids) — 'blood' which was licked up by a dog the next morning. The body had already been lying in the King's Privy Chamber for at least five days and the King's ulcerated leg had been well-rotted before his death, so this lead coffin had been essential before the body could be transported for burial. Catherine Parr had not been present at the death nor did she accompany the coffin, but the story about the dog licking up the blood was told when the cortège reached Windsor. When Jill was at Syon, she was very upset at the memory of this dreadful story. At the time, the event was seen as a piece of karma. When Henry divorced his first wife, Catherine of Aragon, a Catholic friar, Father Peto, had predicted that if the king cast off his wife to marry Anne Boleyn, he 'would be as Ahab and the dogs would lick his blood'. After the event with the dog, which was seen by a number of witnesses, it was believed that this prophecy — perhaps more in the nature of a curse — had been fulfilled. It could well be that Jill had read that story previously; it appears in one version of *The Six Wives of Henry VIII* and is also told at Syon Park, but the exact whereabouts of the ruined chapel in which the coffin lay have, according to the staff at Syon Park whom Jill questioned, been lost. Jill could point to the exact spot. She remembers being there previously, something which is not recorded in history, but as Syon House was a favourite of Henry VIII's it is more than probable that Catherine Parr would have known the location of that chapel.

However, Jill is not the only women to 'remember' Catherine Parr. There a story that involves not only regression but also communication from a dead spirit. Drowsy from an operation, Catharine Warren-Browne said of her visiting priest, 'Here is good Master Coverdale come to comfort me'. When pregnant and feeling depressed she said, 'She, too, died of puerperal fever' and referring to Catherine Parr. When Mrs Warren-Browne was using a ouija board, the Lord Admiral Tom Seymour (Catherine Parr's last husband) apparently communicated to her the fact that Catherine was buried under the altar at Sudeley and that she had had a child called Mary on 17 August. When Mrs Warren-Browne checked out this fact, she discovered that it was on 28 August, but the communicator said it was a case of the Julian and the Gregorian calendars differing by eleven days. Mrs Warren-Browne later claimed to recognise places that Catherine Parr had known well, such as the room in Pembroke castle in which Henry VII — her father-in-law — had been born. Under hypnosis, Mrs Warren-Browne returned to Sudeley and recalled being under the care of a Dr Tahilcus. She mentioned the king's doctor, Dr Herk, and her sister and stepdaughter by name — details which were said to be historically correct.[12] In commenting on this case David Christie Murray points out that it was a story explicable by cryptomnesia with 'perhaps, elements of precognition, inspired by a possibly incubated subconscious fantasy erected on forgotten reading'.[13]

However, Catharine Warren-Browne did not claim to be the Queen, Catherine Parr. She did say that the Lord High Admiral asserted she was the Queen but she herself felt that this idea was preposterous. Under deep hypnosis, so deep that she remembered nothing of the session, a memory emerged which was vivid, detailed and real enough to convince the noted past life researcher, Hans Holzer, that she was indeed that Queen.

Mrs Warren-Browne's 'memories' began in early childhood. She was psychic and precognitive from birth, seeing ghosts and experiencing *déjà vu*. A devout Catholic as a young adult, Mrs Warren-Browne was not particularly interested in reincarnation, although she had discussed the possibility with friends. However, the events throughout her life eventually led her to believe that reincarnation was a distinct possibility.

When she was thirteen years old Catharine had a tutor, Miss Grant, who was given to holding forth on topics which interested her with an almost fanatical zeal. One morning over breakfast Miss Grant spoke about Henry VIII, a biography of whom had just been published. In Miss Grant's eyes, Henry was a monster equal only to Caligula. His syphilitic, ulcerated leg had been a punishment from God. An agitated Catharine told Miss Grant that, on the contrary, Henry was a much misunderstood man. He had not had syphilis but had suffered from high blood sugar and obesity which led to his death — at the time well-brought up young women of thirteen were not even supposed to know what syphilis was, let alone talk about it over breakfast. Some years later came the experience of recovering from an anaesthetic and calling the Abbot Alphege Gleason 'Master Coverdale'. Dr Coverdale was a protégé of Catherine Parr, although at this time Mrs Warren-Browne had no idea of his identity.

The 'bodily karma' connection between Catherine Parr and Mrs Warren-Browne is interesting. Catherine Parr died of puerperal fever following childbirth — this being an infection carried in the blood. Mrs Warren-Browne had a blood condition which led to the death of five of her eight children. Immediately prior to giving birth, she would often suffer deep depression and burst into uncontrollable tears. It was on one such occasion that she was asked by her physician why, when everything seemed to be going well, she became so depressed at this stage in her pregnancy. She replied that although 'she too had been healthy she had died of puerperal fever'. When asked who she was talking about, she said that she had no idea. Following the birth of one of her sons, she was very ill and had a repeating vision in which she saw herself lying in a great, canopied bed, virtually dead. This woman had red-gold hair which was very long. Each time Mrs Warren-Browne came out of the vision, she would be extremely depressed and sorry for the woman, but at the time shrugged it off as a fantasy. It is possible that the karmic memory of that earlier death had imprinted itself not only onto her consciousness but also onto her etheric blueprint and that she carried the repeating pattern of trauma and death around childbirth, a pattern which manifested as the blood condition through which her physical body reacted badly to pregnancy, resulting in the death not of herself but of her children.

When the Lord High Admiral Seymour apparently began communicating with her some ten years later, he told her that he had been waiting for her for a long, long time. He stated that she was the reincarnation of the dead queen, who had become his own wife after the death of the king. She had died having their child and was buried at his old castle, Sudeley. A year after her own death, Tom Seymour was executed.

Shortly after the communications, she contacted Hans Holzer. She did not claim to be Catherine Parr, but said that this was what Tom Seymour was insisting. According to him, after their respective deaths they had inhabited different planes and she had been ready to reincarnate before him. Under close questioning from Hans Holzer she said that although she had never felt she was someone else, there had been many occasions when she had felt she knew places (*déjà vu*) which she had never visited before. Pembroke Castle, birthplace of Henry VIII, was one such place. Hans Holzer suggested regression.

Under hypnosis she began a detailed recall of the last days of Catherine Parr and of her experience as what appears to be an at times earthbound spirit who ministered to the children of the dead king — fulfilling a promise she had made to him. Her experience after death is classic: she talks of seeing a great light which 'speaks' to her and, eventually, of being given a choice to return to earth. But she is told that before she can move on she must stop grieving. It is her desire for Tom Seymour — whom she had loved before she married Henry — that is holding her trapped between lives. She had doubted him, believing him to have been unfaithful with the future Queen Elizabeth — her step-daughter and ward — and she wanted his forgiveness. When she was able to let that go, she reincarnated and made reparation by looking after Polish children during the war. She relived how she came to be queen and the execution of her predecessor, Catherine Howard, for adultery. It was after she had been widowed for the second time and while she was in love with Tom Seymour that Henry asked her to marry him and it was hardly possible for her to refuse her sovereign lord, so her love for Tom Seymour had had to be put on hold. After Henry died, she and Tom married but only had eighteen months together as man and wife before she died. The situation with Elizabeth — whom she herself caught 'romping' with the Admiral — created a rift between them. This apparently had created a situation where she could not move on. Tom too was held there, waiting for her and desperate to meet up. In the regression, while talking to her in the between life state, he assured Catharine he would wait for her. They would be reunited.

Hans Holzer comments that the regression revealed many historical details which were not generally available but which could be verified with careful research. At the time Mrs Warren-

Browne was writing an historical novel based on Tudor England and admits to having read 'a few books on the period'. Notwithstanding, Hans Holzer — a careful and sceptical researcher — was convinced by her regression that she had personal knowledge of the life of Catherine Parr and he was satisfied that unconscious knowledge played no part in the case. He does raise the interesting question of what will happen when Mrs Warren-Browne herself passes to the between life state. It may be that Tom Seymour will get tired of waiting or may be ready for another incarnation soon afterwards, so they may miss each other again. He also points out that as there is a Mr Warren-Browne, it may be somewhat complicated. But as he says, that is speculation and it has not a part in his role as an investigator. In my role as a karmic counsellor, however, it is exactly the kind of situation that creates new incarnations that are full of problems. It would be as well if all three resolved the situation before incarnating again.

Healing the Past

Jill Mayner has had other spontaneous regressions to death in childbirth. An opportunity came to heal this when she was on a workshop with me and was trying to release trauma from a present life relationship. (Her then partner was having affairs with other women and was not supporting her in her life.) Jill was screaming loudly and then suddenly she was giving birth. The labour was vivid. She felt all the feelings of a very difficult birth. The sound reverberated right around the old house in which we were working. The group supported her, each taking a role. One became the errant father who was nowhere to be seen. He was loudly berated and sworn at for having abandoned her at this important moment. Two of us held Jill and urged her on, encouraging her to let happen whatever needed to happen. She squatted down, pushed hard and finally delivered a 'child'. A 'midwife' gently placed a sausage-shaped cushion in her arms. Having cradled her 'baby', the group member taking the errant father role was readmitted to the room and she had the opportunity of saying all that she had been unable to say at her other births — and to all the men who had betrayed her with other women. Having talked with her 'husband' for some time, she was finally able to forgive all the men who had not been present for her. As we worked with her, it became obvious that she symbolically had been giving birth to herself rather than reliving an actual birth, but this was appropriate for her. In doing so she reframed and healed all those other births that had gone before. It also opened the way for her to have a relationship with a man who would be there for her.

To me this is the value of past life recall and regression. I use it as therapy to heal problems from the past. So, for me, it does not matter whether the life is actually, factually true. However, we will look at Jill's story in the next section in the light of some possible explanations for her experiences other than an actual reliving of her own past lives.

Notes:

1. Quoted in *Reincarnation: An East-West Anthology* compiled and edited by Joseph Head and S.L. Cranston (New York, The Julian Press Inc., 1961) p.78.
2. *Reincarnation International,* Issue No. 12, July 1997 — quoted from page 8 but the whole issue is devoted to children's memories. See also Roy Stemman, *Reincarnation* (London, Piatkus Books, 1997); Carol Bowman, *Children's Past Lives: How Past Life Memories Affect your Child* (London, Element Books, 1997); Peter and Mary Harrison, *The Children That Time Forgot* (Kenneth Mason Publications); Dr Satwant Pasricha, *Claims of Reincarnation: An Empirical Study of Cases in India* (New Delhi, Harman Publishing House, 1990); Vickie Mackenzie, *Reborn in the West* (London, Thorsons, 1997); Professor Ian Stevenson, *Children Who Remember Past Lives* (Charlottesville, University of Virginia Press, 1987).
3. Pasricha, *Claims of Reincarnation.*
4. Dr Pasricha quoted in *Reincarnation International,* Issue No. 12, July 1997.
5. Jenny Cockell, *Yesterday's Children,* (London, Piatkus Books, 1993).
6. *Reincarnation International,* Issue No. 12, July 1997.
7. Dr Bruce Goldberg, *The Search for Grace* (London, Piatkus Books, 1997).
8. Linda Tarazi, *Under the Inquisition: An Experience Relived.*
9. Professor Ian Stevenson, *Where Reincarnation and Biology Intersect.*
10. *Reincarnation International,* No. 5, March 1995, p.18. A. J. Stewart's books are available from *Reincarnation International.*
11. *Reincarnation International,* Issue 4, November 1994, p.18.
12. Hans Holzer, *Born Again* (Folkestone, Bailey & Swinfen Ltd, 1975).
13. David Christie-Murray, *Reincarnation: Ancient Beliefs and Modern Evidence* (Bridport, Prism Press, 1988) p.131.

Chapter 2
Explaining It All Away

The possibility of hallucinations and delusions on the part of the subject, and suppression of facts and tendentious reporting on the part of the observer must always be taken into account.

Benjamin Walker[1]

There are many theories put forward to explain away apparent reincarnation memories. Some are psychological, others psychic. All have their strengths and weaknesses. Most could well be true, but there are a few which require as big a leap of faith as a belief in reincarnation may do. What we need to ask, however, is do any of these alternative explanations throw light on one of our fundamental questions: do past lives really exist and, if so, why do people apparently share the same memories?

THE POWER OF SUGGESTION

In my experience this is certainly one to watch. Many people are extremely suggestible. Get them into a nice calm relaxed state and oh so subtly suggest something and they will produce it. This is a way I and many past life therapists take our clients into past lives. We create a scene which will lead into 'another life'. The skill is in knowing when to hand over to the client's own memories — and in differentiating what is a fantasy and what is a real experiencing. I use the fantasy if necessary but always make sure that my client knows we are 'seeing what will happen' rather than working with a 'fact'. If the client has a fantasy about being famous, then this can easily produce a detailed life that seems to be true and yet can have an essential element missing. The reliving will somehow lack an authentic feel even though the words are right. On the other hand, people who ostensibly know nothing about someone's life can bring the most extraordinary detail to the surface — detail which can later be proved to be correct although only after a great deal of digging amongst obscure references. For one of my clients the need to find out involved her learning to read old Russian so that she could actually understand the book she had found about her past life. The picture of the woman in the book was a mirror image of her, and all the details she had already seen of that life, and the roles played in that life by the people with whom she was now involved, were absolutely correct. But she could not verify it until the book was translated. There was no record in English and no way the details could have been suggested to her.

In a similar way one of my workshop participants once regressed into a 'Marat life' (certainly not the only person to do so). She had minor but important details which were confirmed the next day when someone on the workshop brought in a life of Marat. The person doing the regression had not, so far as could be ascertained, even known who Marat was or what he did, much less any details about his domestic life. If there had been any hidden memory from childhood history lessons, it is most unlikely that these domestic details would have been included. There was no suggestion from me that she should go back to any particular kind of life at all and certainly not to one in the French Revolution. Nevertheless, she felt that she belonged in Revolutionary France.

Even here though the power of suggestion could be at work in a very subtle way. I have found that people often identified *in their other life* with a figure who was something of a hero to them at the time. They avidly absorbed details of that life and perhaps fantasised what it would be like to be that person. Their soul took on so much of that memory that it became incorporated into their own. As their life was perhaps dull and mundane, it was much more exciting to be that other person. Then when it is time to go back into a soul memory, the subconscious mind, which has access to all the soul's memories, will bring forward that much more exciting possibility, rather than the dull events really experienced. Of course, straightforward fantasy can also play a part. Most children imagine what it would be like to be someone else; they take on different roles and characters in their play. So too do adults, if only they would admit it. It must pass through many people's minds when they come for a regression, 'I wonder who I was; I've always had an affinity with...' If the person carrying out the regression is not careful, this fantasy can be triggered as a past life.

Language is a very powerful tool. Over the last twenty five years I have learned that you do have to be exceedingly careful in the choice of words and the questions that are asked when someone is in an altered state of consciousness. Certainly many people come to a therapist, or a past life workshop, already believing that they were, or might have been, a particular person. They may well have read up a great deal on that person. They are 'pre-programmed' to that particular person. When the man who thought he was Judas came to see me I knew nothing about him. When we were talking before the regression, he announced that he was Judas. I told him he was not the first person to say that to me. 'Ah,' he said, 'But I am the real one.' He went on to tell me that members of his family had also played roles: one had been the centurion who put the spear into Jesus' side, another Pontius Pilate, and so on. He believed it totally. It did not surprise me therefore that he went back to being Judas. What was interesting for me was that he did not live out the biblical story. As he left, he informed me that he was going to join John the Baptist and the other disciples in Wales where they were currently living. The group had to get back together, he said, for a specific purpose. But how much of this could have been suggestion — 'John the Baptist' had already told him who he was — and how much was he tuning into a different reality? It can be hard to tell sometimes!

This is true of so many people. Once they get the idea that they *might* have been someone famous, they read up on the person and embellish much more detail into their 'seeing'. They incorporate the people around them into the soul drama that is unfolding. The exact details of what they saw in the first place get lost unless they had been recorded by an impartial observer or taped at the time. Many of the more sceptical researchers believe that this process of adding to the basic experience goes on unconsciously in most past life memories. When I appeared on television with Simon Jacobs (whose story we will look at later) Simon made the mistake of saying, 'When I researched...' The psychologist who was commenting on Simon's experience immediately pounced and said, 'That is the problem, he read up on it and incorporated it into his memory, then regurgitated it at the regression'. In fact, with Simon it happened the other way round, he had a recurring dream from childhood which he came to me to explore. Then he went off and researched what he had taped in the regression and was able to verify even the smallest detail of an obscure captain who served in the Second World War. Both Simon and I believe he was that person. We do not believe the power of suggestion comes into his memory. But it could certainly come into many apparent memories.

If we look at Jill Mayner's spontaneous experience of Mumtaz Mahal, there could be the possibility of suggestion at work. She was in an Indian restaurant. There may or may not have been Indian music playing. There could well have been pictures of India around the walls, although she says there were none of the Taj Mahal. The waiters were Indian, so was the smell of the food. She had experienced that previous flash-back to the Taj Mahal at a past life workshop. She was, as it were, pre-programmed for a visit to that particular place in India. But why should she go to Mumtaz Mahal? So far as she can remember, no one mentioned the Taj Mahal prior to her spontaneous experience, which began very quickly after she entered the restaurant. She says she had read nothing about Mumtaz's life prior to this experience. She merely knew that the Taj Mahal had been built after her death. She was not even consciously aware that Mumtaz had died in childbirth. As Jill said to me at the time, why would she go into that particular person, and why when she did the regression did she find herself so unhappy for most of the time, if she was so much in love. It was not what she would have expected.

PARAMNESIA

The definition of paramnesia is the illusion of recognising something that has never actually been part of one's previous experience. It is akin to fantasising and may well come from reading a book or watching a film about someone's life and feeling 'This is all very familiar'. An unconscious identification takes place and one makes the leap to 'This must have been me'. It can also account for past life memories, which the regressee describes as being rather like watching a film. What I think is going on here is that someone has a theme from a past life, whether it be betrayal, great love, loss, unavailability or any of the other central themes that run through our experience. When that person hears the same theme or soul story, then there is an unwitting identification with the underlying truth of that experience. But, the details become 'mine' instead of 'similar to mine'. In other words 'similar things are seen as the same'.[2]

If we look at paramnesia in Jill's case, then we could see her carrying a theme around loving someone but being betrayed by them — something which has come up in other past life recollections she has had. She says that many years ago she watched *The Six Wives of Henry VIII* on television but remembers little about it. However, the biographical details of Catherine Parr were portrayed in some detail, especially how she was manipulated into marrying the king. Jill may well have felt a close identification with the figure of Catherine Parr and what she went through — an identification which lay dormant and then surfaced when she was talking many years later about Tudor times. The difficulty here is that the person Jill was talking to also had memories of that life and herself recognised Jill when they met. Psychologists and sceptical parapsychologists would undoubtedly say that the two women unconsciously concocted and then embroidered the story between them as they went along. Only when two people independently have the same experience — which is documented at the time — and then pick out each other from a group photograph before meeting, for instance (as has happened), could we begin to rule out paramnesia and even then, other explanations may hold good.

Jill's admission that she had seen *The Six Wives of Henry VIII* could also fall into the next category of explanation.

CRYPTOMNESIA

Cryptomnesia means 'hidden memory'. It is something heard, read or seen and then forgotten and brought to the surface as 'my' memory. It is a regurgitating of facts without remembrance of the source. This could certainly account for many past life memories. The subject may have read a history book or a novel in childhood and many years later produce it as another life. This has proved to be the case in one or two of the more famous early past life cases where historical novels became 'mine'. (In other cases, though, historical novels have been constructed from past life memories — the work of Joan Grant[3] for instance.) There is no doubt that we do remember far more than we realise. Hypnosis shows that our memory holds scraps of conversations in different languages and whole scenes from our very earliest childhood that we have forgotten.

Sometimes, however, the 'experts' go a bit far when trying to stretch this particular explanation to fit. Bridey Murphy is a very famous past life memory. Over forty years ago, an American housewife was hypnotically regressed to a life as an Irish woman. She spoke in an Irish brogue and used words that were characteristic of the time. She gave a very precise account of her life.[4] A journalist who went to Ireland found this information difficult to verify due to lack of records but at the same time found nothing could be disproved either, and that much of the everyday detail was correct. Many of the points she remembered concerned obscure details, such as how Catholic lawyers were treated at the time, which she correctly depicted as being rather different to the treatment given other Catholics. The journalist's book was an immediate sell-out. The media launched a de-bunking campaign and brought on experts to say that this woman could have learnt all the details in her childhood from an aunt who was of Irish extraction. There were two problems with this. First, the aunt had always lived in Chicago and could not have had Irish memories, and secondly Bridey had only met her aunt when Bridey was eighteen — hardly a child. Many of the so-called expert witnesses got the facts they were commenting on wrong — to the extent that it makes one wonder if they ever really read the original account. And yet this story is usually recalled as one of the great reincarnation hoaxes.

It is always wise, however, to bear in mind that very specific details and so-called evidence can come from cryptomnesia. What is harder to fake are the deep feelings and emotions, especially the body feelings, that can accompany a true reliving.

FALSE MEMORY SYNDROME

False memory syndrome has been making the headlines, mostly with regard to alleged child abuse. Therapists, usually with the best intention in the world, are bringing memories to the surface in their clients which later turn out to be false. I personally have some theories about what might be going on, but this is not the place to pursue my ideas, except to say that for more than one of my clients, the memories of 'abuse' seemed to have become entangled with apparent past life relationships, and that children are aware of things on an emotional level which may not be true on a physical level.

Notwithstanding, it is extremely easy to induce a false past life memory. Many clients are desperate to come up with something. They may want to please their therapist — and it is worth bearing in mind that some people who bring about past life memories are anything but therapists. The choice of words and images, the emotional ambience, the beliefs of the person facilitating the regression can all create a situation where supposed memories can appear. Questions like, 'What does he look like?' immediately fix the gender unless the regressee is sure enough of what is happening to say, 'No, I'm a woman'. But, as all therapists know, many clients will immediately change the picture because they think they have got it wrong. They *should* be seeing something else — after all this powerful and experienced person called a therapist has just said so and the therapist must know best! Not that therapists do know best; unless they are very intuitive and can enter into the picture with their client, most will have no idea at all of what is going on. If a picture is just coming into focus and the wrong word is used, the picture changes.

Beliefs are also a strong trigger and often unconsciously influence the choice of words. For instance, I was talking some years ago to a pop star turned regressionist. He asked me how many people went back to being animals in my workshops. I replied that very few did. He asked if I believed people were animals *first*. I said that I still had an open mind on this but tended more towards not believing it as happening to everyone. 'Oh,' he said, 'I believe it and people always go back to being an animal when I regress them.' It turned out he specifically did sessions to 'go back and find out which animal you were'. Obliging psyches presented details. I am not suggesting that none of these people had had lives as an animal. I feel it is essential to keep an open mind on this — and to remember that shamans and other initiates had special power animal inductions in which they *became* their power animal and travelled as that animal through many experiences and that this would be imprinted as a soul memory. Primitive man — and those Stone Age tribes that are still around today —

performed rituals of identifying with the animals they were going to hunt or of taking on the animal qualities they would need on the hunt. What I am saying is that the overwhelming experience of most past life therapists is that far less animal memories surface than do human ones.

If we look at Jill's experience, it is possible that false memory syndrome may have been activated by the therapist in America who knew the story of Mumtaz Mahal, but her spontaneous recall came first and could only have been embroidered upon. It was not instigated by the therapist.

Possession by Dead Spirits

This is an interesting idea — and one that presupposes that the human spirit does indeed survive death. The theory is that discarnate spirits, especially ones who are 'trapped' close to the earth following a traumatic death, can communicate through people who are in an altered state of consciousness. Sometimes these discarnate spirits are within the ancestry of the person being regressed, sometimes not. At other times they make contact with someone they have known in their life on earth — as with Mrs Warren-Browne and Thomas Seymour. At times the discarnate spirits actually take over the living — and before we apply twentieth-century rationality to this idea, it is as well to remember that 'possession by spirits' has been seen as a major cause of illness for at least 35,000 years.

In one famous and well-documented case, first published in 1879,[5] Mary Roff apparently took over the body of Lurancy Vennum. Mary Roff was a most unusual girl. All her life she suffered from headaches and epileptic fits and seems to have had an extraordinary level of extrasensory perception. She was said to know the contents of letters which had not been taken out of their envelopes, to be able to read books blindfolded and to use 'far vision'. Mary Roff died aged eighteen, about a year after Lurancy Vennum was born.

For the first thirteen years of her life Lurancy was perfectly normal. Then she had severe convulsions followed by a five-hour trance. After that she had other fits during which she claimed to speak with angels or with people who had died. During one of the trance states which followed a fit, she was hypnotised by a Doctor Stevens who kept an account of her case. Lurancy said that she was being plagued by evil spirits and that one of her angels, Mary Roff, wanted to come into her body to protect her from these spirits. Lurancy assumed the personality and memories of Mary Roff. She moved in with the Roff family and behaved exactly as Mary had done, recognising members of the family and sharing recalled memories with them. She had no memory of herself as Lurancy and did not recognise members of the Vennum family. It seemed that, indeed, Mary Roff was inhabiting this body while Lurancy Vennum was elsewhere. Then three months later, Lurancy resumed her former identify and returned to her first family. Mary Roff retired into the background but would occasionally emerge when Lurancy visited the Roff family. Lurancy had no more epileptic fits and carried on a normal life, eventually marrying and having children.

This kind of 'possession' could certainly be an explanation for people who are seemingly taken over by past life memories for periods of time. It could also be one of the explanations for several people going back to and apparently being the same person. If that discarnate soul does need healing, then it could well appear time and time again until a therapist was found who would do the healing and reframing work needed, rather than simply allowing yet another re-run of the life details.

Certainly if we look at Jill Mayner's experience, she is a very sensitive person who has the gift of clairvoyance. She could well be acting as the medium through which several discarnate souls could tell their story and maybe find healing for an experience which has held them trapped in a particular moment in time. Equally, they could have moved on from those lives but still want to communicate their story. As several people were involved in the Mumtaz story, it could be that all the discarnate souls had gathered together to tell their story to people who happened to be spread throughout the world. It seems, however, that an equally likely explanation is that these people witnessed their own past lives. Most people who go for regression are not at all mediumistic and experienced therapists would be aware that a discarnate soul had 'taken over' their client, as there is a totally different quality to the regression when this happens.

GENETIC MEMORY

The theory of genetic memory says that just as physical characteristics such as blue eyes and red hair are carried in the genes, and predispositions to conditions such as to alcoholism or manic depression can be passed on through DNA, so too can a kind of psychic memory of all that has gone before in all the ancestors who have ever lived (utilising something called the *psychogene* — a kind of 'memory particle' in the genes).

So, for instance, a Canadian woman told me how she had visited Norfolk for the first time. She went to a stately home that instantly 'felt like home'. She 'knew it'. When she mentioned it to her family in Canada she found that her great-grandfather Ezekiel (whom she had never met) had been born there and was a servant at the house before he emigrated. Was this genetic or personal memory? She was unsure.

Here again we may be seeing an explanation for some of the mass relivings that occur. After all, in England, for example, it is not hard to go back to a time when there were far less people around and, if the genetic theory is correct, we will share ancestry with very many other people. We will also share memories of war, famine, plague, religious intolerance and persecution to name but a few of the memories that surface. In Jill Mayner's case, however, as with many other regressees, her genetic background does not fit. Her ancestry is neither English nor Indian. She is Jewish and her racial and family memories come from other countries.

If past life memories are those of a previous family member, then it is possible that such knowledge is passed down through the family. When I did a Talk Radio programme on reincarnation, one man who called in said he had had strong memories of World War I and of driving a primitive kind of tank in which he was killed. When he researched his family history, he found his grandfather had died in exactly the way he himself 'remembered' and he felt he had been his own grandfather — quite a common belief, especially where the grandfather's life was cut short by war. Apparently his grandfather had been given the tank-driving job because he drove early mechanised agricultural machinery in his job on a farm — all of which this man had 'remembered'. Again, was this purely genetic memory or was it personal?

This feeling of having come back into the family is quite a common belief. If we look at Simon Jacobs' experience (also see Chapter 4), Simon had always had strong memories of World War II.[6] As a child he had vivid dreams. He then did some family research and found that one of his father's cousins had died in that war — but at that time Simon had no details as to how it had happened. When he came to me for regression, Simon did a very graphic, extensive and detailed reliving of the life of Miles Henry (the cousin) which he felt was absolutely his own past life. When he went off to research Miles Henry further, Simon verified all the details in the war diaries of the regiment concerned. He said it sent tingles up and down his spine to sit there reading a description that so exactly tallied with what we had taped some months previously when he did the regression. This could be seen as a classic case of genetic memory, except that Simon is not in direct line of descent from Miles Henry and Miles' war history was not known to Simon's own family as they had not been in touch with that branch of the family for a long time.

Where the real difficulty comes in though is when the memories are of a different race and time to anything that is in the genetic pool of our ancestry. So, for example, my own very strong memories of Egypt would be difficult to find in a conventional English background. Except perhaps when we look at my grandmother's claim that her own grandmother was a Romany gypsy (something my own mother and my grandmother's surviving sister hotly dispute!) and there is certainly some evidence to say that the gypsies came from India via Egypt. One of my earliest memories to surface was of a Cathar life — and this was well before Catharism became fashionable a few years ago. On my father's side of the family there are French Huguenots; so this could possibly be the source of this memory. But there are others which seem less and less likely to be genetic.

In my view, one of the strongest arguments against a solely genetic inheritance of past life memories is the number of reincarnated Tibetan lamas now being recognised in the West. While most of them are born into western families who have embraced Tibetan Buddhism, none have the racial inheritance and memories that would enable them to recognise their own possessions — one of the trials by which a reincarnated lama is recognised. Nor would they be able to pick out the people who were with them in their former incarnation — which rarely occurred more than five to ten years before they are found again.

However, I must also say that I have found that ancestral memory and genetic inheritance can be a contributory causal factor in the soul choosing to incarnate into a particular family (see Chapter 5).

Brain Disorders and Psychiatric Illness

When psychiatrists and psychologists look at past life memory — or indeed memory of any kind — they equate it with the brain rather than with the mind. For most of them brain equals mind and mind cannot exist without brain. Near death experiences, where people regain consciousness after having been declared clinically dead and then proceed to tell the people around them exactly what was going on, would seem to refute the idea that consciousness is both physical and dependent on a fully functioning brain, as would the ability to leave the body behind and travel to a distant place and then return and report on what was seen there — something which has been verified under experimental conditions.

Consciousness is rarely understood. In the medical model, altered states of consciousness are an abnormal rather than a normal state. With a few notable exceptions like Professor Ian Stevenson and Dr Peter Fenwick, who was a consultant psychiatrist at the Maudesley Hospital in London for many years, most conventional doctors put forward theories of brain disorder or psychiatric disease to explain these 'abnormal' states.[7] Indeed, Peter Fenwick started out with the intention of writing a book about the neuroses, fantasies, unmet needs and need to be loved that lay behind the delusions of people who claimed to have lived before. He was convinced there would be a rational explanation for all such memories. Suggestion, wishful thinking, hidden knowledge, fantasy and fraud were all part of his 'explanation kit'. When he started to research the evidence, he did indeed find many instances of these, but he became convinced that while a great many could be explained away, there were just as many genuine cases. He and his wife now run a reincarnation project which is gathering together an impressive collection of painstakingly researched empirical data.

By the majority of psychiatrists, however, past life memory is often described as a brain chemistry malfunction or attributed to diseases caused by 'faulty brain chemistry' such as schizophrenia and hypermanic states. It could perhaps be argued that these 'disorders' actually bypass the natural protection against unregulated memories breaking through from other levels of consciousness. There is some evidence that hormones and other natural chemicals within the body can actually stimulate psychic activity.[8] There is also evidence that so called abnormal brain wave states exist during regression with two types of brain waves, which theoretically cannot occur at the same time, synchronised *in both therapist and regressee*.[9] There is clearly a great deal more research to be undertaken in this field.

Brain disorders cited as explanations include temporal lobe epilepsy. For many epileptics seizures are accompanied by, or preceded by, dramatic nightmares or apparent hallucinations. Indeed, quite a few epileptics have found that they experienced flashbacks to other lives, and several have been helped by past life therapy. In this medical view of the brain something physical is malfunctioning, producing hallucinations and delusions. Perceptual malfunction is also cited. In the phenomenon of *déjà vu*, scientists believe that the eye passes messages to the brain, which perceives the signals a few seconds before it registers on consciousness leaving a kind of trace memory behind. When the scene is looked at, apparently for the first time, it feels familiar. What this view cannot explain is how the brain can see round corners. As anyone who experiences *déjà vu* knows, it is not only what is immediately visible that is recognised. Several people have told me how spontaneous memories of lives in Jerusalem enabled them to confidently navigate their way around the maze-like streets of the old city. They could exactly describe what would be around each corner before they got there. I have always found it easy to navigate the rabbit warren that is Rhodes Old Town — until I stop and think about it, at which point I get totally lost. It really does feel like operating on old, instinctive memory.

Multiple Personality Disorder

A recognised psychiatric illness, Multiple Personality Disorder (MPD) is thought to occur when a part or parts of the personality split off due to trauma or abuse. The reappearance of a multiple personality may take place spontaneously as a result of further trauma or shock or a similar situation to that which provoked the split in the first place. It may also be stimulated under hypnosis when several of the personalities will take turns to appear. One such case is documented in *The Three Faces of Eve* — a book (unfortunately long out-of-print) which became a film — where two psychiatrists worked with a woman who had three quite separate and distinct personalities — all of them pertaining to her present life.

MPD usually has its roots in childhood experiences, although any severe shock can set it off. Each part of the personality has a separate and independent life and may or may not be aware of the other personalities sharing the same body. Even when the personality has split off in childhood, it tends to grow up as the 'host' matures, rarely staying as a child. It has distinct memories and a very specific character, which it does not share with any of the other 'parts' of the personality — which can number anything from two to infinity. There may be a central organising personality who will allow the multiple personalities to come forward or the different factions may war amongst themselves for supremacy. In hypnosis it is often possible to use one of these figures to communicate, and integration of the other personalities may occur but is rarely easy. In many cases specific personalities come forward to deal with particular situations; in other words, there is an underlying coping mechanism at work.

MPD is somewhat like pieces of the soul splitting off in other lives or in childhood resulting in soul loss — although in such cases the piece of soul that has split off tends to stay at the same age and does not develop independently. It remains suspended in time. In the psychiatric view, MPD is specifically related to personality not soul. It is a product of a fragmented and disordered mind. Many apparent past life memories are attributed by psychiatrists to MPD. They rely on childhood figures such as relatives, nursemaids, friends, or books and films to provide the external source of material around which the 'life' seemingly lived by that personality is constructed. That is to say, identifiable outside material becomes assimilated and regurgitated as 'my experience'.

Psychiatrists rarely consider that a personality might have been brought in at birth, whole and already formed because it is from another life. Nor do they consider the idea that a deceased soul may 'move in' to share the body. But such ideas are often communicated by different facets of a multiple personality. One women I heard from had several such personalities. She did not see herself as these personalities, she viewed them as cohabiting with her in the same body and coming forward when necessary. One of the personalities claimed to have lived two-hundred years previously and quite emphatically said that she had nothing to do with her host's previous lives and that she had her own reasons for using this body at the present time; in other words, this was a 'possession by dead spirits' case. This is typical of MPD. It is not like a past life memory surfacing or breaking through for a short time and then receding but leaving the person feeling, 'I have learned something more about myself'. It is something *other* that takes over the normal self.

If we look at Jill Mayner's experiences in this context, her memories arose not as a result of shock or trauma but during the course of something very mundane. In one case going for a meal with a friend and in the other feeding the ducks with her son. Those memories did not take over her life. She did not become that personality and lose her everyday persona for more than the time it took for the memories to surface. Even then she was aware of being Jill Mayner and was somewhat sceptical of what was happening to her despite the strength of emotion that came with the Mumtaz recall.

Psychically Reading a Place

This is another of the 'explanations' based on an interesting supposition. This time it is that human beings do have a psychic ability which is beyond intuition. It is posited that places hold an impression of what has happened there previously — especially of traumatic events — and someone can pick up that event. It is rather like seeing a ghost. Indeed, part of the theory is that the 'spirits of the place' communicate. Someone who is sensitive to atmosphere can 'see' the remnants of a soul who has lived in that place previously. It may be put down to too much imagination. Yet many seemingly pragmatic and unimaginative people report such events.

'Reading a place' usually only applies to an experience which spontaneously happens when the person concerned is in that place. It is like stepping back into history on the spot where it occurred. So, for instance, there is the case of two English ladies who went to Versailles on the afternoon of August 10 1901 and found themselves back at the Court of Louis XVI. The two women were teachers, well educated and intelligent but had had no interest in French history until that point. The two walked to the Petit Trianon, a smaller palace which was the favourite place of Queen Marie Antoinette. When the two women walked through a small gate, they stepped back in time. To their right they saw some farm buildings looking empty and deserted, with implements lying about. They looked in, but saw no one. They write that the impression was of great sadness, but it was not until they reached the crest of the rising ground where there was a garden that they began to feel as if they had lost their way, and as if something were wrong.

This feeling intensified as they walked on. They met two men in uniform; a pock-marked man wearing a wide-brimmed hat and a heavy cloak, who seemed most menacing; and then a young girl wearing a 'white kerchief dress down to her ankles'. Finally a young man offered to show them round to the front of the palace and suddenly they were back in the twentieth century. What makes this case interesting is that while this was a shared experience and each saw the same thing, they did not immediately discuss it. It was only when they wrote it up in their respective journals that they then shared the sense of strangeness that had overcome them independently. The two women felt that the place was haunted, that these were ghosts they had been seeing. After doing considerable research, they came to the conclusion that the pock-marked man was the Comte de Vaudreuil, a friend of Marie Antoinette and that they had visited the past on a day in August before the Queen and her husband died in the French Revolution. When they made a second visit to Versailles some three years later, nothing was the same. A small kiosk they had seen had vanished; a meadow had become a gravel walkway. There were no strangely dressed 'extras' and the oppressive, almost dream-like atmosphere had lifted. The two women wrote up their adventure[10] and it was dramatised over half a century later by the BBC and then again more recently by an independent television company. It has been dismissed by many commentators as 'a combination of mistaken identity, overactive imagination, and selective memory.'[11] But, nevertheless, it has a strange similarity with other experiences where the person concerned seemed to step back into a past life at Versailles.

I am presently working with a client who had a much more overwhelming emotional experience at the same place and who feels that she has a past life connection there, but she is not yet ready to reveal the details. In her case there is also an element of connecting with a spirit who appears to be stuck there. Another therapist recently told me of a similar experience one of her clients had had at the same spot. That woman also believed it was part of one of her past lives. I have worked with other people who 'travelled back' to Versailles during regression experiences, one to being the designer of the gardens there, which are set out to a precise esoteric formula. Lee Everitt regressed the actor Keith Michell (who played Henry VIII in the television series) to a life where he seemed to be the architect who created the palace of Versailles.[12] Who is to say whether this is 'reading the past' or re-experiencing an event which may or may not be personal? We will look at another example of 'travelling back in time' in Chapter 4. In this case, the traveller was someone who had had extensive spiritual training and who was able to work on healing the karma of that place.

Many, many people travel to Egypt each year and a surprisingly large proportion find themselves 'back' at the Court of Akenaton or Thutmoses or one of the other pharaohs, acting out the star parts in the drama. *Reincarnation International* editor Roy Stemman wrote about a remarkable group regression on a trip down the Nile. The therapists involved, Janet Cunningham and Dr Ron Jue, members of the Association for Past Life Research and Therapy, believe that past lives should be used to illuminate present experience. Dr Jue says, 'I have discovered that the value of past life images does not lie in the literal understanding of the images but more in the metaphorical aspects. For example, if someone says, "My past life was Cleopatra", that's very interesting but what can you do with it? But if I look at Cleopatra as a metaphor for that person, then it's a metaphor for issues of vanity, power, control, seductiveness.'[13] He does not see the relevance of past lives without an understanding of the metaphor and admits to being somewhat sceptical of his own reincarnation experiences.

Nevertheless, many of the experiences Dr Jue had in Egypt were borne out by 'evidence' of how the priestly duties were carried out. Earlier in a group regression in California he had been seen as both pharaoh and priest by other members of the group and experienced that life for himself. Now as he travelled down the Nile with the group and undertook rituals and regressions, he seemed to be instinctively carrying out what he had done before. He says it does not matter if he was Ramses II or some other pharaoh, the important thing was what it meant for the group to be together doing those things. His group was by no means the first or the last to have exactly those same experiences. Maybe the very nature of Egypt, where magic and ritual is impregnated in every stone, means that anyone who goes there who is in the least intuitive and attuned to the past will experience something of that past.

I myself went to the Temple at Philae in Upper Egypt and found myself back there 'as it was' as part of an initiation experience I had had with Christine Hartley some two thousand years or so earlier. Christine herself had been dead some five years — in the present life — when this happened, but, nevertheless, met me in a most solid and real form at Philae, taking my arm and leading me back into the experience! For me it was a very profound and potent moment — a very personal and intimate reliving of my own past.

There are other accounts of people 'travelling' to places sometimes in a dream state but at other times in waking consciousness. My mother, who is not involved in reincarnation work at all, collapsed in the street some years ago and was unconscious. She says she went to Winchcombe, a place she had never visited in her present life. She walked down a desolate road with a crossroads and eventually came to the town *which she knew well.* I went to check this out and it is still exactly as she described, although the road is now tarmac. It is possible of course that she could have seen it in a film or on television; that is, she was experiencing cryptomnesia, but it still seems a most unlikely place to journey while unconscious in a street in Birmingham many miles away.

Symbolic Reliving

I have known people when in regression to go through the most dramatic and traumatic experiences, complete with intense emotions, and then say, 'That did not feel like me; I'm not even sure which part I was taking, and yet there is something about it that seems important because it has so many parallels with my present life.' I believe such experiences are symbolic of issues that are carried from life to life.

I regressed a present-day monk and he apparently went back to being a family man somewhere in the East who longed to go into the solitude of the desert. However, his family responsibilities prevented this. I felt that he was living out something which was symbolic rather than actual — a certain emotional charge was lacking which would have indicated a real life. His arm twitched during the regression and I asked what that was about. It seemed to express his ambivalence about sexuality and emotions, the inner conflict he was experiencing.

He was an experienced therapist and when we looked at the life he said it was a kind of mirror image of what had happened to him in his present life and yet it contained many of the same issues. When he had been a monk for twenty years things changed dramatically for him. Monks no longer had to live 'by the Rule' in the way that they had. He became much freer. Having been a teacher for most of his adult life, he decided to go and study hypnotherapy and move into counselling. His Order was quite happy to fund this. He chose to go to the States. There he fell in love. The woman concerned was younger than he was and wanted children. He did not feel he was at an age when children were a priority. As he said, he would be old before they were grown. He did not have the energy for both a family and the kind of counselling work he envisaged. So he chose to remain a monk. By being celibate, he felt that he could give more of himself to his work — work he had been called to do. Whereas in the 'other life' he resisted the call and put the demands of his family first, now he was going through the opposite.

Similar symbolic lives surface when the issues are ones of self-doubt, sabotage or betrayal, and when there are karmic patterns that are being lived out strongly in the present life. It is often enough to recognise the pattern so that it can be changed, rather than needing to know all the details of the past. Indeed, if the pattern has been created with people in past lives who are now in the present life, it may sometimes be better not to know the details; so the allegorical life is presented as symbol and metaphor instead.

Soul Fragmentation

Soul fragmentation is a difficult concept which we will look at more closely later. Briefly, the theory of soul fragmentation says that, just as a soul can 'lose' a piece of itself either in traumatic circumstances or in past lives, so too can a soul break into pieces and move into different incarnations or a soul can recombine from souls that have been experiencing different incarnations. What is difficult to conceptualise is whether the 'new' soul should be referred to as a fragmented soul or whether it becomes a soul in its own right. For the sake of clarity, I am referring to each piece of soul as an independent soul — that is not to say I believe that each soul will necessarily remain independent. (This 'fragmentation' idea could, of course, answer that old chestnut: How come there are more souls in incarnation now than have lived previously?) From information from the between life state, the usual interaction is within one soul group, but there is nothing to limit the concept to this, and souls do interact with other groups as necessary.

The simplest split a soul can make is into two — rather like Plato's theory of soulmates. The two pieces then incarnate into separate bodies, maybe at the same time, maybe not. If the souls are in incarnation at the same time, they may well seek each other out as soulmates; although, as we shall see, the traditional view of soulmates as two people who come together to make life complete is far from the full soulmate experience. They may also 'help each other out' as it were. I had the extraordinary experience the other day of meeting 'another part' of a soul I knew well. It was an intuitive recognition on my part, which I shall not pass on to either person. But on meeting the second part, I at first mistook him for the other one. Then I realised that their energy and essence was exactly the same. The only conclusion I could come to was that here were two parts of the same soul (there may, of course, be more). The 'second part' had actually been instrumental in getting the first person's viewpoint heard by thousands of people. What struck me, though, was that each independently told me of his memory of another life, as a quite ordinary person and it was the same person! I don't know whether they have ever shared this memory with each other, presumably not, as it would no doubt have been mentioned.

I have in the past met another two souls who strongly believed they were one and the same but just happened to be inhabiting different bodies. They believed this was for a purpose — mutual aid and support in a situation where one soul would have felt particularly isolated. They assumed that they would reunite at a later stage.

This could work in reverse. We may have one soul in incarnation that was formerly two or more souls. So, if we look again at the Mumtaz Mahal incarnation we followed earlier, we could say that at the planning stage of this incarnation it was realised that considerable strength and wisdom would be required by this particular soul and several souls with the requisite soul characteristics merged to become one soul for that lifetime. Then, after the lifetime was over, the souls again separated and went their different ways. This would account for several people having the same memory. The resonance frequency established between the souls — and others who took roles in this soul drama — could have pulled them all back into incarnation at approximately the same time, perhaps to rework or reframe some of the outstanding karma of that life.

There is also the theory of the oversoul and its 'puppet souls'. In this theory, the oversoul is learning lessons through its satellites in incarnation. Each lesson goes back to the oversoul and gradually the 'puppet souls' are absorbed back into the oversoul. Presumably they can separate out again at a later stage taking all the shared memories with them and then returning again with new memories. A soul group can function in the same way, especially if we consider that all such groups are gradually making their way back to the spiritual oneness from which they all stem.

We will look at ways in which soul fragmentation can manifest later, but in the meantime it is worth bearing in mind that soul may not be the separate, individual and independent entity which our limited western perception assumes.

The Collective Unconscious

As we saw earlier, C.G. Jung postulated the existence of the collective unconscious — a repository for all memories and experiences that have ever been. Many psychologists and psychotherapists, as well as lay people, explain away reincarnation memories as arising out of the collective unconscious.

The archetypes that Jung identified are universal figures cropping up time and time again in the human story: heroes, victims, devouring mothers and the like. Indeed, it has been suggested that there are only a dozen or so stories, which are being endlessly recycled with slight contextual differences. I believe this can in part underlie why people are drawn to 'memories' of particular characters in myth and history who carry a strong archetypal charge, such as King Arthur and his Knights. Figures from history can become archetypes, especially when their tale is told over and over again. This is particularly so when they carry the charge of a specific 'racial' archetype. In England Robin Hood grew out of folk memory to become an archetypal hero robbing the rich to feed the poor. His own hero, 'Good King Richard' carried a glamour and goodness far removed from his actual self, and the much maligned 'Bad King John' became the archetypal villain of the piece.

There is actually nothing in the concept of the collective unconscious which mitigates against personal past life memories rising up out of the ground of that consciousness, either in the person who has individual memory of that life or in a person who 'tunes in' to the memory and experiences it as 'mine'. Where the danger lies is in having no boundary between your self and the collective. Without the filter of a strong sense of self, the collective can rise up and overwhelm the individual, whether with spurious memories or fallacious feelings and emotions.

Thought Forms

I have never seen thought forms put forward as an explanation of reincarnation memories — although this is how my Buddhist correspondent believed lamas reincarnated — but I feel that in some cases it is quite possible that a thought form has been created, which then becomes 'real' to the person experiencing the memories. Such a thought form may arise from a novel or from the historical past or from idle conjecture.

In an experiment some years ago, researchers 'conjured up' a spirit to whom they gave a name and a personal history. They thought about him a great deal, sitting together and concentrating on his story. Then they brought in a medium and 'Peter' came and told his story through that medium, parroting back all that they had included in their visualisation of him. With each sitting, the character grew stronger. But initially nothing was recalled that had not been in the original script. They then experimented with adding to the story, and sure enough 'Peter' then reported back these details. Eventually he began to construct a detailed life for himself. There was a very clear development when the transcripts of sessions were examined. There could be two things going on here. The medium could be telepathically picking up this story and transmitting it, or the researchers could indeed have created a thought form which took on a life of its own. Of course, there is another explanation. A discarnate spirit could have been amusing himself at the expense of all these earnest university professors — but let us look at the idea of thought forms for a moment.

All writers know how characters take on a life of their own. Almost every author who is interviewed about his or her fictional work says, 'That was not how I planned it; it just seemed so appropriate for that character.' Films and books which become classics have a special quality to one or more of the characters. They catch the public imagination in a certain way. The story and the character may be reflecting an archetype or simply be so charismatic that they cannot be forgotten. *The Daily Telegraph* recently published a short sequel to the best-selling novel *Captain Corelli's Mandolin.* This book sold by word of mouth; it received very little publicity and yet the engaging tale which has the taste and smell of the Greek island on which it is set was hugely popular. The novel tells the story of a group of people, Greeks, Italians and Germans on the island of Cephalonia during the last war.

The writer, Louis de Bernieres said in a *Telegraph* interview[14] that one of the characters, Dr Iannis, just would not rest; he remained such a strong imaginative presence over four years that de Bernieres could not get him out of his head. Although he had never intended to extend the novel, he felt compelled to add one last chapter to lay to rest two of its protagonists. He described the characters as a bit like ghosts who keep turning up. When I read this my mind immediately turned to thought forms. After all, half a million people had read the novel and were bemused by the character of the idiosyncratic but good-hearted doctor. They could well have wondered what happened to the 'good Nazi' Gunter, whose story is not resolved in the novel, but who featured in the sequel. He had found himself caught up in terrible atrocities and betrayal, which, in the sequel, he confesses to the doctor seeking his absolution.

This is exactly like a past life personage coming forward because there is an unresolved issue for which he or she is seeking forgiveness. As I have said, I feel that some past lives are symbolic rather than an actual reliving. The past life figure is constructed because of the issue rather than having existed as a real personality. It could well be that the character who comes forward is a thought form, constructed by the subconscious mind out of the lingering karmic thoughts. It could also be a figure attached to the next explanation.

Imprinting

Imprinting is not exactly an alternative way to explain away past lives. It is however an explanation of the way in which souls can share memories. For instance, the Sufis believed that as souls left the earth, they handed on their memories to all the souls who were descending into bodies. So the shared memories became part of the incarnating souls' consciousness.

American past life therapist Dolores Cannon believes that if a soul needs a particular kind of experience which is not in its memory bank, it will go off — usually in the between life state but not necessarily so — to the Akashic Record, a kind of library of all that ever has been, and will be imprinted with whatever appropriate life has that experience. It may well be the life of someone famous or someone who carries that archetype particularly strongly.

It is clear from my clients' regression experiences in the between life state that something similar can happen within the soul group with whom the soul journey is being made (see Chapter 5). Other souls in the group will participate in a 'memory sharing' of a life that has a particular learning experience or which is needed so that its consequences can be played out in a future life with other group members taking key roles. At other times, the regressee's higher self will take the soul off to be shown what is needed, which may include attuning to a past life memory which may not necessarily intimately belong to that soul.

What we Fear

When a life, or a part of a life, does not feel right to me I will ask a client to check out if this is what really happened or if it is what they feared might happen. So often our negative expectations or our deepest fears are imprinted to such a deep level on our psyche that we can then live them out *as if they happened*. Clients too may spontaneously, or with a little judicious guidance (not authoritarian direction!) come to see that something did not happen as they feared.

A client of mine went into a regression that seemed rather like a 'soul loss'. The pictures were hazy; she wasn't quite sure who she was. Her first glimpse was of 'a bundle of rags in the road'. She switched from being under a carriage wheel to watching someone who was run over by a carriage — classic behaviour for someone who had died but had not quite caught up with that fact. It didn't feel right, though. It was a bit too detached. It seemed to me that she was putting herself in someone else's place, feeling how it would feel to be him, and then projecting what she feared would be the consequences. I asked her to rerun the scene more slowly but even then it was confused:

> I can see this man. He's dressed in a shirt and breeches. He's standing by the side of the road; it's only a dirt track. It goes through the village, a miserable place; the houses are very poor. Oh, now a carriage is coming. It's being driven much too fast. It's that young fool. He acts like he owns the road.
>
> *continued ...*

> The man is hanging onto the back of the carriage; he's being carried along on it... He's running away...
>
> Now look, the man is under the wheels. The carriage has driven on; it didn't stop. He wouldn't care. The man is lying at the side of the road like a bit of old rag cast aside.

At that point I asked her whether she was that man in the road. Initially she was confused but then said:

> No, I don't think so; I'm looking down on him. Oh, now he's gone, it's the same place but he's not there. I'm behind a tree, watching. Nat's with me...

Nat was the man she had apparently seen run over. As she flipped very strongly into the past life at that point — and indeed died moments later — I left it until later to clarify what was going on. She had been watching a young man play a 'game'. He jumped and grabbed the bar-like wheel axle at the back, hitching a ride. She feared he would fall. She pictured to herself how it would look and how it would feel. She felt in her body what it would be like when the iron-hooped wheel went over him. She also thought about how she would feel when that happened. And, as she died so soon afterwards, those fears and feelings were strongly imprinted on her mind. So when she came to look at that life, the confused thoughts were the first thing to surface. When she was able to let go of that fear, she could take her own place in this past life; this was followed quite quickly by the totally unexpected trauma of a vicious death. Had we stuck with what she first 'saw' we would have believed she was killed under the wheels. I have taken people through a similar death and it was a totally different experience and this helped me to recognise that it was conjecture rather than an actual reliving.

What we fear may also be something that actually did happen but which we have blocked out. I had a client regress to losing a child. He just did not know what had happened to her. She had disappeared. He was afraid she was dead. We looked for her body, but did not find it. I took him forward to his death and he then tried to meet up with her. Nothing worked. He was clearly very frightened and although we tried everything, he could not find her.

He made up an unsatisfactory ending but confessed that he felt that he was making it up. All we could do was trust that when the time was right, the memory would rise up into his awareness. Sometime later he was on a regression workshop and up popped the memory in its entirety. Yes, it was unpleasant, but somehow he had had time to adjust to the idea that it probably would be and so he could handle it. Later still he went back to that memory with me and we worked on healing and reframing it.

In many near death experiences, people who have moved away from their bodies go into a place which resembles hell — or heaven. Spiritualist literature is full of such accounts from spirits who have passed on and who found themselves exactly where they expected to be. Eventually they realised that they were a prisoner of their own mind and moved on into a different place. So often the place was where they feared they would end up — hell or a place very similar to that which they had just left (see Mac's experience in Chapter 3). When we think of the 'hellfire and brimstone' brand of preaching that has prevailed for the last thousand years or so, it is hardly surprising The same goes for other cultures who have accounts of post-death states.

This shows how strong the mind is and how it can carry a picture over beyond death. Imagine someone who is in fear for their life. They picture how terrible it will be when they are caught. Maybe they are a heretic and know what the Inquisition will do. Maybe they are a spy and have heard graphic tales of how spies are treated when caught. Think what would happen to someone who was so indoctrinated with religion that they were terrified to die unshriven of their sin. Then think of someone who inhabits a fantasy world half the time. Maybe they are merely a little child who has been frightened with tales of witches and goblins or the bogeyman who lives in the woods. It is as much a part of their memory as is what actually happens. There is the man, or woman, who has taken a vow of celibacy but has sexual thoughts which take on a life of their own, 'tormenting the devout', as one account puts it. Lilith, Adam's first wife, was blamed by many a medieval monk for the wet dreams that punctuated his nights. She was supposed to appear 'as flesh and blood', riding the helpless (or hapless) monk to a climax. After death the soul carries these memories and they can be regurgitated as 'a life' just as easily as the memories of things that happened.

Identification with the Past

To these possibilities I would add one more: deliberate identification with a person from the past. I have seen so often a personal identification with a past life figure who is idealised — or idolised — reveal the same kind of hero-worship back in another life that I know it can sometimes be an explanation for apparent memories. It is as if that soul takes onto itself all the qualities which are so much admired — or feared, it can work that way too — and internalises them as 'mine'. However, it came as a surprise to me to know that this kind of identification was actually a religious practice.

Some time ago I gave a talk on reincarnation and mentioned briefly how surprised I was that so many people for whom the American past life seer Edgar Cayce 'read' past lives should have had a life 'in Israel when the saviour walked upon the earth'. I commented that while not wishing to denigrate the experience of many devout and sincere people who believed they had been present at that time, it would have been standing room only if all the people who thought they were alive at the time of Jesus were actually in that small country at that one time. I also said much the same thing in one of my books. David Holton, who is also a karmic astrologer and past life therapist, wrote to me to offer his personal view of why so many people personally identified with characters from the New Testament:

> You put the problem in its true perspective and it is indeed strange that so short a (supposed) historical period should (apparently) contain so many souls in incarnation. The astrological charts of claimants I have encountered all contain indications of significant *medieval* karma. The medieval church encouraged the devout to meditate deeply upon the New Testament narrative and to imagine that they were there, experiencing what is described. This is the essence of the *Spiritual Exercises* of Saint Ignatius de Loyola (1491–1556), the founder of the Society of Jesus, and his work remains to this day as the basic manual for training Jesuits.
>
> *continued ...*

> So vividly were exercises of this nature impressed upon the minds and imaginations of the medieval devout that on reincarnating centuries later, as in the present day, they are recounted automatically *as if* the experiences were actually theirs in New Testament times...

He goes on to point out:

> The whole subject of karmic experience in lst century Judaea begs the question as to whether the New Testament anyway is essentially historical or allegorical. If the latter, then there were no historical experiences had by anyone.[15]

Perhaps the same can be said of all past life experiences! Maybe all apparent past life experience is symbolical and allegorical and there is no 'real past'. It all exists in our minds. As far as I can tell from twenty five years experience of exploring that past through regression, what matters is not whether the details of our other lives are factual but how we lived those lives and how we apply the knowledge we gain from regression to our present life evolution. If we see ourselves as a spiritual being on a human journey, then we can learn from all our experiences, whether personal or arising out of the collective past. In the next Chapter we will explore some of those lessons in greater detail.

Notes:

1. Benjamin Walker, *Masks of the Soul* (Wellsborough, Aquarian Press, 1981).
2. Hypnotherapist Robert Millett-Drew in a personal conversation.
3. Joan Grant wrote six reincarnation novels that are available from *Reincarnation International.*
4. See Judy Hall, *Principles of Past Life Therapy* (London, Thorsons, 1996), and Morey Bernstein, *The Search for Bridey Murphy* (New York, Doubleday, 1956).

5. I found details in a book which is long out-of-print and had no reference notes. So far I have been unable to track down the original source.

6. Hall, *Principles of Past Life Therapy.*

7. Dr Peter Fenwick is looking for reincarnation memories and especially for evidential accounts. He can be contacted at Reincarnation Research, 42 Herne Hill, London SE24.

8. See the work of Dr Serena Rowney Dougall, for example, and her book *Where Science and Magic Meet.*

9. See Winafred Lucas, *Regression Therapy* (Deep Forest Press, 1993).

10. Elizabeth Morrison and Francis Lamont (pseudonyms), *An Adventure*, is long out-of-print. Daniel Cohen, *An Encyclopedia of Ghosts* (Michael O'Mara Books Ltd), gives quite a detailed account, p.74–78.

11. Cohen, *An Encyclopedia of Ghosts,* p.78.

12. Lee Everitt, *Celebrity Regressions* (London, Foulsham & Co., 1997) p.60–62.

13. *Reincarnation International*, November 1995, p.10–15.

14. *The Daily Telegraph*, Weekend section, April 18 1998, p.1–2.

15. David Holton in a personal letter to author.

Chapter 3
A Load of Old Karma?

Our deeds still travel with us from afar, and what we have been makes us what we are

George Eliot[1]

Karma is a very ancient concept. It is found throughout the East, in pharaonic Egypt, classical Greece and early Christianity. In the *Bhagavad*-Gita Lord Krishna says, 'For never to an evil place goeth one who doeth good. The man whose devotion has been broken off by death goeth to the regions of the righteous... and is then born again in a pure and fortunate family.' In Buddhism, the *Skandhas* are the 'carriers of karma' that migrate from one incarnation to another and govern the circumstances of the new life. The Persian teacher Zoroaster explained that: 'Those who, in the season of prosperity, experience pain and grief, suffer them on account of their words or deeds in a former body, for which the Most Just now punishes them.' (*The Desatir)* In the Jewish Kabala (the esoteric wisdom teaching of Judaism) it is stated that: 'If a man be niggardly either in a financial or a spiritual regard, giving nothing of his money to the poor, or not imparting of his knowledge to the ignorant, he shall be punished by transmigration into a woman.' (*Yalkut Reubeni*) In the New Testament, the disciples ask Jesus: 'Who did sin, this man or his parents that he was born blind?' (*John 9:34*) While Origen, one of the most prominent of the early church fathers, specifically stated that each soul 'comes into this world strengthened by the victories or weakened by the defeats of its previous life'. (*De Principils)* Plato warns us: 'Know that if you become worse you will go to the worse souls, or if better to the better, and in every succession of life and death you will do and suffer what like may fitly suffer at the hands of like.' (L*aws, Book X*)[2]

Karma is not conditional upon belief in reincarnation, but it is a part of that doctrine. You do not have to believe in previous lives in order to accept karma. Karma means 'action'. Literally, something set in motion *at some time in the past* has an effect at another time. So, karma can arise from our present life just as easily as from a past one.

Karma is often portrayed as negative and 'bad'. It can as easily be positive and 'good'. Karma is, in fact, neutral. If we view karma as a learning process, subjective judgements such as 'good' or 'bad' are in any case irrelevant and inappropriate. As Ina Crawford says:

> Karma is... a constant balancing of forces between ourselves and the world in which we live. It is a dynamic, self-adjusting system in which there is constant feedback according to the manner in which we accept or refuse experience from moment to moment. Our reaction and attitude in the face of the experience is more important than the experience itself.[3]

Karma plays itself out on all levels of our life. We work through many manifestations throughout our life until we learn the lesson, recognise the trigger and learn to respond in a different way, rather than reacting as we have always done. Our relationship karma, for example, does not just happen with those we love — or hate. An employer can just as easily act the part, or a neighbour, or a stranger we meet just once. If at our deepest level we do not feel worthy of love and this is an old ingrained pattern, we will experience abuse or isolation — which may be physical, emotional or mental — in many different ways. We will play it out with our parents when we are young, the friends we make or do not make as children, the teachers we interact with, the relationships we attract as teenagers and the partner we finally settle down with. We will take that old pattern into our work relationships and may well find ourselves overlooked for promotion and not getting jobs for which our capabilities would seem to fit us. All our old power issues will come into play. We have two choices here. We can retreat into our old ingrained pattern — usually involving resentment and suppressed anger — or we can learn how to love ourselves and change how we interact with the world.

FATE OR FREEWILL?

Some people see karma as their fate or predestination, something inflexible and unmoving. It is mechanistic: a pendulum swings, a wheel turns. There is no movement forward; it is an endless treadmill. Karma here is a question of balance, and what balances is the opposite. You are one thing, then you are the other. You do one thing, and you have it done to you. Punishment is meted out or reward is offered without any personal responsibility. People who take this view offer it as a reason (though perhaps excuse would be a better word) for their behaviour: 'I can't help it, it's my karma' is a crutch many people lean on when they are unwilling, or unable, to change. They see themselves as pre-programmed towards a particular action; in other words they always react in the same way to a stimulus. They may suffer in order to make eternal restitution, believing, 'I must have done something awful to deserve this'.

From this perspective, if you have murdered someone, for example, the only way you can atone for that act is to be murdered in your turn. (People rarely, though, I find, look at it the other way round — if you have been murdered, then you could become a murderer in the next life.) However, if you are unrepentant and see no error, in this mechanistic view of karma, you could well murder again and again.

In the view of those who see karma as fixed and unmoving fate, their life situation will never alter. All they have to do is follow the plan that is laid down for them and they will be aligned with their karma.

Other people see karma as fluid and evolving all the time, arising out of free will. In other words, finding a new way to respond rather than acting blindly in the same old way. Choices and decisions made as life progresses mean that the person is responsible for creating new situations rather than dealing with 'old karma' from other lives. From this perspective, if you murdered in a past life, then you could make restitution by doing something positive for your 'victim' (or someone else) in your present life. In this view you might find yourself the child or parent of your victim, which throws up all kinds of interesting possibilities.

The two views of karma are not necessarily mutually exclusive. We can look upon our circumstances as predestined by our behaviour in the past, but allowing ourselves free will in how we meet our experiences opens up the possibility of change — and choice. As the Dalai Lama has pointed out: 'Once you believe in the connection between motivation and its effect, you will become more alert to the effects which your own actions have upon yourself and others'.[4] I personally believe that we are here to change our old stimulus-and-reaction patterns into an action-and-response realisation that allows us to take responsibility for our life and how it evolves.

A Karmic Definition

Definitions of karma run from the 'eye for an eye, tooth for a tooth' retributive law of the Old Testament, through the 'cause and effect' of Buddhist, Hindu and early Christian philosophy, into the New Age understanding of karma as a vehicle for soul growth. The definition that I found most helpful when I first began to look at karma is by Benjamin Walker:

> Karma is the principle of universal causality, perpetuated by one's actions. Every thought, word or deed and desire, has a dynamic quality, producing good or bad results. Some simple act of charity may change a life or mould a destiny. Actions give rise to effects and the sum total of those actions determines the nature, status and circumstances of happiness or misery of a person in his next life, and so on from incarnation to incarnation.[5]

The more deeply I delved into other lives, the more I expanded upon this basic definition and the more flexible it became. I came to realise that thought, a powerful manifestator, actually created situations — and could create 'past lives'. So, we need not have carried out some terrible act in order for it to rebound — the thought could be enough. (Some people might want to look at this thought as occupying a 'parallel universe' in which all possibilities exist and all permutations of our actions exist. So, although in one universe we have had the thought, in another we have carried out the action and in yet another we have not even had that thought.) Equally, if our higher self decided we needed to develop a certain quality, then the conditions would be manifested in which we could learn about it, irrespective of what had gone before.

One of the most negative pictures of karma is the 'live now, pay later' view. This is a charter to do virtually anything, because you can always pay for it later. Another negative approach to karma is the 'do nothing, then you can accumulate nothing' scenario. Inaction can be just as bad as taking the wrong action, especially when you ignore the urgings of your soul.

Karmic Laws

Personally, I find the idea of there being a 'law of karma' rather rigid and restricting, and somewhat authoritarian. My question 'Who has made this law?' takes me into notions of the judgmental Old Testament God who punishes the slightest transgression. Something a long way from my notions of personal responsibility, free will and soul growth. But after much exploration, eventually I came to see karma as complying to three basic precepts.

- **Desire** — we manifest or create what we want or need.
- **Purpose** — what we are here for.
- **Grace** — an offer we cannot refuse from our higher self.

Desire creates the circumstances in which we find ourselves. It is a powerful force. If we want a particular person, or crave a specific substance or a way of life, or karmically inherit a fixed pattern, then we will manifest a situation which brings what we desire most. This manifestation of desire starts before we incarnate; it is something which is imprinted from former lives. As we shall see, unless we are clear about why we are incarnating and the precise circumstances into which we will incarnate, then our basic desires will fashion our body and our situation.

The strength of desire, and how it carries on after death, can be seen in two stories told by George Ritchie, an American doctor who, during World War II, was pronounced dead from pneumonia only to revive some time later to find himself shrouded in a sheet.

After he 'died', he was led by a guide to the astral realm that interwove with the earth plane:

> I saw a group of assembly-line workers gather around a coffee canteen. One of the women asked another for a cigarette, begged her in fact, as though she wanted it more than anything in the world. But the other one, chatting with her friends, ignored her. She took a pack of cigarettes from her coveralls, and without ever offering it to the woman who reached for it so eagerly, took one out and lit it. Fast as a striking snake, the woman who had been refused snatched at the lighted cigarette in the other one's mouth. Again she grabbed at it. And again... With a little chill of recognition I saw that she was unable to grip it... Like me, in fact [she was] dead.
>
> Then I noticed a striking thing. A number of the men standing at the bar seemed unable to lift their drinks to their lips. Over and over I watched them clutch at their shot glasses, hands passing through the solid tumblers, through the heavy wooden counter top, through the very arms and bodies of the drinkers around them... Furious quarrels were constantly breaking out among them over glasses that none could actually get to his lips.[6]

To Ritchie, this was hell. He goes on to say, 'To want most, to burn with most desire, where you were most powerless — that would be hell.' It illustrates the power of desire that fixates on a substance, in this case alcohol and nicotine, and can think of nothing else. Small wonder that it creates a situation where the object of desire is apparently available, and yet is not attainable, but the soul is tied to the place where that craving can, seemingly, somehow be fulfilled. Over many years, I have seen similar situations when people passed through death from a former incarnation with a particular desire firmly fixed in their mind. It was not merely alcohol or nicotine that were craved, however; a desire for a person could be so strong that it held the soul tied to the place or the person. Similarly, some people would be so fixated on suffering (often considered a virtue) that they would recreate over and over again the conditions of their suffering. Eventually, they would be pulled back into a body, only to manifest the relationship, or the craving, or the suffering once again.

The Tibetans are very familiar with the desire realms that exist after death. *The Tibetan Book of the Dead* not only maps the regions encountered after death, but gives instructions on how to avoid becoming trapped in a particular region. They call the post-death states the Bardo, meaning 'intermediate state'.[7] The Realm of the Hungry Ghosts is the address in the Bardo where strong desires reside, and it is these desires that draw souls towards rebirth. In other words, we incarnate to fulfil our deepest desires.

The problem is, we get what we desire at our deepest, most unconscious level. It may be the complete opposite of what we think we want, and reprogramming our old desires may well be part of our life purpose.

Purpose can override desire. Purpose is what we have reincarnated to do. Our purpose is connected to our life plan: the lessons we have to learn, the reparation we have to make, the potential we have to fulfil. Purpose requires a certain amount of spiritual enlightenment. An objectivity that is acquired by journeying beyond death to other, more refined realms of understanding. It can be found in the 'post-death review' that so many people who have near death experiences recall so vividly. Indeed, many people say that it is this post-death review that irrevocably changes their life after their return. But, from experience of guiding many souls through the post-death states, it is clear to me that there is not just one review. Each stage of growth, whether in physical or spiritual incarnation, requires a review.

Once the soul becomes sufficiently aware, the insights gained from these reviews are incorporated into the circumstances surrounding the next incarnation (and, of course, if we take time out of the equation, we do not need to wait for death or the reincarnation of another part of our overall being, or another life, to have its effect in our present life). Our soul has its purpose of spiritual progress, and karmic purpose is one of the vehicles by which it evolves. However, our ego-self also has a purpose. If this ego-self has been constrained by its desires, then spiritual purpose finds it hard to manifest.

This is where **grace** comes in. Grace can override our purpose, especially where this is not well developed. If our purpose comes from our ego-self, then our higher self may well make us an offer we cannot refuse. Grace, as we shall see, takes strange and multifarious forms, and can come in many guises. Often an apparent disaster is actually a form of grace. It is grace that is operating whenever we look back and say, 'If it hadn't been for that... I never would have... and spiritually I wouldn't be where I am today.'

Grace also operates when we have 'done enough'. Sometimes, it is just not possible to follow something through all the way. If we have relationship karma with someone, for instance, that person may decide to leave the relationship or may refuse to grow or change in any way. The karma of grace says that in those situations where we have done all we can, we can move on. We need not be held back.

Grace can also operate in more subtle ways. It may be that we take on a task that is not really ours, or go beyond what was required. If the task is well done (and that may not necessarily mean successfully in the eyes of the world), then the karma of grace extends to some of our other lessons. We have less to do because we freely did what we did not have to do out of karmic necessity. Similarly, there may be an insight, talent or skill that we have not yet earned but which we need for our particular stage of growth. Grace enables us to draw on the qualities we need.

It is grace that is operating in the Sufi concept of souls departing from the world freely handing over what has been learned to souls who are newly incarnating. Those souls can then capitalise on what has gone before. They can take the lesson, task or insight much further than they would otherwise have been able to do.

There is one further karmic law which shows itself time and time again. If we make **a promise or a vow** in another life and do not specify the time period or rescind it at death in that life, then we have to carry out that promise *at some time in the future.* We can be sure that we will meet the person to whom we made the promise or will find ourselves in circumstances which mirror the vow we made. Typical promises are 'I'll always look after you'; 'I'll always be there for you'; 'I'll always love you'; 'I'll get even with you'; 'I won't forget that'. Often-made promises are of poverty, chastity, obedience and fidelity. If you took a vow several hundred years ago, you may well be surprised to find it surfacing in a past life memory but when it does, people invariably exclaim, 'Oh! So that's why...'. (For instance, many monks and nuns took vows of poverty and chastity.) Poverty consciousness can lurk just below the surface of the present life and can ensure that we never quite get the reward we deserve, that we can never allow ourselves to have abundance. We may seem to be the most sexual being and then we meet someone who triggers that vow of chastity. We suddenly find that no matter how much our conscious mind may desire sex, our unconscious won't let us function sexually. Or we desperately desire someone who was forbidden to us in another life and can never quite bring off a relationship.

THE KARMIC LEVELS

Within the three precepts of **desire, purpose** and **grace**, karma can be seen to operate on different levels:

- **Personal**
- **Group** (soul, family or racial)
- **Collective**
- **Cosmic**

Personal karma is what an individual is dealing with and creating. Some people will be on the 'karmic treadmill', a repeating cycle of action and reaction eternally played out, usually with the same actors in the drama. At this level of personal karma, little insight has been gained and the soul is following an imprinted plan. There are two choices here, to go round and round on the same old path, or to choose a new path, maybe to journey on an upward spiral. Yes, the experiences *appear* to be the same, but each time there is a subtle difference as the soul puts what it has learned into operation. As the soul starts to progress, to recognise, 'Here we go again', changes can begin. Once the pattern is recognised, new choices can be made. Then, the tests come. Has the lesson been fully learned, the insight properly grasped? If so, a different level of experience opens up.

Other souls will be on the karmic growth pathway. New situations will arise, fresh players will be pulled into the story as it develops and calls forth a different response. At this level of karma, old friends — or enemies — may have to be left behind as the soul evolves and moves away from ingrained patterns. New challenges are taken up, which may seem like a backward step, but they are worked through more quickly. Blockages are healed, reparation and restitution is made, and potential is manifested.

Personal karma is usually over-ridden by **group karma**. This may be something that pertains to the soul group to which one belongs. In this case, it is usually a choice which has been made prior to incarnation. If the group has a specific task or purpose, individual karma may be put on hold until it is completed. There is, however, the possibility that by the individual dealing with specific personal karma, the whole group will benefit. In which case, the group may well provide the support, or the situation, in which that karma is worked out.

Family karma tends to pass down through the generations. A soul may well choose to incarnate into a particular family simply because it has the karmic pattern required. This karmic pattern may occur at a physical level (as with inherited disorders or certain genetic propensities), an emotional level (a family ban on having certain feelings, for instance), a mental level (ingrained thought patterns, ideology, beliefs), or a spiritual level (a close soul group). Remember that karma is neutral and does not necessarily have to be negative. In Bali, and other parts of the East, it is taken for granted that a child coming into the family will be a former family member — someone who is welcomed for the qualities that they bring back to the family.

Certain individuals will incarnate into a family with the intention of being a lineage breaker. In shamanic traditions, it is possible to heal seven generations back and seven generations forward by breaking the pattern in a family. Such a healing may require a soul retrieval, or perhaps several soul retrievals going back into the past history of the family (see Chapter 5). It may also require a complete break in the family cohesion, so that a new interaction can be formed.

Group karma can also function at a racial level. Certain racial groups do tend to incarnate again and again within their race:

Australian Aborigines, for example, although I have seen evidence of souls who have had Aboriginal incarnations then moving on into other racial groups and, in at least two cases, then returning to serve 'their people' at a time of need — not necessarily in an Aboriginal body.

Several Jews I have worked with have had the experience of going back into their racial history. Sometimes they will feel they are here to heal past persecution or injustice (as with the Holocaust or pogroms), but at other times they will feel that they have perpetrated something for which they need to make reparation. In one case, the person concerned had been a money lender and had caused considerable hardship to his customers if they could not pay. Now, he was a wealthy man (having 'previously' had a pauper existence in which he learnt what it was to be without money). As a result, he worked actively for charity, concentrating on the dispossessed, homeless and financially challenged. He did not see this as something he did merely for his own karma. He was acutely aware of what he called 'the karma of money' and also the 'karma of dispossession', both of which he felt were particularly applicable to the Jewish nation. In working on his own issues, he felt he was contributing to the karmic welfare of his race throughout time.

Collective karma goes a step further. Here we meet the karma that has been generated over aeons of time. No one soul is individually responsible any longer. It is an accumulation of lifetimes of unfinished business, unpaid debts, unacceptable emotions, pollution, genocide, religious intolerance, persecution and ignorance. It is also the spiritual and scientific progress humankind has made, its technological successes and failures, and its creative and artistic efforts.

War is perhaps one of the best examples of collective karma at work. While it may operate on a racial or group level, its effect is collective and felt everywhere. Recently I had to trace the origins and effects of World Wars I and II for a book I was working on.[8] It became clear that there was no one cause, no single event that was the definitive source of the wars. Rather, it was an accumulation of actions in several countries that went back at least two hundred years. People get swept up in war. Whether or not they believe in it or actively support it, the war rolls over them.

Not only the fighters, civilians too find themselves pushed from their intended path. Just before World War II, the psychics at the College of Psychic Studies in London found themselves seeing sitter after sitter for whom the future was blank. There was nothing to 'read'. It was as though time was in suspension. Life had been put on hold. The collective forces had risen up to blot out individual destiny and karma.

Above and beyond all the other manifestations of karma, there is the paramount need for the cosmos to evolve. **Cosmic karma** occurs at a spiritual level. Spirit has an urge to reconnect to spirit. Souls are propelled towards evolution by cosmic forces. New religions that suddenly sweep across whole countries could be seen as a manifestation of cosmic karma, triggered by avatars who have incarnated to inspire humankind to reach a new stage of spiritual growth (but what particular humans or religious groups then do in the name of that religion creates individual, group or collective karma). So too could our attempts to explore the solar system and beyond be seen as cosmically influenced. Cosmic karma is the urge to push beyond the boundaries of the known world. It is also the need for each individual to recognise personal responsibility, for every soul to acknowledge the part it plays in the whole.

It has become clear, however, that collective karma can also impinge on cosmic karma. If a situation builds up in the collective, it can affect the spiritual evolution of the whole. The sequence seems to include a personal level, a family or group situation, a place where that manifests, and a collective pattern involving several such groups all repeating the same or similar issues. Cosmic karma demands that such patterns be cleared so that the whole can evolve. It may be that one such small group can actually clear the karma for the whole, or it may be necessary for a series of small groups, or possibly a larger group to do the work depending on the type, extent and duration of the karma involved.

Karma in Everyday Life

The principle of karma is operating all around us. Even people who do not necessarily believe in karma, and certainly not in reincarnation, experience incidents which they feel follow on from other actions. For instance, someone I know was driving with her husband late at night. They were two health professionals. Almost home, they passed an accident but did not stop. 'We were just too tired;' she said. 'When I look back, it was awful really because we even had a mobile phone in the car and could have called an ambulance. But we just left the scene without doing anything.' Four weeks later, her own car was hit in the rear by a driver who did not notice she had stopped at crossroads. She was shaken but unhurt. Her young daughter was stretchered off with back and eye injuries. People stopped to help her and called an ambulance. Afterwards she said she realised just how helpless she had felt after the accident, and commented how much she wished she had stopped for that other accident. 'After all,' she said, 'if I had done that, I might never have had my own accident. One thing is sure, I'll always stop in future.' She saw it as karma, even though she did not specifically name it that. But it was certainly an abject lesson for her and she would probably have agreed with Madame Blavatsky who said, in *The Voice of the Silence*, 'Inaction in a deed of mercy becomes an action of deadly sin'.

Sin is a concept that arises out of karma. Sin actually means separation, or missing the mark. (In the New Testament the word is *amatia*, which, according to Maurice Nicholl, is a term used in archery to mean 'to miss the target'.) When we are separated from our sense of self as a spiritual being, we are 'in sin'. Usually, however, in religious terms, sin means transgressing the divine law. In other words, going against God's commandments. As we shall see, karma can arise out of the 'sins of omission and commission', but in my view of karma such 'sins' arise out of ignorance or avoidance of our own personal responsibility.

Let us look now at two different stories where karma may be seen to be operating in everyday life (although, as we shall see, it may not be that simple). Stories where, seemingly, it may not be necessary to go back into a previous life to look for the karmic cause.

In the first, a man left his wife after only a few months of marriage because he had found another woman. He took with him the family car, which had been a wedding present from his wife's father. The car, containing all his belongings including his computer and the manuscript for a book he was working on, was stolen the next day. Although the car was recovered, the computer and the manuscript were not. During the divorce, he began to pressure his wife for 'his share of the house' — although he had not put money into the house. When his ex-wife rang him to remonstrate, he was at the police station. His wallet had been stolen that morning.

On a television programme about Aids, a group of community leaders had come together to spend a week with a group who were HIV positive. The aim was to improve understanding of what it was to live with Aids. The group included drug addicts and haemophiliacs, as well as gay men. One of the community leaders (a devout Christian) came across as extremely intolerant and bigoted. He was a local county councillor. He said that 'such people' should be isolated on an island, 'away from decent society'. He saw Aids as a punishment from God for being 'unnatural' (in his opinion, normal people did not contract Aids).

One of the Aids sufferers, a drug addict, explained in very moving terms what it was like to suffer from an addiction, and to know that he had passed the disease on to his wife. The councillor refused to listen and was extremely abusive. Although all the other people in the community group changed their attitude dramatically by the end of the week, the councillor was the only one to remain obdurate and intolerant.

At the end of the programme it was stated that the drug addict had managed to kick his habit. And that the councillor had been killed in a car crash the week after the programme was filmed.

We could see the first story as a straightforward example of instant karma. The husband's actions were 'rewarded' by an 'appropriate punishment'. But this might be too simplistic. There could have been a great deal going on under the surface. He may have been repaying a karmic debt from another life to his wife: he may have agreed to come back with her to give her that experience. He may also have been 'doing as he had been done by'. Or he may, as was suggested by regressions she did to look at the cause of the problem, have been part of an old pattern into which she had once again fallen.

Equally, we could see the second story as one man accepting an offer from his higher self to grow, and the other failing to grasp the opportunity. It could well be that this man's soul decided that his extreme intolerance was never going to change, and therefore opted out of incarnation. But here again, much more complex factors could be at work. He may, for instance, have needed that experience of just touching upon the Aids problem to 'seed' something for his next life. His death at that particular age may have been fore-ordained in his life plan. It is virtually impossible to assess karmic situations, if indeed they be karmic, from the perspective of earth.

TYPES OF KARMA

As we have seen, karma operates on several levels, and there are many types of karma. Some, or all, of which can be engaged by present life situations. Many karmas overlap and it can be extremely difficult to assess exactly what type of karma is operating at a given time. The following pages outline some of the various types of karma, but it is not a definite list!

Shared karma can arise out of past causes and can continue over into present-day relationships. It is specific to the two or more people involved. That is, it is a continuation of an old interaction. The purpose may be to change the pattern, to develop work that had been undertaken, or to provide an ongoing learning experience. So, for example, if one person has cheated another in a past incarnation and the other has allowed him or herself to be duped, then they may come together in a situation which has the possibility of deception but the potential for an honourable settlement. It may also be a situation that provides a framework in which one or more of the following karmas may be worked out.

Retributive karma is the 'boomerang effect', whereby something rebounds on us. We perform an action, and reap what we have sown. This is the 'eye for an eye, tooth for a tooth' level of karma. At its most simplistic level, if we put someone's eye out in an other life, in the present life we could well have eye problems; if we cut off someone's hand, we could have a withered hand, or one affected by a stroke later in life. If we ignore someone in pain, then we may well suffer a pain; if we avoid those in trouble, there may be no one to come to our aid in times of need.

In my experience, retributive karma of this kind is a 'karma of last resort'. The soul would rather learn, and the higher self prefers to teach, lessons in a much more subtle way. Someone who had been an alcoholic, for instance, may now find him or herself counselling alcoholics or experiencing the destruction that addiction in a close family member can create. But, if repeated efforts fail, then it may be necessary to experience an exact retribution.

Retributive karma also has another manifestation. It can be called 'what goes round, comes round'. What we do unto someone else, gets done unto us. We are on our spiritual path, and we digress. Perhaps we become envious or jealous. We wish someone ill, and then find that we ourselves suffer from what we have wished on another. Or, we refuse to help someone else because we are too busy or too involved, and we find that when we need help, nothing is forthcoming.

Organic karma occurs where there has been abuse or over-indulgence of the body in a former life, or is the effect of an old injury or an ingrained emotional state. Injuries and emotions imprint themselves on the karmic blueprint from which our body is made. They either manifest immediately as a physical deformity or lie undetected as a site of karmic weakness until an event in the present life triggers them once again. A woman who was hung in a past life found that she experienced recurring back and neck pain whenever her relationships became 'stuck'. This was directly related to the situation immediately before that hanging.

If we take just one illness, asthma, we can see how it can have different past life causes, which could lead to a predisposition towards over-sensitivity to industrial pollutants and natural allergens — in other words, creates a karmic weakness in the lungs. In asthma, breath can be drawn in but it cannot be fully let out. The gaseous waste products cannot be released. The underlying causes may be physical or emotional. I have seen several cases of asthma where there was severe guilt from a past life. Although it was an emotional sensation, it felt physical. It pressed down on the chest so that the person found it hard to breathe. It was brought into the present life, and in some cases manifested immediately as infantile asthma and in others grew more slowly as childhood illnesses left their mark. In one case, the woman was fine until a death happened which exactly mirrored what had occurred in her past life. It triggered enormous guilt once again. She developed full-blown asthma in days. In another case the problem was compounded by someone having been killed in a previous life by a horse which rolled on her and crushed her chest. The gaspings as her life ebbed slowly away in that life exactly mirrored the desperate attempt to breathe during an asthma attack. Smoke and fumes can also create a similar situation, as can choking. The choking may not necessarily be physical. We can choke on our words if it is not appropriate to utter them or if we are not free to speak them. If fear or expediency holds us back, then we have to swallow our words. There may be times when we wish with all our heart to speak out but someone else will suffer if we do. Such things can also create conditions where cancers flourish and other states of dis-ease prevail.

Organic karma can underlie cases of anorexia or bulimia. If someone has consistently overeaten in a past life, the body image may be so strongly imprinted as 'wrong' that this is carried over into the present life — so too may be the desire to punish oneself for having overeaten. What is seen in the mirror is not the present life body shape, but that 'bad body' image from the past. In the same way, not so long ago, women were supposed to have eighteen-inch waists. They starved themselves, laced their body into a corset, and fainted and swooned their way through social engagements. Similarly, the medieval monk or nun was taught that abstinence was a virtue. Over-indulgence was a sin. They fasted and subdued their body. The new body may well carry such a memory which may result in chronic diseases. If you were poisoned or ate bad food in a past life, and did not heal that condition in the between life state, then you could well find yourself with something like chronic heartburn, or 'gas' as an American friend of mine calls it. Again, the condition imprints itself so firmly that the 'new' body manifests a condition which resembles it.

The conditions that arise out of organic karma are often referred to as illnesses, but they could more properly be called dis-ease. There is something not quite right, something out of sync, something incomplete or damaged about the blueprint from which the present body has been manufactured. A very good example of this was a woman who hanged herself, rather ineptly, in another life. She jerked and twitched for some time before she finally died. In her present life, she occasionally had epileptic fits, which exactly mirrored the movements of her body in that other life. She also had neck and shoulder problems. Problems that disappeared once she had 'seen' her other life and done the necessary healing work both on that body and on the blueprint for her present body.

Attitudinal karma may well manifest physically. It arises from tightly ingrained attitudes and emotional stances. If someone has had a chip on their shoulder in a former life, then this may well manifest in the present life as scoliosis or a 'hunchback'. The person looks as though they are carrying that chip around still. Equally, a hard-hearted attitude may manifest itself in heart problems; long-seated anger may emerge in liver dysfunction; ancient grief in a chronic lung condition. The possibilities are endless.

Symbolic karma occurs when someone suffers from a condition or situation which reflects what they did in the past. So, Edgar Cayce, the well-known psychic and past life reader, said that someone who had a problem with bedwetting in the present life, had been a witch-ducker in a past life. The bedwetting problem stemmed from forcibly immersing other people in water. Now, the person would awake to find himself surrounded by his own water.

Cayce also mentioned that people who were deaf or suffered from tinnitus, should 'no longer close their ears'. Certainly this is something I have encountered across quite a wide expanse of clients' 'lives'. People have been asked for aid or for alms, only to refuse — consistently. Other people have refused to listen to someone else's point of view, arrogantly believing that they knew best. Still others were too timid to reach out to people; their fear kept their ears 'closed'. It can happen at all levels of society: the statesman, the rich man, and the very poorest person in the meanest circumstances who feels 'no one else could possibly be this badly off' and who refuses to recognise that other people share the same situation. Karma would accrue from holding onto a piece of mouldy bread, for instance, and refusing to share it with the person who had lost the scrabble for it in the dirt. The organic manifestation in the present life could be a wheat allergy, which did not allow someone to eat bread, but the symbolic manifestation would be ears that rang with constant noise (the cries of the hungry one).

Symbolic karma can sometimes happen in circumstances which appear from the outside to be very different. Amongst the many people I have regressed to monastic lives, when looking at the reason for entering the enclosed life, several have said they could not bear the suffering they saw around them; so they went into the convent or monastery to pray for people's souls. One even went to get away from someone's constant complaints when, in fact, she could have made that person's life so much better had she listened. So, the real reason behind these apparently spiritual lives was a selfish one, although it appeared to be selfless when looked at on the surface. Now, out in the world, the hearing difficulties also shut out what is around.

There are many similar situations, some a matter of attitude, others of employment. I have seen more than one person who acted as a gaoler in another life imprisoned within a body that did not function well, and someone else who then had to care for one of his former prisoners when she became paralysed in her present life. The working out of attitudinal and symbolic karma can be very subtle at times.

I believe that many apparent past life seeings are in fact symbolic; the story shows you the karma, but it is not necessarily the case that you actually lived that life. In such cases people will say, 'I don't think this is real, but I know exactly what it is telling me.'

Relationship karma is very wide reaching and will be explored more fully in Chapter 5. It operates across all our relationships, no matter how tenuous, and starts in childhood with family interactions. Bearing in mind that what we set in motion in the past comes into our present, our relationship karma can have many strands. We may be perpetuating an old pattern — such as infidelity or betrayal or very deep love — or we may be experiencing the exact opposite as a kind of balancing experience. People who have betrayed their partner in a past life do sometimes find that this time round it is they who are betrayed or moved on from. But they may also find themselves in a position where they are making some form of reparation for that betrayal.

Power issues are common in relationship karma. People get drawn into symbiotic and dependent relationships where one person holds all the power. It may well be time for the other person to take back his or her power. We may also be closely bound to someone by an old vow. That vow may need playing out, but it could also need releasing. We may need to reframe our whole attitude to loving and being loved. It often happens that once we have worked on this in a love partnership, we then have to take the learning out into other aspects of our life.

The karma of work: If in the past someone has displayed a lack of integrity and trustworthiness, has lied and cheated, believed that expediency was allowable because it enabled them to have their own way, honed sharp practice to an art form, or abused the workers in any way, then there will be one kind of 'business karma'. If, on the other hand, someone has been the victim of sharp practice, lies and dirty tricks, there will be a different kind of work karma. If someone has been lazy and feckless, refused to take responsibility for themselves and their family and looked to other people to support them, then yet another kind of work karma is born. If someone is a workaholic, never allowing anyone else to step in and always demanding to be in power, especially when over-exacting standards have been set that have driven others to the point of exhaustion, then a different work karma accrues.

Positive work karma, on the other hand, entails a succession of lives where a skill or ability is being developed. We can look at child prodigies as having developed a high degree of skills over several lifetimes, but many children show early talents and abilities. Whether it is developed or not is often down to parental care — or lack of it — and even that situation may have been set up before birth as part of the karmic intention of the life. Not all such talents are showy; many seemingly mundane skills such as needlework or carpentry may well have been learned in another life.

I have a German client who makes the most beautiful furniture and does wonderful carvings as a hobby. It was not challenging enough for him to develop it as a career. A few generations back in his family is a famous woodcarver. We can wonder whether he carries that talent in his genes, or whether he was that woodcarver. If it was something he had intended to develop in this life, then he might well have chosen that family because the talent was in the genes — although he would perhaps have selected a family where the skill was in his father or other close family member. He actually drifted into being a teacher and a writer, something his father was extremely good at. He was able to develop this skill through his family but despite being a gifted teacher, this was not enough for him. He is now a full-time writer but is looking for another challenge.

Ideological or **coercion karma** occurs when strongly held personal beliefs underlie a course of action which forces, or enforces, that belief system onto others. The force used may be psychological, but it frequently embodies violence in one form or another, and underlies many a war. Such a course of action presupposes that those who see things differently are inferior or 'have it all wrong'. Such karma can occur on both a personal and a group level. Religions are particularly prone to forcibly converting, or punishing, unbelievers or 'heretics', but ideologies of all kinds use force to 'persuade' others to their point of view. Communism, for example, outlawed religion.

To have felt that strongly about something is powerful indeed. One of my friends died recently. When I first did a karmic reading for him over twenty years ago, I 'saw' him as a powerful Jesuit missionary priest, who was engaged in forcibly converting his flock. He really believed it was the only hope for their immortal souls. His will was so strong that he almost mesmerised people into accepting what he said. Mac had me told after the reading that he had strong memories of being that priest — a life which was confirmed later. When I was regressing someone who knew him slightly, she suddenly said, in a voice full of fear, 'Mac's here. He's a Jesuit priest with piercing eyes. He can see right through my soul. I am just a small child and I am absolutely terrified. No wonder meeting him had such a catalytic effect on me.' In his present life, Mac was a powerful healer. He still had that ability to see into someone's soul. When meeting this woman, he had suddenly looked deep into her eyes and told her a great deal about herself. Unpalatable truths, but truth indeed. As she said, 'He changed my life.' In part, his healing work was making a reparation for what he had come to see as using unreasonable force. But, there was something of a contradiction; in his present life, he could be equally forceful when propounding his New Age beliefs.

Mac went through some difficult times, some from choice as he wanted to identify with other people's suffering, but many were seemingly beyond his control. When he came to his second Saturn Return (astrologically, a time of reassessment of how we are doing in our life), he developed throat and then lung cancer. He said it was his karma, from the Jesuit life. 'It was symbolic of all those "poisoned words" he had uttered.' He believed he had chosen the cancer to make reparation and purify himself. We can argue that he got the cancer because he believed he deserved it, or that he felt that he deserved the cancer he got (what we cannot do is judge him for it). Either could well be true. But the bottom line was, Mac felt it was just and right. He chose not to have treatment. Fortunately, he wound up in a nursing home where he was wonderfully looked after and where the nurses understood him — a situation which he said was his good karma coming out (which we can look at as him drawing some merit karma out of his karmic bank account). He chose to take some of the suffering out of the world with him, performing a Tibetan ritual to do so. But, as his dying grew closer, the Jesuit life took over.

I sat with Mac while he was dying. His body had almost given up, but his spirit and will were enormously strong. Although ostensibly in coma from the drugs, he seemed to be holding on way beyond what was reasonable. Indeed, he appeared to be catatonic, rigid, rather than comatose. He lay with his staring eyes firmly fixed on a picture of his guide. When I went into his world with him, it was the Jesuit fear of hellfire that held him. That powerful belief had risen up and nothing could shake it. Despite a great deal of reassurance, he was desperately afraid. In his view, the fires of hell were literally around him in a circle from which he could not escape. A friend spent hours reading *The Tibetan Book of Living and Dying* to him, especially the practice of *phowa* (transfer of consciousness):

> *Through your blessing, grace, and guidance, through the power of the light that streams from you:*
>
> *May all [Mac's] negative karma, destructive emotions, obscurations, and blockages be purified and removed,*
>
> *May [he] know [him]self forgiven for all the harm [he] may have thought and done,*
>
> *May [he] accomplish this profound practice of phowa, and die a good and peaceful death,*
>
> *And through the triumph of [Mac's] death, may [he] be able to benefit all other beings, living and dead.*[9]

We used flower essences and breath work to help cleanse his fear and aid him in forgiving himself. Despite his deep coma, he was able to breathe with me. Gradually, he let go. When Mac died, I journeyed with him as far as was possible. It was quite an experience. First of all, the 'flames of hell' that had surrounded him opened out into a long corridor. As he progressed down this, so his karma was burnt away and purified. The Jesuit was left behind. At the end of the corridor, intense light awaited him. By this time, he was rushing forward with great speed, released from all his fears. While I was able to step into this light for a little while, I had to leave him there with his guide — whose picture had fallen off the wall the moment he died.

In *The Tibetan Book of Living and Dying,* Sogyal Rinpoche quotes one of his pupils who was living with Aids:

> ...when fear becomes so obvious to you, and so predominant, and you feel like you are being swallowed by the fear, you must take your mind in hand... that's what happens in the bardos, when and if you see a vision coming at you that might be frightening, it's not coming anywhere other than from you! All those energies we have kept damped down into our bodies are being released.[10]

The energies may not only be from our present life; our bodies hold past life memories too. For Mac, that 'old life' as a Jesuit had taken over his mind as the cancer spread throughout his body. The karma of coercion was very strong, especially so because he believed so implicitly in it. But in handling his death, he negated that karma.

The karma of mockery arises when we deride someone's suffering, laugh at afflictions, or have enjoyed seeing someone made the butt of cruel humour. Ridiculing or despising another person makes a tight karmic link with that person.

Gina Cerminara, who based much of her research on Edgar Cayce's work, has pointed out that 'someone who laughs at the affliction of another is condemning a set of circumstances for which he does not understand the inner necessity... he is despising the right for every man to evolve through even the meanest form of folly, he is deprecating the dignity and worth and divinity which inhere in every soul, no matter how low or ridiculous the estate to which it may have fallen'. She goes on to point out that, in addition, in laughing he is 'asserting that his own selfhood is superior to the one he mocks'.[11]

Cayce himself told a polio victim that he was paralysed because he had been in the audience in the arena in Rome. He had joined in the mockery of the early Christians, and the chant for their death. I have seen similar cases, people going along with what everyone else is doing and ignoring a small voice which says, 'This is wrong, this is inhuman'. It seems as though the soul tries to make the point, but the ego-self may not be listening. It is too busy ridiculing someone else in order to feel good. In another life that soul may become an object of ridicule or disgust, or may make reparation for past mockery.

The karma of hypocrisy has similarities with the karma mockery. It involves anything from the 'anything for a quiet life' approach, where someone conforms to society's norm without necessarily supporting it, or pays lip service to a belief or act they do not condone; to someone who deliberately acts in a specific way to curry favour or find personal power; from someone who covertly hides their own beliefs in the furtherance of ambition or to be thought a 'good person'; to the person who says one thing in public, and acts in a very different way in private life. So often fawning and cringing are part of hypocrisy. In *David Copperfield*, Charles Dickens made his character Uriah Heep 'ever so umble', His hypocrisy, like so many others, in fact, concealed great ambition.

Hypocrisy can also be a form of debasement, personal or other-orientated. Such hypocrisy has no spiritual conviction, and therefore lacks connection with any kind of inner truth. Feeling so valueless, because of lack of inner worth, such a soul will either debase itself or those it comes in contact with. This definition of hypocrisy is perhaps best expressed as having fallen off one's spiritual path, as having lost the sense of karmic purpose that gives us a sense of connection with other people. Then, in another life, that soul may well find itself evolving through just the kind of life that was so despised.

Vocational karma carries over from one life to another. This is especially common when a life has been cut short, but it also occurs when one life is simply not enough time to do everything. More than one life is necessary as a preparation. Child prodigies may well be continuing an old vocation but many seemingly less talented folk also continue work or develop their skills from another life.

I had one very clear case, a consultant doctor who specialised in blood cancers in children. He knew he had to be a doctor from an early age, despite his family being non-medical. Much of his training had taken place a century or so earlier, at a time when grave robbers were taking corpses for the dissecting rooms. This was how he learnt about circulation of the blood — an idea not yet accepted by the medical establishment. Other lives had educated him in pollutants and subtle causes of dis-ease. Unable to pursue his present life work in England because his ideas were too unorthodox, he moved to America so that he could integrate his knowledge at all levels.

While not exactly karma, **pacts and promises** can have strong karmic repercussions. If we promise to do something, and fail to keep that promise, karma accrues. If we make a pact, we may have to meet its karmic implications in another life.

In one regression, a woman went back to a time when she made a pact with her lover that, should one of them die, the other would follow. Word came that her lover had died. However, when she took poison to join him, it didn't work and although she was ill for a long time, eventually she recovered. In the regression, it was clear that her lover was 'hanging around' and was extremely angry because, as he saw it, she had failed to keep her promise. In the end, he stormed off, saying, 'Well, that's it, finished'. She had gone into the regression to see why someone with whom she could see the present possibility of a very strong and loving relationship kept himself aloof. The lover and this man were one and the same. At a soul level, the man in incarnation now somehow did not quite trust her. We had to reframe the experience, talking to the lover after death to explain that she had tried, but that it had not been possible to join him. They had to dissolve the pact.

Similar things happen when people say: 'Of course I'll always love you'; 'I'll always be there for you'; 'We'll never be parted'. For ever is a very long time indeed, and the promises and pacts may well need re-negotiating as we shall see.

Technological karma arises from ethical choices concerning the use of technology. Many people feel that the fall of Atlantis, that legendary land chronicled by Plato, was due to technological overload. People from that time who have incarnated feeling that they failed then to stop the destruction now feel compelled to combat pollution, campaign against genetic abuse, work to find clean energy sources, etc. In regression several people have gone back to being the victims of medical experiments from that time. Sometimes this has resulted in a long-term dis-ease, at other times it has left a feeling of 'I must prevent this happening again'. I have also seen people who felt that they had been part of the technological failure of Atlantis now wanting to make reparation. No doubt there are many scientists and others out there who want to continue the work they started, but they are unlikely to consult a karmic counsellor.

But, we do not have to go so far back to find a time when the introduction of technology brought about some horrific incidents. One hundred and fifty years ago in England, children as young as four or five were crawling under machines to clean and free them; factory owners were insisting on unsafe machinery being used by tired, malnourished people; chemical processes were used which slowly poisoned those who worked with them. Such things still go on in the world today, not just in 'underdeveloped countries' but in so called developed nations. Every time we collude with this process by buying the products, we share that karma. Half a century ago the world was horrified at the experiments carried out in German death camps, but equally horrific experiments go on throughout the world today in the name of medicine and science. Technological karma is accruing all the time. At all times and by all nations weapons of war are being developed. Comparatively recently, the potential for mass destruction has been unleashed, but this may not be the first time in earth's history that such an event has occurred if regression experiences are to be believed. All of these events have karma accruing to them.

The **karmic treadmill** occurs where someone has become caught up in destructive patterns, situations or relationships. Alcoholism, for instance, can be a recurring pattern. The desire is so strong that it pulls the soul back into incarnation time and time again. Instead of fighting it with will power, it may well take a total surrender of will to a higher power to break the cycle. The karmic treadmill is particularly visible in relationships. Quite often one or other partner will simply not let go. The desire is so strong, that it pulls all the parties back in exactly the same interaction or experience. These recur time after time, becoming more and more entrenched. Eventually the pressure becomes so intense that 'something blows' be it physically, mentally or emotionally. At which point the pattern can be changed.

The sins of omission and commission are karmic. They arise out of 'those things we have done that we ought not to have done, and those things we have not done that we ought to have done'. If we have lusted improperly or been over-proud, then we will meet the consequences in another life. If we have failed to take action, we will meet the opportunity time and time again until we accept the challenge.

Karma is not always active. We simply cannot work on everything at once, and there are certain karmic situations which would conflict with each other, so **karma-in-suspension** has been put on hold while we experience other aspects of karma. If we deal with everything on our plan, then we might go on to some of the suspended karma. It may also be that we need to learn another karmic lesson before we can handle some of our karma. When we learn the lesson, then the suspended karma comes into play. It may be useful to bear in mind here that the lessons might not be part of the present life process. It could well be that, *in some other lifetime*, we make a breakthrough and this affects our present life, bringing the 'new karma' into play.

Karma-in-the-making arises in our everyday life. We have already seen how karma is an ongoing process. We have the potential to create new karma all the time. Some of this karma might be very positive indeed, while other aspects of karma can be self-destructive. We have the choice!

Grace is something we have already looked at, but the **karma of grace**, says that we only have to do enough, and, what is more, we can reap the rewards of our past endeavours. This means that we do not have to remain in untenable situations. So long as we have genuinely done all that we can and are not merely running away from a lesson — which can be difficult to establish — then we can leave the situation with good grace. It can be useful to look upon such situations as an opportunity to neutralise karma by applying forgiveness and then letting go.

If we have helped others in the past, been a karmic Good Samaritan, then we may well have **recompense karma** due to us. Our acts of charity are money in the karmic bank as it were. We can draw on this as and when we need it.

Recompense karma may well arise from a life of self-sacrifice or a situation where we have assisted a soul partner in learning some difficult lessons, sometimes putting our own growth on hold in order to do so. We may have given a life of great service without seeking any acknowledgement or reward. The karma can be personal, so that the person concerned then 'repays' the debt in some way, or it can be impersonal, in which case life seems to offer us an unsought reward or a situation which enables us to make enormous headway very quickly.

Merit karma arises from the things that we have got right in the past. For some reason, human beings seem more programmed towards believing in 'bad' karma than 'good'. But merit karma is another kind of karmic bank account, one with a longer time period. It is all the breakthroughs, insights, rewards that we earn, through our spiritual evolution. It does not necessarily mean we have an easier life, or one 'free from karma'. But it does mean that we will reap the benefit of all that positive karma we have generated.

Redemptive karma is perhaps best described as a calling or a vocation. It is a decision, taken before incarnating once again, to make reparation, to perform a sacrifice, or to clear collective karma. It is not necessarily based on the repercussions of a personal act somewhere in the past (although there may be an element of that). So, if the chosen pathway is reparation, it may not be for an individual act. It can be on behalf of the whole. We could look on Jesus allegedly saying that he had come to take away the sins of the world as an act of redemptive karma, for instance.

Many of the Tibetan lamas are committing an act of redemptive karma when they incarnate once again. They have reached a state of enlightenment that is beyond karma, but choose to come into the world once again to help others move closer to that state. In this respect, it is interesting to note that the high lamas were told prior to the Chinese takeover of their country that this invasion of their ancient land would happen. It was necessary, the Oracle said, so that their ideas could be more widely disseminated in the West. Since that time, several lamas have been identified as incarnating into western bodies, a new departure for a lineage that had formerly tended to stay within its own race.

It may well be that the Panchen Lama is undertaking redemptive karma to bring the plight of his people to the world. The Panchen Lama is second-in-command to the exiled spiritual leader of Tibet, the Dalai Lama. The last Panchen Lama (the tenth) spent a great deal of his life in what amounted to political custody in China. To many observers it appeared he had 'sold out' by cooperating with the Chinese aggressors, who had forcibly taken over his homeland. After his death it was said, however, that he had tried to work with the Chinese to ensure the safety of the people who had had to stay behind in Tibet, at great personal cost to himself.

As the Panchen Lama is the person who officially recognises the new incarnation of the Dalai Lama, it was most urgent that the new incarnation of the Panchen Lama should be found as soon after his death as possible. Agents of the Dalai Lama found the young child in China in 1995 and took him to a monastery in Tibet. Unfortunately, however, the Chinese government announced that they were taking this child into 'protective custody' as he was an imposter and they had found the 'real' Panchen Lama by the drawing of lots. Nothing has been heard of either child since, but it has focussed the attention of the western world on the whole question of Tibet in a way that no other atrocity — and there have been many — has done. There is no doubt that these young children will be suffering greatly through their incarceration and separation from their families. Is this yet another act of redemptive karma on the part of the Panchen Lama?

There is another aspect to this story. If a bogus Panchen Lama, under the control of China rather than Tibet, has to seek the new incarnation of the Dalai Lama after his death, there is no guarantee that the real *tulku* will be found. A chain that has stretched over fourteen incarnations will be broken and Tibetan Buddhism destroyed. Such an event would greatly benefit China. It will not be the first time political expediency will have destroyed a belief in reincarnation. If an apocryphal story is to be believed, Christianity followed the tenets of reincarnation until the wife of the Emperor Justinian in the sixth century suddenly realised that she might have to come back to pay for her misdeeds. It is said that she persuaded her husband to support the anathema against Origen, which officially ended the Christian church's belief in the pre-existence of the human soul. It was Origen who said:

> The soul has neither beginning nor end... Every soul... comes into this world strengthened by the victories or weakened by the defeats of its previous life. Its place in the world as a vessel appointed to honour or dishonour is determined by its previous merits or demerits. Its work in this world determines its place in the world which is to follow this... (*De Principils*)

The Christian Church's answer was, 'If anyone assert the fabulous pre-existence of souls, and shall assert the monstrous restoration which follows from it: let him be anathema.' Political expediency may well be a whole karma in its own right. It has certainly been practised often enough down the centuries.

Genetic or inherited patterns may well be karmic. As Craig C. Downer says, '...the genetic stamp of heredity is the manifestation of the acquired abilities of the individual, of the lessons learned from all his past experiences.'[12] Genetic memory encodes ancestral experience, but it also provides a framework for an incarnating soul's experience. Within that framework, the genetic instinct is manipulated and directed by the soul according to the soul's need.

While not necessarily 'personal karma', genetic and inherited patterns often belong to a family group and may be taken on by an individual for a variety of karmic reasons, some of which can explain why, while all individuals within a family with an inherited genetic problem have a propensity for that condition to manifest, it is usual for only one or two members of the family in any generation to actually manifest it. In other genetic disorders, it requires two people to come together who carry the defective gene in order for a third person to be born with the physical manifestation of that problem. So, if an incarnating soul wanted to experience a certain condition, then he or she would choose a family that carried that propensity.

In one case, for instance, a haemophiliac felt that he chose to be incarnated into his family so that he could be part of research into the condition which would lead to a cure (redemptive karma), but he was also aware that in another lifetime, he had shed considerable blood and wanted to 'atone for that' (retributive or organic karma). The blood shedding had been ideologically based, so he could also have ideological or coercion karma. He did not feel he was being punished, either by himself or an outside agency. He felt that, as part of his unfolding pattern, he was going through a cycle of incarnations, in one of which he needed to have haemophilia. It was his karmic choice.

Phobias and fears may well have a karmic cause, or be firmly rooted in another life. Phobias are karma in the sense that they have a cause, which has had a result: the phobia. Uncovering that cause may well heal the phobia.[13] Fears are slightly different. Fear can arise out of what we have done in the past or out of what has been done to us. We can carry a fear over from life to life. So, fear is also karma, but there are as many reasons behind that fear as there are fears themselves. We will look at this more closely later

If you feel that you are always misunderstood, that people twist your words or ignore your opinions, or that you are never there when that important phone call comes, or that significant letters go missing, then you are probably suffering from **communication karma**. The ability to speak your truth is essential for your soul's growth and yet there are many situations which prevent that. It is also possible to weave such a web of lies and deceit that it can trap both the soul who wove it and those who become caught in it for several lifetimes. We have already looked at hypocrisy, saying one thing but meaning or doing another, and at mockery, making fun of someone else. We have seen what can happen if you coerce someone to your point of view or subvert another. We have seen what happens when you do not hear the pleas of those who cry for aid. However, there are also many opportunities in other lives to pervert the truth or justice, to lie under oath, to be economical with the truth, to speak about someone behind their back, to break an oath or simply evade being straight with someone. All of these situations and more can lead to communication karma.

In a regression to find out why important letters always went astray, there was a neat piece of retributive karma. The man had been a mail coach driver. One day it was particularly miserable, wet and very cold. It would clearly snow before nightfall. He was taking his coach over high moors and knew it would be easy to get stuck. He was supposed to deliver an important package to a house that lay somewhat off his route. It would add many miles to his journey. He looked at this package, weighed up the inconvenience against the thought of getting home, and tossed it into a ditch. The loss of that package had severe repercussions in the life of the family who awaited it. His conscience was pricked when he heard the result. In his present life, he manifested the karma with amazing exactitude. Despite being sent recorded delivery, his packages would go astray. Compensation was not what he required. He needed the contents — his manuscripts — to reach their destination. In his regression he had a great deal of reframing and reparation to do before he could release that karma, but it worked. His book was a best seller.

Having talked with — and regressed — many authors, I begin to think that **publishing karma** is a karma in its own right. Many have found that they are carrying over something which created blocks or difficulties. One, for instance, had published a very revolutionary and contentious broadsheet and had been imprisoned as a result. Whenever in her present life she was about to publish, she would become ill with a rerun of the 'prison fever' she had developed in that other life. Another had produced a salacious scandal sheet with all the latest gossip and felt that he was reaping the karma of that as he was finding it extremely difficult to be taken seriously as a writer. As we will see in another chapter, I had to go back and revoke a vow of silence that was affecting my own writing. I have also found that a desperate desire to write often stems from having been prevented from doing so in the past — sometimes by force, but at other times by lack of education and the means to communicate.

The karma of place is a situation where a specific place holds an imprint of a karmic condition. Such a place may be a house, a town, a village or a whole country. People who reside there will be affected by the karma — and may well be drawn to that particular place to work out that karma for themselves.

The karma of place is nothing new. Four-and-a-half-thousand years ago an Egyptian text informed readers that:

The miserable Aam it fares ill with the place wherein he is...
He has been fighting ever since the time of Horus...[14]

The Aam were an Asiatic people who inhabited Southern Palestine, a pretty troubled land even in those far off days. They were traditional enemies of the Egyptians, who fought more than one war on that territory. Not so long after the text had been written, Palestine would be invaded by the Hebrews, who believed it to be their 'promised land'. Once they established themselves (having fought the indigenous people for supremacy), the land would be invaded by the Babylonians, and the Hebrews would be taken into exile. Historically speaking, they had not been back in occupation long before the Romans took over. The fight over the land of Palestine has continued ever since, with all sides claiming it as of right. Feelings run high, emotions are powerfully engaged, bloodshed is everywhere. The Israelites saw it as 'the promised land', the Egyptians as a cursed land.

It was indeed a land that fared ill. Those who fought over it, reaped the karma of the place. Nebuchadnezzar, the Babylonian king who took the pick of the Jews into exile, had a powerful dream. The priestly Daniel — described in the King James version of the bible as a 'magician' — was called upon to interpret the dream. He warned the king of what would befall him and, sure enough:

> ...he [Nebuchadnezzar] was driven from men, and did eat grass as oxen, and his body was wet with the dew of heaven, till his hairs were grown like eagles' feathers, and his nails like birds' claws. (Daniel 4:33)

Eventually, the king was reinstated in his land, but we could look upon his fall, in which according to Daniel the god of the Jews played no small part, as reaping the karma he had sown. We could also look on it as a shamanic initiation, a completely different kind of karma. The Jews he took into exile were treated well; indeed, they were selected for their excellent qualities and their learning, and so were valuable assets. So we could see the king as being inflicted by the 'bad karma' of the place or as offering the Jews an opportunity to grow away from that 'cursed land'. (In Chapter 4 we will look at one woman's experience with another 'cursed place': Dachau.)

Reward and Punishment?

It has been said that karma may be a 'murderer's charter'.[15] In other words, someone can do a deed in one life, and then come back and pay for it again — and again if necessary. It is rather like the medieval malfeasant who sinned and sinned, and then bought an indulgence on his death bed, had perpetual masses said for his soul, and died happy in the belief that his immortal soul was safe. Personally, after having witnessed so many regressions, I think he was in for a big surprise. Similarly, anyone who murdered or committed some other act in the full knowledge that it would have karmic consequences could well find that karma is much more subtle and wide-ranging than he anticipated.

In my view, the incoming soul may be 'loaded with karma' when it arrives on earth. The conditions into which it incarnates, the people surrounding it, and the attitudes and patterns it brings with it, will shape that person's life. What ultimately directs how that life will develop, however, is free will. Free will is the ability to choose — to make a decision without compulsion, reaction or fear. Someone operating from free will is not afraid to risk making a mistake, simply because in this view of karma there is no such thing as a 'mistake', only a learning experience. On the other hand, someone who understands about karma is not about to do anything that will create negative karma to be dealt with in the future, which is why the idea of karma being a 'murderer's charter' (or anyone else's charter, for that matter) is absurd.

Notes

1. Quoted in Head and Cranston *Reincarnation: an East-West Anthology* but no attribution given as to source. A similar sentiment: 'Our deeds determine us, as much as we determine our deeds' is found in Chapter 18 of George Eliot's *Adam Bede*.

2. All the quotes in this section are taken from Head and Cranston, *Reincarnation: an East-West Anthology* and associated sources.

3. Ina Crawford, *A Guide to the Mysteries* (London, Lucis, 1990).
4. The Dalai Lama in a television interview in 1996.
5. Benjamin Walker, *Masks of the Soul* (Wellingborough, Aquarian Press, 1981), p.21.
6. George Ritchie, *Return from Tomorrow* (Eastbourne, Kingsway Publications, 1978), p.57–61.
7. Venerable Lama Lodo, *Bardo Teachings: The Way of Death and Rebirth* (New York, Snow Lion Publications, 1982).
8. Judy Hall, *The Hades Moon* (Maine, Samuel Weiser Inc, 1998).
9. Sogyal Rinpoche, *The Tibetan Book of Living and Dying* (London, Rider, 1992), p.215–6.
10. *Ibid*., p.384.
11. Gina Germinara, *Many Mansions* (New York, Signet, 1950) p57ff.
12. Craig C. Downer, *The Spiritual Evolution: A Book on Reincarnation and Evolution* (New York, Vantage Press, 1981).
13. See Judy Hall, *Principles of Past Life Therapy* (London, Thorsons, 1996).
14. Sir Alan Gardiner, *Egypt of the Pharaohs* (Oxford University Press, 1966) p.37.
15. Ongoing correspondence in *Reincarnation International*, issues 9, 11 and 12.

Chapter 4
Some Other Time, Some Other Place?

Have ye not confessed to a feeling, a consciousness strange and vague
That ye have gone this way before and walk again your daily life...
Hath not at times some recent friend looked out, an old familiar,
Some newest circumstance or place teemed as with ancient memories...

Martin Tupper[1]

Whenever something becomes fashionable there is a potential for tragedy and error. As more and more people develop an interest in past lives, so a larger number of people and organisations cater for that need. Past life workshops are becoming increasingly popular. There are people leading large-group workshops who have years of experience. There are individual therapists who have been around for a long time. However, many of the people now advertising themselves for past life exploration are untrained or have a year or two's experience at most. Few realise just how damaging a day trip into the past can be, even in the hands of an experienced guide. As psychotherapist Mary Swainson says, 'Idle curiosity is a dangerous incentive.'[2]

Day Tripper to the Past

Some years ago I went to one of the first past life therapy seminars in England. Two hundred and fifty people were told to write down three places which they particularly feared or disliked. Then, with a snap of the fingers, they were told to pick one of those places and go back to it. After fifteen minutes or so, we were told to return.

I played safe. With more than ten years experience behind me, I knew there was no way I was going into something which could clearly be traumatic unless I was in a one-to-one situation with an experienced therapist. I picked India, a place I have no particular fear of, although whenever my partner suggested we visit India, I had no enthusiasm; there was always somewhere else I would rather go. I see pictures of India, especially the buildings and say, 'Yes, that looks really interesting' and then off I go to Egypt again or somewhere else that catches my attention much more strongly. In the mass regression, I was rather surprised to find myself not in India but in Tibet. I feel a great affinity with the Tibetan people and have met some extraordinary Tibetans away from their homeland but had not considered going there. I have always felt very strongly that the Chinese invasion of Tibet was wrong and stories of the extreme suffering the Tibetan people, especially the monks and nuns, undergo under Chinese rule always brings tears to my eyes, but I had had no inkling of any life in Tibet. Nevertheless, there I was, standing in a red-walled Tibetan monastery, quite young and feeling absolutely and utterly bored. Strangely enough my partner's brother was also there, equally bored. It was an endless round of chanting, learning and very little fun.

I have to say I was not deeply into this regression and it never felt like 'my life'. There was no gut recognition of 'this is me'. I had never felt that I knew my partner's brother in another life and this did not feel like a genuine past life connection. Only the boredom felt real. I was viewing a film which was of some interest but no particular relevance. When we came out of the regression I told my partner and he laughed and said that his brother always said he would hate to be in a monastery like that because it would be so boring.

I thought nothing more about it. We went downstairs for coffee and there was a client of mine, looking extremely agitated. 'Thank God you are here,' he said, 'the man next to me went back to having both legs shot off and is in shock. I've talked him out of it a bit by doing what I did with you when I had a regression, but he still can't feel his legs. I couldn't catch the attention of anyone on the stage and they've gone for coffee. Please come and help.' Off I went to talk the guy back, complete with legs. We had a lot of healing to do in a very short time. Since then I have met several people who were also at that seminar and had similar experiences. Some felt the ill effects for years before they found a therapist who could help. Others were brought into past life therapy by finding that they could talk someone back instinctively. When I talked recently to the man who ran the seminar, he said he never does mass regressions now. I am not surprised. He was an experienced therapist but did not realise quite what he had set in motion.

I have always tried to avoid mass regressions. On two occasions I have found myself in a situation where my limit on numbers has been ignored. On walking into the room I was faced with sixty eager and expectant faces. On such occasions I find myself choosing my words very carefully indeed, 'Go back to a happy life, one of joy and fulfilment...' Nevertheless, one or two people have gone into traumatic events which have needed work afterwards. I spent an hour out in the car park at one of the venues, as this was the only place where we had the space to deal with what had come up. Earlier that day someone had said to me, 'I was asked if it was safe to go to your demonstration. I said I'd had two years' experience as a past life therapist and I wouldn't run a group like that.' My reply was that I had had twenty year's experience and I wouldn't do a group like that given the choice! The organisers had sold treble the number of tickets I had specified. I have never done one since.

Past Life Perils

There can be problems with both spontaneous recall and group recall that are brought about by someone who is either too inexperienced or who simply has too many people to deal with. It happens in one-to-one sessions too. Many hypnotists, and some hypnotherapists, believe that simply rerunning a memory and coming out of it will heal any trauma involved. But that is emphatically not so. Nor is simply denying that a past life is taking place enough to banish it — as happens when the therapist does not believe in past lives or finds something too traumatic to handle. It may disappear back below consciousness again, but it will fester there until dealt with. As we shall see, traumatic memories need reframing and healing, in the past life and in the post-death state. Emotional entanglements and blockages need a release. Such incidents leave an imprint on the etheric body which can result in dis-ease, whether emotional or physical. If a memory is stirred up, then it needs to be worked with.

A typical example of 'something being stirred up but not dealt with' came when I went up north to work. I was scheduled to teach a training course for potential past life therapists and was offering a past life workshop at the weekend. Another past life healer, a very charismatic figure, then organised his own workshop the weekend before. Naturally this affected the bookings for my workshop. However, I decided to go ahead because we had the past life therapy training group already set up and the organiser for my workshop said she had a strong feeling I would be needed, as she had been to one of his earlier workshops.

By the time I arrived, the other workshop had taken place. I had said I could be available for one-to-one sessions the day before the training commenced. I found I had a queue! Everyone was coming with unfinished business from the workshop. The last woman, whom I had squeezed in because she sounded so desperate, told me that the people on the workshop had been told first of all that they were part of 'the Wallace-group' — the book and film about William Wallace had just come out — and then that they had been at the foot of the cross when Jesus was crucified. She had coped with her 'memories' of being Mrs William Wallace — unknown to her she was the third that day — but was finding having been Mary Magdalene very difficult. Indeed, she had phoned me because she was suicidal and had found herself deliberately slipping under the water of her bath. She had had to leave her car at home and take a taxi because she felt so unsafe. She had first phoned the workshop leader, who was still in town and asked for a healing session with him but had been refused. (He described her as too emotionally attached to him.) 'Well then,' she said, 'I shall go for a session with Judy.' 'I wouldn't advise you to do that,' he said, 'You have obviously done quite enough past life work for a while, take a rest.'

We spent two hours working with her picture of herself clutching the foot of the cross. She was sobbing and sobbing. Her world had ended, she too wanted to die. The only way to work with her was to enter totally into her reality, in other words, to assume that she was Mary Magdalene. Eventually I helped her to move on — incidentally producing an interesting 'confirmation' of the heretical theory that Mary Magdalene and Jesus were married.

(She was unaware of this theory until I gave her details afterwards.) We then healed and reframed the image. She was sure she had been Mary Magdalene, just as so many other people have been. The workshop leader initially encouraged her in this, and then failed to support the result, which was more than she could cope with — especially as in her, and quite probably in his, eyes he was the Christ, her partner for much more than that one life. (He did actually claim to be William Wallace and therefore her 'husband'.)

What is interesting is both these men, William Wallace and Jesus Christ, died for a cause they believed in. By seeing herself as a woman who was abandoned by her men, it seems that she was setting in motion a pattern of not being supported by a man — epitomised by the workshop leader — when she needed support. In all cases she had been left to cope with the residual emotional trauma alone. When I worked with her, we healed that pattern and connected her to her higher self from which she could gain the support she needed. Had she been left without help following the workshop, however, she could well have succumbed to that initial desire for suicide.

A Fantasy in Fancy Dress?

There are dangers and delusions in past life work. I know them all too well having led workshops for so many years. It is so easy to get caught up in 'this is who I was' and forget what that 'memory' is telling you. Sometimes it is hard to tell whether it is delusion or fact. Is someone merely enjoying a fantasy in fancy dress, or is there something more? As we have already seen, this is especially hard to determine when someone is not the only person to have that memory. But, as we will see, there are also past life experiences which are extremely valuable. The difficulty can be in recognising which is which.

A good friend of mine, an American with little knowledge of English history, came to one of my workshops. She went back into what we came to call 'the oranges lifetime'. She had detailed memories of Nell Gwyn, courtesan to Charles II. As so much was left unfinished in the workshop, she followed it up with two one-to-one sessions in which much more material emerged and several of her present life hang-ups were explained. When she researched the story, which she had written down in great detail immediately following the regressions, she concluded, 'I just know it was me. It is all there.' I sent her a tape of a TV programme on Nell; it confirmed her feelings. She kept saying: 'Look at her portrait, this is me.' There was certainly a close resemblance. She was emphatic that she had read nothing about Nell Gwyn before that regression and that she had gone back to a genuine past life. The problem was, it gave her a sense of being 'someone special' — which she may well have been, of course. Certainly all the emotional feeling was there and a great deal of historically accurate information. It was nothing, however, to the amount of information another 'Nell Gwyn' had already brought back from the past.

In a chapter in *Encounters with the Past* entitled 'Read or Remembered?'[3] Peter Moss recounts the regressions Liverpool housewife Edna Greenan did with hypnotist Joe Keeton (who conducted over eight thousand regressions during his long career). In over eighty hours of regression Edna 'became' Nell Gwyn repeatedly and with great congruency. She could consistently return to any period in Nell's life and accurately recount what was going on at that time. She would assume the mood of that moment, the memories the historical Nell would have had, and the ambience around her. As the author says, analysing this information was a formidable task. There were inaccuracies, but there was also the most minutely accurate detail from birth to death. Much of the material could not be substantiated either way. Edna Greenan left school at fourteen. She categorically states that she has never read a book or seen a film or TV play about Nell Gwyn. Joe Keeton checked this under hypnosis by asking her to give him details of everything she had read or seen. There was nothing. There is just so much detail that the alternative explanations, some of which Peter Moss considers, simply do not fit. As he says, it remains one of the most enigmatic of all regressions, 'unless one more or less whole-heartedly accepts that some element of the immensely strong personality that was once Eleanor Gwyn is now embedded in Edna Greenan.'[4] Is it any coincidence, I wonder, that the American Nell was equally strong-minded? Did they both inherit a part of Nell, or is it some other phenomenon entirely?

DOING IT YOURSELF

I find the proliferation of 'do-it-yourself' past life tapes and books rather alarming. These seem to me to cater to the curiosity level and to ignore the dangers that can lie in wait for the unwary. Several suggest that the subconscious mind or the higher self will only give what can be coped with. But! The subconscious mind's definition of what we can cope with may not accord with our conscious mind's, and does not necessarily take into account that we will be alone and vulnerable. It is our strongest and most traumatic memories that lie closest to the surface waiting to break out. Despite the care with which some of these tapes are recorded, and the effort to put healing in place afterwards, it is all too easy to be so deeply immersed in the life which has emerged that you miss being talked out of it. I have used the following story before[5] but make no apologies for using it again because it is still the most graphic example I know of why one should not take unchaperoned trips into the past, especially out of sheer curiosity:

> I put on the tape and lay on my bed. It took me on a journey and eventually into another life. Everything was going along fine until suddenly a tree fell on me. I was paralysed, couldn't move. The pain was excruciating. I shouted and shouted for help until I was exhausted. No one came.
>
> Then I realised that somehow the end of the tape had come and gone. I had no idea how to get back to my present life. I was trapped. I prayed and prayed for help. I managed to reverse the process I had gone through to get there. That brought me back into my bedroom. I opened my eyes.
>
> But, when I tried to move to my horror I was still paralysed. My chest hurt, I could not feel my legs at all, and I could not speak. I lay there for hours and hours. Daylight faded. I cried and cried, and could not wipe the tears away.
>
> Suddenly there was a knock on the door. I realised it was a friend with whom I was supposed to be going
>
> *continued ...*

out for the evening. I tried to shout but nothing came out. The house was in darkness. Would she think I had simply forgotten and gone out?

Fortunately she had a sixth sense that something was wrong. She came in through the back door and shouted for me. She came up into my bedroom and saw me there on the bed. I managed to indicate the tape recorder with my eyes.

She ran the tape back and played the end. It made no difference. So she talked me through it step by step. I had to go back into that life and tell her what was happening. She told me to ask my guide to move the tree. But I was still paralysed. She told me to leave that body behind, to let go of the sensations. To come back into my present life whole and healed. Gradually I was able to let go and the feeling began to come back into my body. She massaged me and then brought me a cup of tea.

I sobbed and sobbed as I told her how lonely and helpless I had felt stuck on the bed. It seemed like an eternity. I don't think I will ever forget that experience, it has scarred me for life.

The woman who did that regression was highly intelligent and aware, she had had years of experience of working in a therapeutic setting, but she still got stuck simply because of the deep emotion and trauma of her situation. She was fortunate that her friend was intuitive enough to help. Had she not been able to, the experience would probably have faded gradually; the woman would most likely have come out of it after a night's sleep, but she might well have been physically as well as emotionally scarred for life, as she would have done no healing work on her organic karma. Her 'etheric blueprint' would have carried that paralysis over to the present life and by remembering the trauma, she could well have activated a physical condition as a result. She would doubtless have developed back and leg trouble — sciatica or disc problems that affected her legs would be a hot contender, as would the more subtle condition of fibro-mialgia. She could well have found herself stuck in her life too — a kind of symbolic karma occurring in which she could not move forward. She had reactivated a deep feeling of helplessness and powerlessness as she lay there unmoving for so long with no one to hear her call — something which she said rang bells for much of her present life. And, of course, in her present life she had the added discomfort of not being able to call out for help as she had lost her voice. That could well have developed into throat problems and a difficulty in speaking out had it not been cleared.

Triggering the Past

Regressions do not have to be deliberately induced to be traumatic. I was on a course with a Tibetan lama who is an incarnation of the healing buddha. For once I was 'off duty', there purely for my own learning — or so I thought! One afternoon there was an exhibition of Cham dancing, a sacred dance form which until the exile from Tibet had only been performed in the monasteries. A group of young monks were touring Britain to introduce Tibetan culture to a wider audience and they had accompanied the lama. They offered to perform both the dance and overtone chanting for us. As with all things Tibetan it was an amazing mixture of high spirituality and great humour. They began with a long chant to change the level of consciousness. We had already been through several initiations with the lama and so were already in a heightened state. After the chanting, the dancing began. Almost immediately I was aware that one of the women on the course, who lived in a Tibetan Buddhist community, was having problems. Tears were running down her face and she clearly felt faint. As she was sitting with another lama and several of the English monks, I turned my attention back to the dance, telling myself firmly that this was none of my business. The healing lama was there and was clearly aware of her situation. I even refrained from offering Rescue Remedy when someone went out to get her some water.

After the dancing was over, we all went out onto the lawn for coffee. It was wonderful summer's day and I sat chatting with friends. Up came a woman I knew, who had helped to organise the course, bringing with her the woman who had been having problems. 'Lama Ganchen says please take her away and do what is necessary,' I was told. I took her to my home, which fortunately was close by, and regressed her. All she had been able to tell me was that she had been overcome by this terrible wordless sorrow as soon as she saw the dancers emerge in their exotic masks and colourful costumes. 'It was all so familiar', she said, 'and so so sad!'

In the regression, she went back to being a young boy dancer in one of the monasteries. He was very good, highly talented, in fact. He took such pleasure in dancing, it was literally what he lived for. All he wanted to do was to be the best cham dancer ever. The monkish studies were an irrelevance as far as he was concerned. He took great pride in this ability to be the best dancer and saw no need at all to be a good student. Unfortunately, the abbot of the monastery took a very dim view of all this. As a form of spiritual discipline, he forbade the young monk to dance, and condemned him to watch others do what he could not do. It broke his heart. Lying there in deep regression, the present life and the past life were one, she sobbed and sobbed. We clearly could not leave her in this state. I asked her what was needed to heal that life. She said that she needed to dance. We went back to the abbot to ask him to revoke his ban so that she could dance in her present life. She also explained to him that she had been studying Tibetan Buddhism for several years now and had caught up on her neglected studies from that life. He agreed to release her, but cautioned against such pride again. She came out of the regression feeling much freer. As it happened, with great synchronicity, the woman was about to go for an interview for a performing arts course. She had always had a compulsion to dance and finally had the opportunity to become a mature student. She had to prepare a dance routine for this interview. I suggested to her that the monks who had been doing the cham dance might be able to help her. They taught her the hand movements they used and explained the sacred meaning. By the time they left, she had her routine.

PAST LIFE PLEASURES

There are, of course, past life regressions that are most pleasurable. They may throw light on the present life or they may seem like a beautiful fantasy:

> I can't see my feet because I'm wearing a long skirt that sweeps the ground. It's a beautiful shade of blue and I have made it myself. It is my favourite dress and I am
>
> *continued ...*

wearing it because today is a special day. It's a bit heavy for this beautiful spring day but I want to look my best. I feel so good. I am walking in a garden. I can smell the flowers and hear the bees buzzing. It is beautiful here. I'm so happy. I 'm collecting herbs and then I'm going to get the rose petals to strew in my bed. I have made a posy to give him. Rosemary for remembrance, sweet bryony and heart's-ease, celandine and violets, the promises of spring. Soon he will be here.

[Having been asked who 'he' is] He's my beloved, of course. The man I am to marry. He's so handsome. I haven't seen him for three years but I know he won't have changed. Today is the day we will be handfasted. Then later the priest will come and our union will be blessed. But from today he will never leave me. He has been away to make his fortune and now he is returned.

[Skipping forward a few hours.] He is late, he should be here... oh, it is all right. He has sent word his horse is lame and he is walking. He will soon be here. It is hot and I must make myself ready again. I bathe my face with rosewater. It smells so fresh. I bite my lips to give them colour. I want to look pretty for him. I picked this dress specially for him ... [she prattles on for a while in nervous excitement] ... He is here! Now I must wait. My father has to greet him first and they must talk. Then they will call me. Oh, I can hardly wait. Maybe I can peep through the stairs ... [whispering] Yes, there he is. He still looks exactly the same. Nut-brown from the sun and sea, but he is still my handsome one. He is with my father. Soon they will call me.

Now I am walking down the stairs. I go into the room. He is there. My father has the contract ready. His deep blue eyes gaze into mine, 'Are you ready to be my wife?' Oh yes, yes! But I must not seem so anxious. Mother always said I must have more decorum. I look down and peep at him from beneath my eyes. He laughs and tells me not to play games. He knows me too well! My father smiles and they sign the contract.

continued ...

He takes my hand and I give him the posy. Now we are one.

We walk in the garden. He tells me of his travels, the places he has seen. Once the ship was overrun by pirates but they fought them off. He was able to get enough goods to sell at a good price in Bristol. He says that now he is home, he never wants to leave.

[She moves forward a few years] We are still very close. The priest never did come, so our union was not blessed. [It seems they were secret Catholics.] We have children now and he goes to town on business from time to time. But we spend most of our time together quietly at home. I don't travel far. Sometimes a trader comes with cloth and gee-gaws. The knife sharpener and the pot-mender come with the spring. I prefer to stay here; I don't like the busyness of the town. My father is very old now. I look after him and we are happy.

[Many years later] Our children are grown now and my father has died. We live alone with just our two servants. My husband lets the estate and the tenant farmers come to pay their rents at Michaelmas. Once a year we have the harvest home for all the farms. It has been a good life. My only regret is that the priest did not come. [Wistfully] I would have liked our union to be blessed by God. Maybe next time...

With that, the scene fades. As she returns her awareness to her present life she smiles. 'I met him again you know,' she says, 'He was my first boyfriend. But somehow I did not want the life he offered. We lived in a very small village and he was content to stay at home. I wanted to see the world so I left. Now I know that we have been together before and that then he had seen the world before we became man and wife. This time it was my turn.' She commented that she had sometimes wondered what would have happened if she had stayed in that small village. She feels that she would have become discontented. She can look back on a happy memory knowing that they had a good life 'before'. She is content with that.

Some Other Time?

We have looked at whether past lives are personal and unique and at the karmic reasons why we might need to remember them. We have also looked at some examples of possible 'fantasies in fancy dress', and some of the perils and pleasures of past life memories. But we also need to look at *when* these lives are occurring. Are they really way back in the dim and distant past? Are they strung out like beads on a thread with definite beginnings and endings? If so, why are so many memories so vibrant and alive?

I have always felt that time turns inside out whenever I go into another life. It is as though time does not exist: it is all part of my present experience. I do not see 'past' lives stretching out behind me in a fixed, chronological and linear fashion like staging posts on my journey. They are all around me. I well remember teaching on a karmic astrology workshop with Howard Sasportas and hearing Howard say, 'Somehow it is all happening *now.*' I nodded my head emphatically to support what he said, and Howard said, 'And Judy will now explain that because I can't!'

Just how do you explain a gut feeling, a sense of such rightness about a statement that it makes you want to shout 'Yes!' at the top of your voice and yet when you stop to look at it logically it seems to be impossible? As I explained in the Introduction, my usual practice is to say that time as we know it does not exist. It is all part of the eternal *now*. Nevertheless, people do feel that they go 'back in time' to other incarnations. They need a sense of history to give them a sense of moving from there to here. But, as we shall see, 'the past' can so easily be part of the present.

Meddling with History?

Several years ago now one of my clients asked me a question that was to set me thinking even more deeply about time — and about the effect of Past Life Therapy. I know from experience that 'going back into the past' and changing something in another life has profound consequences in the present life. This question however made me wonder quite how far those consequences extended:

> **Since the past, present and future are all happening simultaneously, by altering one's action in the past,**
> *continued ...*

> and thus the desired outcome, is one not in fact meddling with history. Is there a danger of depriving another person of learning his lessons in life. There are many reports of miraculous occurrences and we hear about divine intervention. Could this in fact be an aspect of our future self undergoing a 'past life' therapy, changing the outcome, so to speak, from a future stand point?[6]

It was a fascinating thought. While the idea of going back into the past is slowly gaining credence, little work has been done on our self in the future coming back to the 'past' that is 'now'. Progressions to the future have been done by people like Chet Snow — an American hypnotherapist — but these are gloomy affairs linked to the end of the world as we know it. There was little sense of evolution and improvement for the human race or for the soul. In the few progressions my clients have spontaneously gone into, two 'futures' at least had been apparent. The fairly gloomy prognosis would be glimpsed first and then the higher self or guide who was accompanying the journey would say, 'That is one choice; if you do not change (or if you follow such and such a path) that is how things will go. But if you do change (or take a different pathway) then this is what would happen...' And a much brighter future would be revealed.

It is interesting to speculate that somewhere in that future, perhaps in the gloomy one, our self could be directed 'back' to our present in order to make some changes that would enable us to participate in our own evolution. This is, of course, assuming that we look at it from a linear time perspective. From the perspective of the eternal *now*, it is much easier to imagine another part of our self reaching in from another part of the wheel or the spiral to tweak us onto the right path. After all, this apparent travelling back into time is what happens in a present life regression to childhood, when our adult self can go to the aid of the child who is trapped in a painful situation, or in a past life regression, where we retrieve a part of our self or change the outcome of a life, rescind a vow or any of the myriad possibilities Past Life Therapy offers us.

When I worked with Simon Jacobs (recounted later in this chapter) he went back into a recurring dream of his 'past'. He did nothing to change the outcome of that life. He simply wanted to understand this dream that had haunted him all his life and his sense of having another identity. Recently, I asked him what had been the value. He said he had had to go back in order to go forward. Knowing where he had come from, the kind of man he had been, had helped him to establish his purpose in his present life.

However, as we shall see from the next story, there are ways of actively changing the effect of the past, not just on a personal level, but also on a collective one.

WHERE DO I GO FROM HERE?

We have already seen that a place can hold memories. It can be very difficult to establish whether a memory actually relates to a place, whether it is personal or collective, or whether it is an intimate entwining of all three. A short time ago, I was asked to look at an experience a woman, Roz, had had when visiting Dachau in Germany. Marjorie, the friend who asked me to do this on her behalf, said Roz had also asked specifically, 'Where do I go from here?'. She was about to move back to England having lived abroad for a long time, but could see no future for herself. Before I had time to do the reading, Roz returned to England and died of a brain haemorrhage — on my birthday, which seemed rather significant. Her friend asked me to continue with the reading and to use it where possible to honour Roz's experience and so that others might benefit from it. I have already used it in *The Hades Moon*[7] but feel that it is appropriate to use it here also.

Roz prefaced her account of her experiences at Dachau by saying that initially she was not sure whether she was tapping into the shared memories of the collective unconscious or whether it was a personal reliving. As she worked with the material, she came to believe that being caught up in the collective memory had taken her to one of her own past life experiences. Roz had a strongly developed psychic ability and, as we shall see, considerable experience of spiritual work. Astrologically speaking, Roz had a strong karmic purpose in incarnating. With a need to work on behalf of society, she was trying to reconcile the past with the present and to find the karmic point of balance. However, it seemed that she might also be practising redemptive karma and in her dying taking some of the collective darkness out of the world.

Her story is best told through her letter to Marjorie and extracts from the journal she kept at the time:

Postcard from Munich:

Love it here in Bavaria — lots of trees and green space and food and beer are great.

Letter to Marjorie (a week later):

When I was in Wimbledon I bought a book called *Rune Power* by Kenneth Meadows. It went into the history of the Runes and especially into recent history, and specifically the misuse of the Runes by the Nazis. So, there I was, taking to Germany this book which chronicled the Nazi involvement, and also spoke of one of the German Runic authorities having spent the war years in Dachau so that he would not speak about the involvement of certain Nazis in occult work.

When I got to Kathy's I discovered that she had just bought and begun to read a book by a Jewish guy called Daniel Jonah Goldhagen, who had written of ordinary Germans and the Holocaust. In *Hitler's Willing Executioners* he puts forward a very convincing and well-documented argument that Hitler did not 'force' the Germans to discriminate against and vilify the Jews, that those feelings were already there; he simply fuelled them. The extermination came later, but was also in the main, carried out by ordinary Germans who did not lose sleep over what they did, firmly believing that the Jews were the origin of all that was wrong in Germany. Well, of course, I began reading this book too, and there were many graphic accounts of the atrocities both in and out of the concentration camps. Dachau was mentioned quite frequently.

My trip started in Munich. I didn't know that the Nazi movement began in that city. I thought it was Berlin or Nuremberg. But Hitler went to Munich from Austria when he was nineteen and lived there for many years. It was where he wrote *Mein Kampf* and did his

continued ...

plotting! He was tried and sentenced in the courthouse there when in the 1920s he tried an abortive attempt to impose his Nationalist Socialist Party.

And Himmler, who created Dachau in 1933 (the first of the camps) was the Chief of Police in Munich.

Now we come to my visit to Dachau. I had no idea, initially, that Dachau was anywhere near Munich, but in fact it is only about 10 or 15 miles away. The town of Dachau itself is a delightful place, really pretty, with a river and lots of greenery. Dachau the camp was originally an armaments factory in the First World War and fell into disuse afterwards. It was this ready-made site which Himmler decided would make a good venue for incarceration.

Well, I was *very* keen to go to this so-called Memorial Site, thinking that it would be quite something different to do — and how!! Kathy took me on the Sunday. The main feature of the place is the huge museum, housed in what was one of the original buildings. The museum is a pictorial history of the coming to power of the Nazis and the formation of Dachau and other camps, together with what went on in them. That in itself was harrowing enough, but then there was the original, unrestored building which had been the prison block where prisoners were tortured, etc. The site itself is still surrounded by barbed-wire fencing, the ditches and sentry towers. Just outside the site 'proper' are the ovens (I found this most distressing) and the gas chamber, which was never actually used (prisoners were sent elsewhere to be gassed) but plenty were killed at Dachau by other means. What I found quite strange and also made me angry were the several small churches and religious memorials which have now been erected on the site of the camp itself. I just thought, 'And where the hell were all you lot when this was going on? Turning your faces to the wall!'

Walking around the museum was horrific, and I felt quite nauseous at times, and sometimes near to tears.

continued ...

But walking around the grounds, where there were less people, was in some way even worse. I kept looking at the sentry towers and imagining being a prisoner and perhaps being so desperate that one would want to walk on the forbidden grass strip near the ditch and get mown down by the sentry's gun. But the worst of all were the buildings with the ovens in them, and it was one in particular which made me feel awful, and that was the oldest and smallest of them, with a tall metal, old-fashioned type of chimney. It was really weird to be walking about where such terrible atrocities took place. It made me grateful that I'm alive now.

When we left we went back into Munich to the Olympic Park (made from the war-rubble of Munich) and sat outside in the sun for cakes and a drink, and hopefully for some of the awful vibrations to disappear from us. But that night when I got into bed my mind went straight back to Dachau and I couldn't clear it away. Also I developed pains in my lower back and legs, which I didn't at that time associate with my visit to Dachau.

The next morning I went swimming and I put my neck out in the most painful way. I was quite ill for a couple of days, and then it eased a bit, but I knew that I really needed some treatment as I was still having awful headaches, etc. My friends found this very nice chiropractor-acupuncturist-homeopath. I had two treatments from him and on both occasions he gave me six injections at the top of my spine where it went into the base of the skull. These consisted of a dental anaesthetic and some homeopathic preparations (more on the relevance of this later).

After my injury I set about looking at Dachau and my reactions to it, as I felt that what had happened to me in the pool was a result of my visit in some way.

What I felt most strongly was that by making a commemorative site out of Dachau, those awful

continued ...

vibrations, and all the terrible things that happened there were not only being kept alive but being *strengthened* by all the people who go there and experience what happened.

I did quite a long visualisation in which I pulled the whole place down, burnt what was burnable, broke up into small pieces what wasn't and made sure there was nothing left standing by bulldozing the whole site. Then I planted trees everywhere and scattered grass seed and wild flower seeds, and imagined the whole place being taken over and cleansed by nature, until the perimeter of the camp was no longer distinguishable; it was all just one natural site.

Then, I thought I needed to look at my own life and see where I have made commemorative sites in my mind and emotions of things from the past which needed to be completely obliterated from any sort of 'remembrance'. I needed to bulldoze those to the ground and return them to nature to be recycled.

Roz then returned to her home to pack up ready for her return to England. She was part of a spiritual group, a group which felt that they 'belonged together' and had come together for a purpose in this life:

Anne asked me to tell the Thursday Group about Dachau, which I did. Then Melinda, who had been in the process of doing my astrological chart, using it to look at the past lives and had felt there was something else she needed to access and couldn't, suddenly said that I'd been in Dachau myself, and had been with Greta [Roz's daughter, a heroin addict] who had been my twin. We had been experimented on, and had been injected as part of these experiments. (Hence my reliving those injections this time around with the chiropractor, and Greta with her heroin addiction.) Anne said that she also felt this was so. She also said I had been there with Natasha. Natasha had been told on two previous occasions that she'd been a Jew and

continued ...

had been persecuted. A kinesiology guy had asked her whether she was allergic to dental anaesthetic as that had shown up in his testing, she said 'No'. On further reflection he said that it was the nearest thing to the cyanide gas used in concentration camps, and he felt that her brain still carried memories of that!

Diary extracts:

Thursday: After having so vividly in my mind and emotions the dreams in Germany and being sure that I needed to do some inner work to find out the connection with Dachau, I was switched completely to Greta after Melinda's comments. I felt that my meeting with girl twins yesterday and talking to their mother, and reflecting myself on what it must feel like to be a twin, and how they coped apart, etc., etc., was a confirmation of what Melinda told me.

Saturday: By the afternoon I was 'connected' again and started to work on Dachau, full of feeling.

First of all querying the dates. I was born in 1936 — there was only three years of Dachau before that — and I wonder when the experiments started? Research shows: 'The experimental station of Dr Rascher was set up in early 1933 in Block 5 where high pressure and exposure experiments were practised on defenceless prisoners... many of these experiments resulted in death.'

Comparing this to my symptoms in Germany this time: great pressure on my head and top spine caused by cold water — and the doctor emphasised the factor of the cold which ' infected' my structure; injections in the base of the skull; felt out of control in the doctor's surgery because of the language barrier (I was 'helpless'); great fear before each visit — because of the pain I was in and also because I was going into the unknown and to an 'alien' doctor and practices.

Did a visualisation with Greta and the camp and went into the infirmary block where the experimental station had been. Also visited the crematorium where

continued ...

I had been particularly horrified by the older and smaller of the ovens. Again I come to the time factor — could I perhaps have been aware of Greta's cremation there after 1940? If she had survived me, then perhaps part of my consciousness had stayed with her and registered all that happened to her and I had experienced her pain, fear and suffering too? Is this why I 'came in' this time around with those ghastly nightmares which persisted for much of my lifetime and still occasionally visit me, although the content is different but the fear remains — also the migraines.

Visited Irene in hospital. This took me back to the fear and pain of my own similar experience. I was dreading this as I have a fear of hospitals anyway... and especially of hospital machinery, e.g. bone scan. With the work I had just done re Greta and me and the experiments, I was led to look at my visit to Irene in a different light. I thought it might be an opportunity to change some of my energy and connection to past fearful experiences...

Sundries:

When I was twenty I spent some time in London and lived with some German Jews who had come to England before the war began. At the same time I worked for Victor Hochhauser's wife (he was an impresario). They were orthodox Jews and I learned quite a bit about the religion and became very interested in Zionism.

Although there was so much of the Nazi past in Munich, I liked the city very much and felt happy and at home there.

Greta:

I have been involved and connected to her while she was injecting heroin, and also when she was doing 'cold turkey'. Both of these situations were traumatic. She has said to other people that I had 'abandoned' her

continued ...

> when she was about thirteen (I had left home for about six weeks). This quite understandable feeling in this lifetime may, of course, also be linked to the past if I died before her.

If we look at Roz's experience in the light of some of the alternative explanations we have already explored about past lives, it is, of course, possible that she set herself up for this experience. She was already deeply interested in the Jewish question and had read those books about Dachau. So it could have been a question of suggestion. She could also have been 'reading' the events that took place there fifty years previously. Or one of the souls trapped in the horror of that place could have been wordlessly communicating with her. Hidden memory from previous books or films could have surfaced, as could the collective unconscious. But that there is so much emotion in Roz's diary account, and so many 'coincidences' would seem to point to a personal level of experience as well.

It is common for a visit to a place where a past life took place to trigger body memories. Roz's back and neck pain could well have been reflecting an old injury, as could the treatment she was given by the chiropractor. The kind of research carried out at Dachau certainly fits. The story did develop as she went along; one of the strongest criticisms about 'past life memories' is that as each new bit of research and information comes along it is added into the original experience to swell the memory. However, we can also look at it as the story unfolding as she was ready to accept each piece. Had it all flooded in at once, she would have been overwhelmed. In her diary, initially, Roz is not so sure that it was 'her' life. Then when she did the work with her spiritual group she became more certain. But Roz did keep an open mind. One of her reasons for asking Marjorie to contact me about her experience was that she wanted me to check it.

When I did the reading, I felt that she was correct in her assumption that she had been interned at Dachau when it was first set up but had died early on, leaving her twin (now her daughter) behind. The astrology certainly reflected this and so did my psychic vision. As she and her twin/daughter were powerfully connected the contact did not end with Roz's death. Part of her did indeed stay with her twin and witnessed all that she went through.

Roz's consciousness registered this as strongly as if it had been her own experience — which was horrific enough in any event. I felt that in going back to Dachau she had retrieved that part of herself, but it took some time to integrate and pass on the messages it had for her. I also felt that Roz had, in that previous life, died some time after she was born in this present life. It sounds strange but twenty-five years' experience tells me that this is possible, especially when the last life has been particularly traumatic. When it does happen, it leaves extremely strong 'cross-threads' between the two incarnations. It can result in a child prone to horrendous nightmares and strange fears. Roz's fear of hospitals and hospital machinery, which had been with her since she was very young, would also link into this kind of cross-memory. I also felt that Roz had incarnated again quickly so that she could be mother to Greta at the appropriate time — in response to a vow she had made to her twin before death in that other life to look after her and help her heal the aftermath.

In my psychic vision, I also saw Joseph Mengele — one of the most notorious of the concentration camp doctors, who was particularly interested in twins. I felt he was in some way connected with Roz's experiences. Subsequent research showed that in 1930, age nineteen, he had entered Munich University. Interestingly enough, he had first thought of becoming a dentist but opted for medicine with a particular emphasis on human evolution, anthropology and genetics. In Munich at that time the theory was being developed that some human beings afflicted by specific disorders were unfit to reproduce and even to live, which led to genocidal programs, the first of which started at Dachau. Mengele studied under the leading exponents of the theory: Professor Mollinson and Drs Rudin, Hioche and Bindong. Rudin firmly believed that doctors should destroy lives deemed to be of no value and was one of the architects of Hitler's 'Law for the Protection of Hereditary Health'.

With their 'laboratory', Dachau, only twelve miles up the road conducting research into twins, which was to become the core of Mengele's own work, it seems unlikely that he would not have taken advantage of the research facilities there, but I have so far been unable to verify his actual presence. Certainly in his later work at Auschwitz he performed experiments on twins that had much in common with Roz's memories. The children would be strapped to slabs of marble where their spines, eyes and inner organs were injected with chemicals and many other atrocities were performed as he sought to probe their joint hereditary 'secrets'. In 1935, the year after Roz believed she went to Dachau, Mengele was awarded a Ph.D. for his work in heredity and 'racial hygiene'. Mengele then qualified as a doctor and moved to Leipzig. In 1937 he joined the newly founded Institut fur Erbbiologie and Rassenhygience (Hereditary Biology and Racial Hygiene) at Frankfurt. The rest is history but does not concern us here.

Roz was fortunate in that she had considerable metaphysical experience and was able to resolve her traumatic experience at Dachau by looking deep into her own life to make appropriate connections and changes. By using imagery and visualisation to heal and reframe not only the Dachau site but also her own life experiences, she was able to put healing into the collective. When her task was complete, she moved on. It may well be that as an act of redemptive karma, she undertook that karmic clearing for humankind. As so many people have memories of being in concentration camps, and as so many were killed or scarred for life there and could well bring the memory forward, applying Roz's method could heal the pain for both victims and persecutors alike. It will also help to heal the collective. As Roz said, making a memorial does perpetuate the horror, while applying forgiveness to the memory helps it to heal. When Marjorie asked me to publish this material, she asked that it should encourage us all to make of Dachau a garden of remembrance and forgiveness instead of focussing horror and negativity there. She said, 'I am continuing to visualise Dachau as a place of peace and love, festooned with wild flowers in full bloom.' Please do likewise.

Pieces of a Jigsaw

Simon Jacobs is an ex-Army officer, intelligent and level-headed, well trained in observation, down-to-earth and personable; he is not the kind of person you would expect to have memories about living in another time. But that was what brought him to me. Ever since he was a child he had suffered from a recurring dream. One that is still absolutely crystal clear. As he says, he only has to shut his eyes to see it again. In the dream he was in camouflage uniform. He was wearing a helmet and a rucksack. He had lots of kit, webbing and ammunition pouches strung about him. He was in a large glider and the back of the glider, which was empty, was open. Then he was running around woods somewhere in Northern Europe. There were leaves on the trees. He was aware of panic, urgency and a sense of drama. And then, nothing. Things went blank. His dream was in black and white. Initially, it was like a smooth photograph. Then it would distort. As he describes it, it was as though someone moved the contrast button.

In childhood, Simon simply knew it was a war setting. He wondered whether it was the First World War or Second. Now, with the benefit of hindsight, he knows that it was not prior to 1945 because no one wore camouflage before then, and it couldn't have been after that date because of the gliders. Gliders were last used in a battle situation in 1945. So that focussed the time for him.

When Simon came to see me, several years ago now, he wanted to go back into that dream to find out what it was all about. He had been researching his family history and had come across a distant relative, Miles Henry, who died in action during the Second World War. He knew that this man had a wife and daughter and he had discovered where he was buried, but that was all. He had no further details, not even, at that stage, the date of death. He had no regiment, no place of death, nothing. But he felt a shiver of recognition at the very name. He was sure this was who he had been.

I do not use hypnosis in regression and, as Simon had a starting point, I relaxed him until he was able to re-enter the dream in a most graphic way. Initially he went back to the wood. He was wearing the same uniform. There was enormous confusion, panic and lots of running around. He commented on the noise — gunfire and shouting. He and another man were looking for someone who was injured. When they found him, they picked him up and starting taking him to safety. Then Simon simply blanked out.

I took him back to an earlier time, before the dream began. He had many small details — which he was later able to check. We covered his basic training. Then he was in Palestine on a secret mission. He had a wife and child and we saw some details of his time with them. But most of all he was aware of waiting — the boredom and tension of it. It was foggy which delayed things. Then he was in the glider going over the Channel. He felt that he was on his way to Arnhem and would parachute in. When he did land there was all the rushing about and the noise in the wood. He was wounded going to the aid of a comrade and blacked out. After that, he looked back at things from beyond his death. We did notice that he did not do much fighting himself; that was not his role. As it turned out, he was the intelligence officer of the unit.

Simon was keen to research and confirm what he saw. Initially he went to the Museum of Army Flying but drew a blank. They suggested that he should go to the Parachute Museum. There he discovered that Miles Henry had been a Captain in 10 Para and had been killed at Arnhem. They confirmed that he was buried in Holland. But they said that the only way Simon could get details of the actual death was to read the War Diaries of the regiment which were at the War Museum. Simon went to the War Museum where the diaries were ceremoniously presented to him. He says it sent shivers and tingles up his spine just to see them. But more was to come when he read the account. He found the reference to Miles Henry. He had been in Palestine but came back to England to train in 1944. Then he was assigned to be the Intelligence Officer for Regimental Headquarters at Arnhem. The flight out had been held up by the fog for two or three days before they used the gliders to take them to where they jumped in. Sure enough, Miles Henry had been with another man, trying to take a wounded soldier back to the Aid Station when he was seriously wounded. He died that night without regaining consciousness. As Simon said then, 'I just know it happened. I know it was me. I can't not believe it; there are too many pieces of the jigsaw that come together for it not to be believable.' Having done further research on the family and confirmed other details seen in his regression, he remains utterly convinced to this day.

A traumatic death often lingers in consciousness. It makes an impact. Especially when, as with Miles Henry, life was cut short at a young age. As we have already seen, many people remember their death in the First or Second World Wars and I have had other clients who remembered Korea, Vietnam and other conflicts. It is as though they got caught up in the collective karma of the day and their own was put on hold. Then they have an urge to return and complete the unlived life. In Simon's case this entailed going back into the Army. He, as with Miles Henry, was a career soldier. It was only when he left the Army and started looking at his purpose in life that he wanted to know more about his past. He felt that the man he is now had grown out of the man he was then.

As we shall see, death does play an important part in many past life seeings. The following experience is no exception.

Bones of Contention

One hundred years before Columbus 'discovered' America, Sir James Gun was buried in the New World. This is the earliest known European medieval burial in the USA. His effigy is incised on a rock near Westford, Massachusetts.[8] The Gun, or Gunn (sometimes spelt Gunne), family is an extremely old — and very small — Scottish clan. The name has a long connection with the American continent. In AD900 Icelandic records tell us that 'Gunnbjorn' — meaning 'born of Gunn' — reached North America. Over a thousand years later, Gunn is a common surname amongst the Arrow Lakes people of Western Canada. So it is not surprising that when Northumbria-born Celia Gunn went to live in Canada and came into contact with these people they should think her 'one of ours', that is, married to one of their clan rather than being a member of the Scottish Gunn clan who had strayed a long way from home. Celia herself had long felt a connection with the Native American peoples. She had been fascinated with them as a child growing up in England, but it was not until she had lived in British Columbia, Canada, for twelve years that she first met Bob (Laughing Thunder) of Arrow Lakes descent. Little did she know just where interest in the native culture would take her:

> I got involved with the Arrow Lakes Band [the Canadian term for 'tribe'] basically because one of their descendants singled me out at a Medicine Wheel Gathering in 1987. He told me about his ancestral lands and that his people had been officially declared extinct. He also told me about an archaeological dig that had taken place at a two-thousand-year-old ancestral village, and how ancestral remains had been dug up and taken off to a museum. As well as being excited by being singled out by this very handsome and charismatic man, when I heard about these bones

> being removed it really affected me. I had never ever thought about bones before. I've seen them in museums but never bothered about it. Now, just the thought really hit me deeply. I was filled with a deep sense of outrage. My thought was 'It's so offensive to them; they should be put back if that's what the people want.' And that's how my involvement began.

As we shall see, although Celia did not know it at the time these bones were to become most important to her as they hooked straight back into a very powerful past life memory which had not yet surfaced. This memory seems to have been influencing her strongly, pulling her into a scenario which not only had elements from her past but which also brought in a promise she needed to keep. As is so often the case, the story spread over several years and became visible to her piece by piece. Having felt that the bones needed protection and the people needed aid in getting them back, Celia became deeply involved with the Arrow Lakes site and its people:

> Not long after, an unrelated job opportunity led to my relocation right into the heart of the Arrow Lakes ancestral lands. I wasn't yet consciously aware of the magic of synchronicity, but knew I was there for another reason than the job. I got involved with the actual village and burial site, initially as a volunteer. It was by now a designated heritage site and I got onto the Board of Directors of the local Society who were stewards of the site. We were all non-Native people because the descendants were fragmented; some were located south of the Canadian border in Washington State on the Colville Reservation, others on Reserves in British Columbia and still others scattered over Canada. The site was going to be developed as a tourist attraction and my feeling was that the Indian people should be the ones to decide what would happen there. I kept Bob informed about what was going on and this led to him and another Arrow Lakes descendant turning up at a crucial meeting with British Columbia Heritage representatives, as a 'voice of the
>
> *continued ...*

Elders'. The local people responded really well, but the heritage officials seemed determined to ignore them.

There were two issues. The Arrow Lakes Elders wanted their ancestral remains repatriated and they wanted a say in what happened to their ancestral village.

I was appointed as a coordinator for the management plan for the site, because as it happened I was the person who knew the most about every aspect of the place. I had been researching avidly. Incredibly, I remembered everything as soon as I read it, all the archaeological and ethnographical information, as well as all the cultural teachings Bob and others told me from the oral tradition. I was also an invited guest at Band meetings on the Reservation.

When we discussed this, Celia commented that she had felt it was more like a recognition than a learning process. At a deep level she *knew* all about Native American practices.

The situation escalated into a big political issue because no Native people had ever asked for bones back for reburial before, and this Band had been declared officially extinct, although they were anything but! At the same time, a road was suddenly ploughed next to the designated site which caused concern about disturbance to more burials there because no further exploration had been done. In this way the descendants of the Band were called back home — to take care of their ancestors' resting-places. It was the first time that some of them even knew how they came to be Arrow Lakes people. (They were called the Lakes Indians, but that didn't make sense to them because there were only a couple of small lakes on their Reservation).

A crucial meeting was called to discuss the road and after that meeting Auntie Vi, an Elder who became my closest friend, said to me, 'I know who you are!' She

continued ...

then told me the story of Green Blanket: 'A twelve-year-old girl was stolen from us by the Blackfoot and taken over the mountains into Montana. She was desperately unhappy. At the first opportunity she ran away. It was winter and she spent four months walking back over the mountain to her people. All she had was this green blanket which she would tear up to wrap around her feet. When she got back, the people couldn't believe she had done this. To cross the mountains in winter is a physical impossibility. Green Blanket said, 'I have a story to tell about Old Man Coyote.'

Auntie Vi had to go then and she said she would tell me that part of the story another time. 'But', she said, 'if I believed in reincarnation and I'm not saying I don't — well, the story reminds me of you. That girl, Green Blanket, came back and because of the miracle of her return, she led them back onto their spiritual path, and you are bringing us home, back onto our spiritual path.' I never asked her about the rest of the story as, out of respect, I always waited to be told.

It wasn't until later that I remembered how when I first met Bob, at the end of the Gathering I had agreed to help organise the next year's. I had gone to a core meeting — late because I'd been feeding my kids supper — and my idea was to have it multi-cultural. I waited until there was a break and the guy who was leading the meeting (not a Native American, although he looked like one) turned on me and rudely said, 'Oh I hate it when people come late and start talking about what has already been settled.' It was embarrassing, but at that moment I felt a blanket being put around my shoulders. It was Bob. He had seen what had happened. He put a green blanket around me and my kids and sat down beside us. Everything changed because he was the key person there.

At the end of the meeting I was going to give the blanket back but he said, 'No you keep the blanket.'

continued ...

> The next morning he came by and I insisted on giving him the blanket back. I told Auntie Vi about this incident because it had been a *green blanket*. She said that in the old ways when a man gave a woman a blanket, it was a proposal of marriage and she added, 'Good job you didn't keep it because he's already got three wives and seventeen children!'

In this case, Celia did not actually experience herself as Green Blanket but the essence of that girl was recognised in Celia by one of the Elders. It seems that Green Blanket had promised to return should the tribe need to step back on to their spiritual path again. We have already looked at various possibilities which could be operating in this story. Celia could be living out the consequences of the Native myth, whether at an archetypal or personal level. It would have been told and retold, perhaps creating a Green Blanket thought form, who watched over the tribe. Had Celia herself relived the Green Blanket story then we could have said that hidden memory might be operating. (The myth has been published although so far Celia has not traced it.) But it was not Celia who identified Green Blanket, it was an Elder of the Band. She, of course, knew all about the story and felt that, in a way, history was repeating itself. The discarnate spirit of Green Blanket could have been influencing Celia, especially if she had remained in the spirit world to watch over her tribe. Celia is certainly mediumistic enough to pick up that kind of subtle direction. Celia could also have a fragment of the Green Blanket soul in her soul ancestry. There is also the possibility, of course, that Celia was a direct reincarnation of Green Blanket. However, as Celia says, whether or not she is a reincarnation of Green Blanket is not the issue here. A past life connection was to surface which was so real that it seemed indisputably Celia's — no matter how much she tried to resist it at first:

> To go back to the bones, which for me is the important bit of my story... While I was working as the coordinator I had a dream. It was so powerful. I was sitting on a floor beside a fire and there were shadows on what I realised was the interior of a tipi. A Native man was on his knees. He was elderly, in his sixties,
>
> *continued ...*

> skinny with thick grey hair and he had a woman in front of him whose buttocks he was holding. He was making love to her from behind. I remember her gleaming buttocks and his head thrown back in ecstasy. I woke up with a feeling of awe and wonder. It really stuck with me, especially the features of the man and I thought, 'One day I'm going to draw him'. Normally, I'm not much good at drawing people, but one day I just took a piece of paper and a pencil and as I began to draw, a little shadow appeared in front of my pencil, so I followed this shadow and I outlined this man. But he wasn't old and skinny, he was muscular. He had black hair with all these things coming out — like eagle feathers — and instead of the woman he was holding Mother Earth. I kept that picture and put it in the scrap book of all the things that were going on at the site. (By this time there had been a blockade and the matter went before the Courts.) One psychic actually told me this Indian was my husband from a previous life, but that he was staying on the other side where he could help me better. I was most disgruntled, as he was such a handsome man, but it somehow didn't really feel that was right, as I didn't feel I'd make that kind of arrangement. But I just let it go.

As we shall see in Chapter 5, these kind of agreements are possible, but it is likely that Celia could equally well have agreed to meet a husband from another life in her present one. However, as we shall see, things were not quite what they seemed. Psychics do not always pick up correctly on past life connections. Past life contacts need careful interpretation, especially in a situation where someone as sensitive as Celia has become so enmeshed in the past — although at this stage she did not realise just how much the past was manifesting.

> Time passed, about two years, and I did some rebirthing sessions using chaotic breathing. It was very difficult and I only succeeded in breaking
>
> *continued ...*

> through the resistance my body put up two times. The first was brief, but the second time I flew through into this other space. I felt nothing in my body and I didn't breathe. (The psychic healer who was taking me through it said I 'hovered'.) I had this flash of grey hair, skinny arms with dark freckles, a strong smell, a flash of light. A keening wail burst out of me and I felt like there was this black stuff oozing from my vagina, and I shot back into this life.

However, it seemed that life was inexorably pushing her towards understanding her other lives and their effect on the present:

> Six months later I was at a fascinating workshop where we were doing all kinds of inner work with this brilliant man. One of the things we did was with mirrors. You had to look into your own eyes for some minutes, and not break the concentration. Not an easy thing, but the third time I tried it, it was as though my face was being erased and other faces gradually appeared. After a succession of faces, some Indian, others I could not tell, I guessed that I had the ability to look down my past lives. I knew there had to be a Viking and asked to see him; he was ugly and unkempt and that convinced me because if I had been making it up I would have made him handsome. The workshop leader confirmed my ability to look down my past lives 'at the drop of a hat!' I thought this was fun and never thought about how dangerous it might be. I practised at home and within a very short time only one Native man kept coming forward — very handsome with black hair. Similar to the drawing, but not the same. The woman I did the rebirthing with said it was a 'carry-over personality' who was influencing my life and that I should do a regression.

A carry-over personality is something which seems to come entire and complete into the present life from the past — rather like one of the multiple personality persona which is 'just there' from birth, awaiting contact. Such personalities can lie quietly in the background but they can also be very powerful indeed. Under their influence people dress like they did in the past, have the interests they had then, and revert to emotional patterns and desires which belong to 'back then'. To release such an obsessive contact may need regression and soul work at a very deep level.

> I put the idea of regression to the back of my mind. Then, in 1992 I was visiting my mother in Northumbria and I met up with my friend and mentor, an elderly lady called Eileen Churchill, and told her about it. She was a Jungian psychotherapist, and she said she did regressions and would love to do this with me. I put it off until two days before I was due to return to Canada — that's how much I didn't want to do this. I realised that I was afraid, and my excuses to avoid doing it were pathetic! By this time I had also realised that my feelings about the Native Americans had become obsessive, even fanatical — to the point where I couldn't stand to look at men of my own race. It made me nauseous. They smelled so strong and I hated to see the stubble on their faces and their pale blotchy skin. I had been trying all kinds of ways to get onto the Reservation to work and live.
>
> So we did this regression. It took almost two hours. What we accessed was incredible. It was in a cave; somewhere down in front was a slash of light that was the cave entrance. I was sitting there, a dirty smelly scraggy old man, not handsome at all. I had been away from the village and had come back to find it wiped out; I had a quick flash of men with muskets and Davy Crockett-type hats. Eileen asked me to describe what I could see in the cave and I described a hide-wrapped, bulky, odd-shaped and somehow ominous presence on a ledge behind me. Eileen sensed the relevance, asking, 'What's in the package?' 'It's *not* a package', I blurted tensely, affronted by her speaking of it as if it were an inconsequential brown paper parcel. 'It's a *bundle*.' There was an infinitely precious feeling to the
>
> *continued ...*

dirty lumpy thing and I realised I could not bear to think of the reason for that preciousness. Eileen was persistent, 'What is it?' 'It's not... I can't... I don't...' Something jammed in my throat. Nausea tightened in my chest as I sucked a deep shuddering breath into my trembling body and wailed. '*It's the bones*!'

I'd taken the remains of my grandchildren and my wife to the cave, but I couldn't do any more because it was the place of the women Elders to sing the song that let the spirit go. I was in deep despair. Eileen said, 'Well, there's no one else there to do it. You have to do it.' And then I sang it. It was incredible. It just burst from me. I repeated it four times and I remember thinking, 'How brilliant, I've got a tape going. I'll have this song'. But, of course, I hadn't put the tape on properly, so it didn't record!

When the song was over, I just lay there and this incredible hot grainy feeling passed through my body in waves. Somehow I knew to let it pass on down into the earth.

Then Eileen said, 'Well, that's it, you've done it. You can go outside.' And I said, 'No, there's nothing to go for.' So she said, 'Pray to your Creator, or whoever you make your peace with, and go outside.' And I said, 'I'm not going to pray to the Creator. It's all gone. There's nothing there.' She pushed me again and I snapped out of it. But what I felt was that he had sat there till he died. In other words, he committed suicide, which is not the way of the Native people; you go when the Creator says it's time. I wasn't sure what had happened to the parents of my grandchildren — presumably my son or daughter. But in those times it was nothing unusual for the grandparents to bring up the children.

This kind of situation is tricky. It needs very gentle but persistent handling. Too much pushing will make the regressee jump out of the experience, as Celia did. Eileen Churchill, whom I knew well, was a strong character. If she had an idea of how things should be handled and felt that she was right, she could push hard. Clearly in this situation she felt it needed reframing (that is, changing the ending) by getting the old man to go outside. But he, and Celia, were not ready for this. It would perhaps have been better to have let him go through his death and then done some healing work with him — although it is impossible to know without the benefit of hindsight just how to handle something as tricky as this! It sounds very much as though part of that soul could well have been trapped after death, still sitting in the cave as it were. If that was so, that soul fragment would need retrieving, something that can more easily be done in the post-death state. However, as we shall see, the regression had loosened the grip of that past life on Celia and helped her to see why she had become so obsessed with the Arrow Lakes people and their ancestral remains. It is, of course, possible that she regained that part of her soul simply by going through that experience. In other words, she 're-membered' herself. The change in her was noticeable immediately:

> When I went back to the reservation, Tom, the Arrow Lakes pipe carrier I worked with on cultural preservation projects, said, 'There's something changed. It's almost like there's a wall there, or you've left part of yourself behind.' Which I thought was really astute because from then on my obsession seemed to fade away and I could gradually walk away from the Native American world, the whole thing — and look at who I'm with now, a blonde Englishman — my husband!!

Nevertheless, that regression was crucial to her understanding of what had happened:

> What grabbed me first about the Band was their predicament with the bones and there was that old man with the bones. I can't verify any of this, only tell you what I went through.

It is not always easy to get into such a deep regression, especially when there is such trauma. Celia found it extremely difficult at first, but Eileen Churchill was a tenacious old soul and knew a trick or two to overcome resistance:

> When I couldn't get into the regression, Eileen asked me to look at what I was wearing and I thought 'OK, I'll make this up'. So I made up fine clothing — buckskin, soft and supple because it's so lovely on the skin — and long black hair, and I'd just got this description of the man who was in the mirror right when suddenly a terrible smell went like a warm cloud into my nose. It was an awful smell of that old man with his unwashed body on his way to death. It took me over then and my mouth started saying this stuff almost of its own accord, as the images came in. I became aware of a sensation, a rough scrap of material that covered my groin area. No soft tanned buckskin this, but a filthy, scraggy, hardened piece of material that scratched and chafed. Then from the corner of my eye I caught a glimpse, not of a sleek fall of black hair, but twisted, matted grey ropes like filthy dreadlocks lying untidily and stiffly over the knob of my bony shoulder and my skinny naked chest. My skin was dark and coppery, smeared with dirt and soot. This was a far cry from the image I had thought to call up. I felt cheated, angry and then a great despair at how everything seemed beyond my control suddenly caught hold. At times I hated Eileen. I wanted to say, 'Go away old woman' and stuff like that, but she made me stick with it, and I believe it.[9]

This is classic regression. It just feels so right — no matter how uncomfortable — and the detail is so acute with body feelings and emotions, and sensory experiences like that awful smell. After a regression like that, you cannot help but believe in reincarnation. You really do feel it is you.

As Celia found, once you have discovered the reasons for compulsions that are tied into past life experiences, the obsession goes. The 'past' no longer intrudes into the 'present'. When you have carried out the task that you reincarnated to do, to keep your promise, you are then free to develop your life in a different way.

For Celia this meant moving away from her Native America psychic heritage and returning to England. This involved her in a soulmate meeting, but it was far from straightforward. She first met her husband-to-be on a trip home to Northumbria sometime ago. Both were in a relationship with someone else and she was in the middle of her obsession with all things Native. As her now-husband said to me some time later, 'We clocked each other, recognised there was something, but that was as far as we could go.' When both their relationships had ended and Celia had done her karmic work, they met again — briefly. It would be another year or two before they were able to spend more time together. She then returned to England to be with him.

What we need to look at now is exactly why we incarnate with the people who are in our present life and how they may be linked to our past.

Notes:

1. Martin Tupper, *Proverbial Philosophy: On Memory,* quoted in Head and Cranston, *Reincarnation*.
2. Mary Swainson, *Light,* Winter 1985, p163.
3. Peter Moss with Joe Keeton, *Encounters with the Past* (London, Book Club Associates, 1979), p.135-158.
4. Ibid., p.158.
5. Judy Hall, *Principles of Past Life Therapy* (London, Thorsons, 1996), p.125ff.
6. In a personal letter to the author, the writer of which wishes to remain anonymous.
7. This account has already been published in my book *The Hades Moon* published by Samuel Weiser Inc, Maine, 1998. See this book for further explanations of the astrological connections.
8. For a picture of this effigy see Michael Bradley with Deanna Theilmann-Bean, *The Holy Grail Across the Atlantic* (Ontario, Hounslow Press, 1988), p.144. See also Andrew Sinclair, *The Sword and The Grail* (Century, 1993), p.150.
9. This account is taken from a personal conversation with Celia Gunn and from her book: *A Twist in Coyote's Tail.*

Chapter 5
Have I Seen You Somewhere Before?

I tell you of a truth, that the spirits which now have affinity shall be kindred together, although they meet in new persons and names.

The New Koran

A very large part of my work is concerned with relationships. How and why, who and what, are all words that feature prominently in people's questions about relationships. They want to know why they met their partner, what the purpose is, why their partner has left them, or why they continually meet the wrong sort of partner, what they are 'doing wrong', why they incarnated into the family that they did, how they can meet their true soulmate and who that soulmate is.

For this kind of work I do a karmic reading, both astrological and psychic. I tune into the past lives that are impacting on the present. For example, when Anna wrote to me asking me to look at her parental patterns, I saw a life in the English Raj. Her mother in that life was living very frivolously. Intelligent and creative, in Ceylon she found very little to occupy her time and turned to gambling and drinking — which got out of hand. Her daughter was left with servants to be brought up, so there was very little contact. Even after her mother's death, the child was left while the father continued his dissolute life. In Anna's present life, her mother had died when Anna was ten months old and Anna had been brought up by her grandmother and an aunt — although I did not know this when I did the reading. When Anna wrote to me afterwards she said:

> Your description of the mother figure who gambled and wasted money really struck a cord in me. As a young child I never saw anyone playing cards, but I vividly remember the visits to the cinema with my aunt. Whenever there was a supporting feature in which cowboys, or the like, gambled, I felt physically sick, and the apparent waste of money really horrified me. I used to wonder, as a child, if I had gambled in a past life and thought it unlikely... I do feel that those parents in Ceylon were probably my parents in this life. My father came from a poor family of Welsh origin. His mother, his sister and he all left school at the age of twelve and disapproved of anyone sitting down reading. My mother's family were educated, talented, and Irish.

She went on to tell me how her parents had met just after the First World War and had secretly been engaged for eight years while they saved up to buy a house outright. As she said, 'That was difficult but they seem to have learned their lesson and never drank or gambled. In fact, my mother kept account books in which she recorded every farthing she ever spent.' After her mother's death, her tyrannical father was a widower for forty-two years and would have nothing changed. He stayed in a time warp. It is quite common to find that you are either caught up in exactly the same scenario, or in one which is the opposite. In the present life, Anna's parents were obviously working on balancing out that gambling karma and went to the opposite extreme. But the pattern of being 'abandoned' by her mother held strong. She was brought up by people who, despite being blood relatives, were alien to her in every way.

Karma and Emotions

Many of the karmic lessons we have to face around relationships are to do with our emotions and strong feelings carried over from the past. It is clear from people's experiences in the post-death and the between life states that earth is the only plane where 'emotional games' can be played and where emotions can be kept hidden. Many communicators 'from the other side' report that once out of the physical body, the subtle bodies wear their emotions plainly for all to see. I see earth as our emotional learning ground. So, all those people who believe we are here to 'transcend our emotions' would seem to me to be on the wrong track. From both my own and my clients' experience, it is important to accept our emotions, not push them away. If we reject them, they fall into our shadow and return to plague us in new guises. Many of the characters in our karmic drama are acting out our unaccepted and suppressed emotions, and ingrained patterns, for us. We can change the patterns by finding a new way to deal with the person projecting the pattern to us, or by acknowledging the part of us that has those emotions. We can transmute these by fully accepting our emotional self and then choosing not to be bound by our emotion. This is a very different matter to analysing them away in therapy or rejecting them. If we fail to deal with our emotions and their consequences, we get pulled back into incarnation time and time again by the unfinished business.

Relationships are where our ingrained patterns show up — and our unlived life. We may endlessly recreate issues of abuse, abandonment, rejection, smothering, manipulation, power struggles and other compulsive 'love' sagas. We may find ourselves embroiled in victim/martyr/persecutor/rescuer scenarios, or acting out a dominance/submission scene, or a dependence/collusion, betrayer/betrayed, enabler/enabled theme. We may enter back into an older seducer/seduced tale, or freedom/commitment dilemma, or guilt/reparation epic. We may continually put partners on a pedestal, idealised and idolised, only to find them fall off and expose their feet of clay. We may also find ourselves time and time again wondering: 'Why can't I have fulfilling relationships?' or 'Why is it everyone I want a relationship with already has someone else?' We may have fixed ideas that rigidly control our lives, holding us back from growing emotionally or spiritually. We may be in a destructive cycle of addiction to something we call love but cannot move out of. We may also find ourselves with the most wonderful partner, but something prods us to move on. We may be looking for conditional love but need to learn the art of the unconditional. We may be seeking love from outside ourselves when the challenge is to love ourselves. The answer usually lies in other lives.

Reworking the Pattern

When Grace consulted me she told me that her mother was very rejecting — and abusive. She had spent a great deal of her young life in a children's home along with her siblings. Her father had left soon after her birth and her mother could not cope. When she was at home her mother 'displayed a fairly virulent hatred of me — as the outsider in the family'. She subjected Grace to violent abuse about her colour, which wounded her self-esteem. Eventually, the mother committed suicide. As a result, Grace found it hard to form relationships, and particularly difficult to deal with rejection on the part of a partner. Separations were very traumatic for her. She had already got in touch with several past lives, which had shed light on this, but she wanted to know more.

Astrologically speaking, there were aspects in her chart which indicate a great deal of 'mothering karma' and many issues around abandonment and rejection. One of her greatest needs was to learn to love herself instead of relying on anyone else to give her love. (The situation with her mother provided the ideal setting for this.) I read a past life for her in which she had been a beautiful small boy who was petted and pampered — and yet who was the son of a slave. Like Grace in her present life, he was a mixed-race child. He was brought from Barbados to England by a woman whose children had all died from a fever. She herself returned to England for the good of her health bringing this substitute son with her. He appeared to be the son of her husband and one of the slave girls. Taken away from his natural mother, he felt she had abandoned him. A black woman had been brought over to be his nanny, but she resented the child deeply. She was looked on as the lowest of the low while the child was elevated to high status. Hating England, she blamed the child for her predicament and went into a deep depression. Eventually she simply pined away and died. I felt that this 'nanny' was the previous incarnation of Grace's mother and that all this resentment had been brought back into the relationship.

The child was well educated. He was handsome and well liked, but in the society that he found himself no family would allow him to marry their daughter. He was extremely conscious of both a class and colour barrier. After his surrogate mother's death he returned to his homeland, where his natural father was happily ensconsed with his real mother. While his father would have given him a place on the plantation, having given him his freedom when he was taken to England, his mixed race made him even more of an outsider than he had been in England. He was socially unacceptable both to his father and his mother's people, so he went to America. There he started up a business and found a niche he could occupy according to the strata of society to which he 'belonged' in the thinking of the day.

However, with going back to his birthplace and being rejected, something had died inside him; he thought he had no place in the world. He felt very unloved, despite having a wife and children. Although he had been petted and pampered in England, he had not been loved for who he intrinsically was. This was a pattern which Grace was to transfer to her present life.

In New Orleans, he had many affairs with white women. With his striking appearance he was considered quite a catch — in the amusement stakes. He was passed around a group of bored women who found him most entertaining as a lover, but with whom he could not be seen in public as an equal. This further crystallised his sense of not belonging anywhere and reduced his sense of worth still further. Many of the issues he faced then, Grace would have to deal with again.

Had I been working with Grace in regression, I would have asked her to trace the line of her relationships back until she found one in which she had had good relationships. By reconnecting to this, she could have learnt once again how it felt to be in the right relationship — both to herself and others. As I was working psychically to find a way to heal this, I had to look for a life at its root. I wanted to find a life where Grace knew how to have good relationships and was in spiritual balance (another part of Grace's initial question to me). Ironically, in that incarnation she had spent her life counselling others who had problems. Because she herself was in a happy relationship, she thought to herself, 'I don't know about jealousy, pain, lack of self-worth, etc. I need to know because how else can I help people. I cannot feel it from my heart because I haven't been there.' So she had made a conscious decision to learn about these things at first hand. This had led to many incarnations in which she experienced the whole gamut of emotions and painful relationships. But she had not intended to get trapped in that cycle for so long.

Now in her present life she was trying to break out of these deeply ingrained patterns. She had become aware that she had an addictive need to fill the inner void in herself with any relationship which would distract from her sense of empty incompletion. When I checked back with her some two years after doing the reading, she was working in a spiritual way — using *A Course in Miracles* to heal that need and find her own inner self. As she said:

> If it is true that we create our own inner reality, that people simply mirror back to us our opinion of ourselves and trigger us where we are still damaged, then my mother offered me the gift of journeying back to self-love through childhood adversity... What is important to me is that I've found a path to empowerment, I've begun to sprout and refine a Good Mother inside me, and she will extinguish the generational legacy of maternal wounding, a belief my future children will one day hopefully testify to.

As she grew older, so Grace's sense of identity grew less split and the less attached she felt to it. She began to value her self as she was.

Whether the lives I saw for Grace were symbolic of her past experience, or actual, did not matter. They epitomised the splits and the patterns that were in essence her soul story. They showed where her difficulties in relationships had their roots. Knowing that it was her choice originally and that she had done it out of a desire for compassion and empathy with others, helped Grace to heal. She then began to look forward to finding her true mate with whom she could have a fulfilling and rewarding relationship.

SOULMATES

I have already written in depth about soulmates[1] but make no apologies for returning to the subject here — albeit briefly. Relationships are where we learn our fundamental lessons in life. Families and soulmates are the vehicle for this. That your soulmate is not quite what you expected is, I feel, the norm rather than the exception. But the desire for a soulmate lies behind many of our relationship sagas.

Experience leads me to believe that our soulmate is not singular, neither is it necessarily the man — or woman — of our dreams. A soulmate is someone who shares our soul group — part of that original large drop of soul essence that separated out from the whole and began its journey through incarnation. A soulmate is someone who helps us to grow — in the way we need, not the way we would like. So often a regressee will go to the between life state and find that an agreement has been made before incarnation. That agreement is to help us learn the lessons or experience exactly the conditions we need for our spiritual growth. These things are rarely comfortable. We may also have made an arrangement to fulfil something while here on earth, to take on a task with our partner. That task may have nothing to do with sexual matters, and yet it is usually sex that rears its head first when a past life contact is renewed. Old soulmate contacts begin with a wave of lust as the base chakras open up in recognition of an old lover. Indeed, so many people fall instantly in lust rather than in love that it is hardly surprisingly that soulmate connections do not always end happily. This wave of lust may well obscure the real reason for meeting again.

We may also find that a soulmate is not in incarnation with us. He or she may be acting as a 'guide' for our present life, helping and encouraging us from the other side. There are occasions, however, when this seemingly disparate being is actually a part of our self that we need to reintegrate so that we can make the inner marriage of our own masculine and feminine selves. This 'projection' of the masculine or feminine can occur in or out of incarnation. Some people do it with a partner, others with a guide, or an imagined soulmate for whom they eternally search instead of looking inside their own self.

While we may believe that we are looking for someone to make us complete, to love us for ever, and to be completely and utterly *ours*, it seems that the spiritual purpose of partnership is to learn to be whole within oneself. To be totally bonded to someone else on all levels is unusual, and may even be spiritually unhealthy. It is certainly psychologically so, as it can create dependence. Many relationship issues centre around regaining autonomy and taking back one's own power. There are times when it is appropriate to be joined on the physical, emotional, mental and spiritual levels. This is the ancient 'mystic marriage', some of which still survive today. But there are also times when a spiritual divorce is called for, a separation back into the two individuals. In such cases the union is on one or more of the levels but not on all. A regression back into the between life state often shows that people choose a relationship that will enable them to grow into and learn how to complete an incomplete bonding on a particular level — and also how to break free from a too suffocating bond that has formed previously.

There may be bonds left over from any previous relationships, which exist and function on a physical, emotional, mental or spiritual plane — and sometimes all four at once. It depends on how many of these bonds are appropriate to the present incarnation, and how they are developed, as to whether we will have a loving, fulfilling soulmate relationship in this life or a struggle to free ourselves from those bonds.

For many people the connection to someone else is purely physical. But it is worth remembering that even a physical act, especially the sexual act, can take with it a part of our soul — if we allow it to. I have done so many tie cuttings with clients where they realise that they have given their heart or soul into someone else's keeping, even in the most fleeting contact, that I now look out for this. If this occurred in a past life, the act will carry over into the present. When we meet that person again, he or she can 'reel us in' through the karmic bond that was created. Ina Crawford says of karmic bonds that 'the action of one person needs a reaction on the part of another on the mental and emotional planes before a thread is formed'.[2] If one person is truly detached, that is not hooked into an old pattern or engaged in an emotional game, then no karmic link can accrue. I would add, unless, of course, that person is deliberately holding back from a situation or intimacy into which it would be more proper to enter. We have to bear in mind that karma arises just as much from inaction, the things that we have not done that we ought to have done, as it is does from the action we take.

Many relationship problems only arise once the marriage or other bond has been in place for some time. People do not move or grow at the same pace. If one person develops on a spiritual level but the other does not, this means there will be no link at that level but strong feeling will still feature in lower levels. If one person detaches emotionally, but the spiritual development of both keeps pace, it will lead to a situation where they feel like soulmates — born to be together for ever — but find a sexual relationship frustrating, as intimacy will be lacking. People may well be on the same mental wavelength but have no physical attraction or spiritual understanding. 'Imbalance can lead to unhappiness, suffering and sometimes tragedy.'[3] This is perhaps the core of karmic relationship difficulties.

It is often the case that someone comes for karmic counselling because what has been a good relationship has turned stale or feels stuck. The other person is not growing or moving. It may be that the lesson is to stand aside placidly and let that other person develop in his or her own time and own way. So often a degree of spiritual understanding is accompanied by the need to prod partners into finding the same understanding for themselves. Part of the definition of unconditional love is the ability to stand by and allow others to make their own mistakes and to develop in their own unique way, no matter how much we can see what they could be. If we love them *as they are* this allows them to be what they must be. If we impose any conditions or try to change them in any way, then the love is not unconditional. Similarly, if allowing them to do what they must do entails them walking all over us, the 'love' is martyrdom or victimhood, not unconditional love. So much of relationships is sorting out this kind of confusion — and learning to do for ourselves what we feel we should do for others.

It may also be, however, that the time has come to move on, to look for a way that enables us to part without acrimony and further karma accruing. Letting go in this way can present an enormous challenge when the physical or emotional bond remains strong. It may be that if we love someone, we must love them enough to set them free. We may want to hold on to the relationship; we may feel it is not complete, that there is more to do — we maybe believe that even more bonding is necessary. But if we can open our heart and let them go, then our soul as well as theirs can grow — and who knows what will happen then when we meet again?

In these kind of circumstances, I have my clients perform a 'tie-cutting' which loosens the bonds of the past. It removes negative conditioning and karmic expectations, all the 'oughts and shoulds' that build up, and releases any vows or promises we might have made. That way each person is set free to be his or her own self. Such work does not cut off the unconditional love from a soul level, but it does allow a new beginning to be made in whatever way is appropriate for the highest good of each person concerned.

The Karmic Mirror

We can look at our relationships as mirroring our own inner psychic reality. We create the situations we need to play out our karmic scenarios, to meet our ingrained expectations. The actors in the drama have often been known to us in the past. But this is not always so. New characters can be drawn into our 'unfinished business'. Indeed, we may choose to work through something with someone with whom there is no karmic charge from the past so that we may learn the lesson and then apply it to a relationship where there is a karmic link. In what appears to be a repeating past life situation, the cast may change from incarnation to incarnation, but the underlying theme will be the same.

Ina Crawford reminds us that our surroundings and companions react to us in a way that responds to what and where we are at any given moment. In other words they 'tune in' to us and respond consciously or unconsciously, to our frequencies, just as they are at a particular moment in time. If we or they fail to understand and adjust to these frequencies but react to them instead, a further chain of reaction is set up. This chain of reaction then carries over into another lifetime. However, by going back into the past, we can sever that connection and change the interaction — and we can also change it by tiecutting in the present life.

A prime example of that comes from the experience of one of my clients. She found that she had said, 'I hope you rot in hell' in response to some particularly nasty behaviour towards her in a past life. However, as she said, she was most surprised to find that she had to do another life with that person, to watch and be part of that hell. She had thought the hell was nothing to do with her. She was suffering by seeing the suffering of this other person, whom she had loved — and whom she desperately wanted to leave but felt a duty towards; so how could she have set all this in motion?

But, as she realised during the regression, she had actually set this in motion by her thoughts and words in that other life. By forgiving that person 'back then' and taking the words back, she was able to set them both free. Although the person who was suffering would continue to do so (he was working through his own karma on this), she did not need to stay in the situation which had been exacerbating things. She moved out and he became much less bitter. Both of their lives improved. Things are rarely what they seem at first glance.

Many other vows, promises and pacts have present life significance but stem from the past. Even comments like 'I'll always be your mummy' can go horribly wrong when the relationship is not physically one of mother and son, but when it is emotionally, and this is how it shows itself at a more subtle level. So many women — and men too — say 'I don't want to mother him or her, but somehow I always do.' The reason lies in the past but the challenge is to change the interaction. By detaching from the past, cutting the ties with the scenario, the present is affected for the better. A new relationship is possible. The dynamics of any relationship are rarely what is seen on the surface.

Family Ties

Families too are rarely what they seem. We may rant and rail against a parent for treating us badly, but when we look at the astrology of the situation we learn that we arrived into incarnation expecting exactly that kind of experience. Our parents have mirrored the right ambience for us, even though it may be hard to acknowledge — or indeed to see the reason why. On the other hand, we may have chosen a family because they enabled us to flower and encouraged us to develop our skills and talents in the right way for us. We may well have chosen that particular family because they carried an emotional or a genetic imprint that we needed to interact with. Or we could be working out personal karma with them. Ancestral memory too is a contributory causal factor in the soul choosing to incarnate into a particular family. That we would incarnate into a family with whom we have had no connection at all anywhere in the past is rare, although we may well only have a prior connection with someone like a grandmother, for instance. But our family is by no means always our soul group — and this may be one of the insights we have incarnated to make. We also make agreements to come so others can learn a lesson. We may be the representative from our soul group who incarnates to pass on what our group has learned to others. This can occur in the family, in our relationships, or in other spheres of life.

There are times, however, when we need the close ties of a family that is both our soul group and our family of origin to support us.

Richard Metcalfe was an amazing young man. He cooked to *cordon bleu* standards, was a champion hurdler and an exceptional scholar about to take six A levels and assured of a place at one of the top British universities. Richard was a gentle person, a peacemaker who really cared about the boys he was at school with and who was liked by everyone that knew him. A well-rounded person who organised 'Renaissance Man' contests for his fellow pupils. Despite the unpromising start of being the product of an ugly rape, he was extremely close to his parents and his younger brother and sister. He had a brilliant future ahead of him. Why then did he commit suicide just ten days after his eighteenth birthday?

Well, his mother Carolyn believes it had a great deal to do with the stress he was under at school. Not only were those six A levels looming, but he had also had to contend with the death of the father of his best friend and the pressure of a drama festival. And the school had, unbeknown to his mother, put him on a lethal cocktail of Prozac and Diazepam because he had been suffering, as they saw it, from depression. Both Prozac and Diazepam are medically recognised to have the side effect of depression; so this was perhaps not the most appropriate treatment for a young man who was under such stress.

The month Richard died, four other boys from Dorset also committed suicide or disappeared from home without trace — a pattern that was being repeated all over the country. It had the makings of an epidemic. Having found out that many other boys at Richard's top public school were also on this cocktail of drugs, his mother decided to speak out. She appeared on several television programmes, including prime-time national news, and the story was written up in a wide array of newspapers and magazines. The school was not at all pleased. They withheld his medical notes and his personal belongings. But it did bring the dangers of these so easily prescribed 'panaceas for all ills' to the notice of those who might otherwise have blindly continued to follow medical advice that could well lead to their death.

Shortly after his death, Richard appeared several times to his young sister (with whom he had had a very close rapport) who saw him as solid and real as when he was alive. His mother too was aware of his presence. Knowing that Richard had died in the library, his favourite place at school, and aware that there was a strong possibility that he had expected to be found before the pills worked, she felt that he might have been regretting his action. So she told him that if he wanted to, she would be his mother again. He could come back and be part of the family once more. Within a month, she was pregnant.

The birth was a particularly difficult one. Having gone into premature labour, Carolyn was sent back to her isolated home by the hospital because 'the birth was not imminent'. Within an hour, she was on the phone to them saying that the baby was coming. They told her to hold back, to put herself in a position which would hinder the birth until a midwife or an ambulance could get there. Eventually Carolyn heard a voice saying, 'I'm dying, I'm dying, you have to help me'. She delivered the baby herself. He had been inhaling muconium, a very dangerous condition, and was blue and barely alive. They were rushed to the premature baby unit.

Rufo, as he was quickly christened, died several times and was revived. Mother and baby were sent off to a special baby unit in another county. No one expected to see the baby alive again. But somehow he pulled through the toxic conditions, the chest infections and specific disabilities that his premature birth had created (helped no doubt by the flower essences and homeopathy for past life trauma I had smuggled in to Carolyn and with which she surreptitiously treated the baby whenever the sceptical nurses were out of the way). The hospital were sure he was brain damaged. I sent in more potions. They decided that he was fine after all. When my partner, Rob Jacobs, who is a complementary doctor, saw him sometime later he commented that all the medical conditions were the exact mirror of the way Richard had died.

Unbeknown to Rob, Carolyn had already come to the conclusion that this was Richard reincarnated.

She had checked this out with a Tibetan lama who had the ability to know such things. Indeed, while we were waiting for Rob she had been telling me this very thing and the baby kept looking at us both, nodding his tiny head and quite clearly saying 'Yes, here I am again!' Although, as Carolyn said, she also felt that Richard was somewhere else as well; that, in some way, he was in several places on various levels at the same time: part of him was working on a spiritual level, part of him had incarnated as baby Rufo, and part of him was somewhere else again (possibly still as Richard in the post-death state). This 'fragmentation' was something else that the Tibetan lama had confirmed. In his way of looking at the world, this was nothing new. The lama had another part of himself reincarnated in Tibet (the spiritual home from which he had been exiled by the Chinese) and yet another part that was not in incarnation. It was quite normal.

Talking to Carolyn over a year later, she was still of this same opinion. The baby wasn't out of danger. He had been rushed off to hospital several times. His breathing still caused problems, he was asthmatic and allergic to just about everything. All these conditions could have carried over from that previous death. With such a quick turn-round, there was little time for healing his etheric blueprint. But he handled this well, never protesting even at some of the more invasive procedures that saved his life more than once. He had the same sweetness of nature that Richard had had, and the same bond with his sister. When he was taken to Richard's old prep school at six months old, he had looked at the headmaster and several of the teachers 'as though he knew them well'. He was happy to be in the school Richard had loved.

Carolyn commented that in the past she thought that Richard's mixed-race colour might have caused him some problems; he had the dark skin, deep brown eyes and curly hair of his blood-father. 'Now', she said, 'he's just the opposite. Very delicate white skin, pale blue eyes and light blonde hair. Just about as different as he could get.' And very like the man who had accepted him as his own and fathered him for eighteen years.

It remains to be seen how far Rufo will take his present life. Sometimes when someone has died a violent or precipitate death, they need to come back for a time to adjust and then they leave again. At other times, they want to live out all that was left unlived the last time. Certainly Rufo has an extraordinary will to live and is already presenting the quick intelligence and brightness of Richard despite the slow physical development that his birth created. He may be suffering from soul loss; there may well be a part of himself that is still Richard going through the after-death process. He may need to regain this part of his soul or to reconnect to the part of himself that is in the spiritual world. Only time will tell.

Soul Groups

As we have seen, soul groups can have complex interactions. A soul group is a band of souls that we travel with — loosely. We may spend a great deal of time with many of our soul group, a little time with one of them, a lifetime or two with others. It is rare that all of a group are in incarnation at once. And as we get deeper into incarnation, we find that we have strong karmic links with some of the band and not others. Indeed, it may be a new member of the group coming in that changes the whole pattern. Such catalysts can have a profound effect on the consciousness of the whole group or a devastating impact on just one soul. Carolyn felt that she and Richard, her other children and her partner, and other close associates, all belonged to a soul group that had incarnated many times together. She traced many of their interactions and recognised the lessons and the patterns. She felt like they were working through a vast 'net' of karmic connections.

This is a common experience. While it is not always within a family group, there is, nevertheless, a strong sense of a group forming and reforming over many incarnations. Jill Mayner and the 'Taj Mahal group' (see Chapter 1) are just one example of how souls feel they are drawn together again. Those drops of water return to the puddle more than once before being splashed out again.

Such soul connections are not always conscious or obvious. I have one client for whom I do a great deal of work. He is the centre of a web of people all of whom, we feel, have a karmic task to carry out. In most cases, he is the only point of contact. Few of them know each other. When we looked at the dynamics of the situation, we felt that it was the linking up of a healing group who were not working on the physical plane. So, they did not need to meet up again physically but did so on a soul level through this man's connection with each one of them.

In other cases healing bands are drawn together again to work in a much more concrete way. They have trained together in the past and now make use of that training. Along the way they may well be working on karma that has been generated in another life; power issues are common in such cases, for instance.

I personally see no reason why discrete souls should not incarnate into one body if the situation calls for it. Whether they will necessarily be part of a soul group — or a group soul — is a moot point. If the soul for the incarnation separates out into its 'droplets' again after that incarnation, then several souls could carry the memory of what seemed to be one soul. This may well be one of the explanations of why so many people remember being that one person.

Groups may well come together for other purposes. It is in these groups and in their interaction that archetypal patterns and the kind of 'historical group' lives that we looked at in Chapter 1 most often surface. I know of one New Age centre run by such a group. So many of the people there told me confidentially that their leader was King Arthur reincarnated and they were his knights. Very few seemed to have shared this feeling with the others and as people are continually coming and going there is a constant recycling of the image. Suggesting to any of them that they might be seeing things symbolically led to vehement denial. This was who they were! It has been fascinating to watch the same old power and betrayal scenarios play themselves out over the years. Of course, this scenario needs its Guinevere. There have been plenty of those offering themselves on Arthur's altar. Interestingly the leader believes he was an English king and has his court around him once more — but not that particular king. This one is rather less saintly and certainly indulged in more than one power battle during his life — battles that have endlessly been repeated. No doubt they will continue being played out until someone takes hold of the dynamics behind the projection, deals with the realities of the karmic interaction — and faces the leader's power complex.

As with so many past life dramas, Arthur and his Court will no doubt be reworked many times in the course of history as soul groups continue to unite and reunite. If such groups can accept that they are playing out an archetypal drama, the people caught up in it have a much better chance of not becoming embroiled in personal karma. They may well be part of a genuine soul group, in which case they will go onto other things, but in many cases they are simply pulled into the drama because of their own issues. And, of course, there is a group ego just as much as a group soul. When the soul group goes its separate ways, those souls may have a choice as to whether they continue to incarnate together.

The Poet From the Underworld

For a soul relationship to go on, both parties do not need to be in incarnation at the same time. If there is a task to do, one may elect to be here on earth, while the other remains in the spiritual realms. This may sound far-fetched, but I have encountered many such cases. One of the most fascinating concerns the First World War poet, Wilfred Owen.

Wilfred Owen spoke for a whole generation of young men. While being bitterly opposed to war, he volunteered because he felt it was his duty — pushed by a tyrannical father who thought his sensitive (and homosexual) son should 'be a man'. As a young officer, he was sent to the trenches where he found himself in hell. Wilfred was buried alive several times and he saw unspeakable horrors. He came to realise that his task was to portray the pity and horror of war. His poems certainly capture the horror and beautifully illustrate how the soul can leave its body in moments of terror:

My soul looked down from a vague height, with Death,
As unremembered how I rose or why,
And saw a sad land, weak with sweats of dearth,
Grey, cratered like the moon with hollow woe,
And pitted with great pocks and scabs of plagues.

Across its beard, that horror of harsh wire,
There moved thin caterpillars, slowly uncoiled.

It seemed they pushed themselves to be as plugs
Of ditches, where they writhed and shrivelled, killed.
...

I saw their bitten backs curve, loop, and straighten.
I watched those agonies curl, lift, and flatten.

Whereat, in terror what that sight might mean,
I reeled and shivered earthward like a feather.

And Death fell with me, like a deepening moan,
And He, picking a manner of worm, which half had hid
Its bruises in the earth, but crawled no further,
Showed me its feet, the feet of many men,
And the fresh-severed head of it, my head.

The Show

Wilfred's severe shell-shock gave him an opportunity of moving to light duties away from the Front but he chose to return to be with his men. (He was a Pisces and as such was willing to sacrifice himself for others.) He was killed with them, trying to cross a river on a suicide mission, just days before the war ended. When he died, many fragments of his poems remained. His 'work in progress', as with so many war deaths, had been interrupted.

A solicitor friend of mine, Robert, originally sent me Wilfred's birth data and his photo and asked me to describe this man's last few hours, and to do a synastry reading for the two of them — despite the fact that Wilfred had then been dead for seventy-five years. When I did the reading, I told Robert that he was living something out for this man. Something that had been incomplete had needed completion; so Robert agreed to do it for him. I was also sure that they had been close in a previous life — and in a joint death.

Robert wrote back to say that he was working on performance versions of the unfinished and fragmentary poems that Wilfred had left behind — with Wilfred's help and, indeed, at his insistence. Wilfred was most anxious that these should be completed. Robert was allowed no rest until the work was finished — a period of several years. This was not a possession by a dead spirit (Robert's boundaries are strong enough to resist that) but it came close. Wilfred 'spoke through' Robert in the poetry they made together. Robert was the scribe, the amanuensis for Wilfred's genius.

Robert himself is sure that he too had died in that war. He has always had powerful memories of that time and very strong feelings about that war. He believes he knew Wilfred Own well, that they were close companions. This is why Wilfred chose him to complete the poems. This is not some strange fantasy. As a solicitor, Robert is used to weighing up evidence. Despite his sensitivity and artistic interests, he is not the kind of man given to vivid imaginings. His scholarship is meticulous and is of such a standard that Oxford University have lodged the finished poems and performance versions in their archives. He is convinced that he and Wilfred, having been together in the trenches, were soul companions. And, as soul companions, they made a pact to complete this work.

When the work was over, Wilfred was reluctant to leave. This was where I came in again. I had been doing work on the astrology of Wilfred's life and was aware of his presence from time to time. It became clear that while not exactly trapped, part of Wilfred's soul was still fixed in the horror of war (although the majority of it was vicariously enjoying life at the end of the twentieth century). Robert and I joined forces to help this soul reunite and move on. As Wilfred was particularly devoted to his mother, we asked her help in taking him to the light. In the end, Wilfred went willingly — having left a last-minute 'final gem of a poem' with Robert. When I was writing up Wilfred's story for *The Hades Moon*[4] Wilfred returned. A delightful man, he was most helpful. I would be directed to exactly the right poem and just the research information I needed on that war. It was as though he was saying thank you, but more than that he wanted the story told. It was his contribution to the end of the astrological Age of Pisces. A great deal had been surfacing from the collective around the First World War — which has been in some senses the forgotten war. It is very much 'in the air'. As we have seen, many people are incarnating with memories of that time and, of course, while there are only a handful of men left who actually fought in that war, the generation who were children at that time are now leaving earth. It is as though the memory of those men who sacrificed their lives needed to be honoured, and then let go of. In doing this, the collective karma of war would be cleansed.

The Continuing Perils of a Handsome French Stranger

Although Wilfred Owen's story seems to end there, at least for the time being, whenever I write a book, I am aware that by writing about something I 'fix it in time'. So often the story goes on, expands, changes as it takes its life course. But my readers do not know this. What they read is, for them, as it is. One story in particular needs an update.

In *Hands Across Time*[5] Christie and Tyrell told the story of their relationship from their different perspectives. The two accounts were so different that several people asked me if some text had been missed out. Had I gone on to something else? No, I had not. These were the individual accounts of that joint relationship, even if they did seem to be living in totally different worlds. And, perhaps not surprisingly, by the time the book was published, Christie and Tyrell had separated. As I said in the book, initially they did seem so right together even though Christie in particular showed enormous resistance to committing to the relationship — but projected this out on Tyrell. But it was not to be. Examining their relationship so closely for the book only brought the inevitable split forward. I had suggested to Christie that perhaps Tyrell was not the handsome French stranger she believed she had fallen in love with but who had abused her trust in a past life, but she was adamant. Tyrell was, in her mind, indissolubly connected to a man who had in the past caused her to live in the 'darkness of losing the love and acceptance of a community' [her tribe]. She felt he was responsible for all her ills. She could not forgive him, blaming him for all she could not own in herself. When they were divorcing, she took her revenge. Taking everything that she felt was owed from that previous life, she drained him dry of energy and resources. So ill did he become that he sought the counsel of an intuitive diagnostician who said that he was on the verge of becoming terminally ill as a result of his ex-wife's wrath. He needed a considerable degree of healing to overcome the effects of the present life contact. As I saw it, all he could do to counteract the past was to continuously forgive her so that the relationship would not need to be taken into another life.

This is another peril of the past intervening in the present life. Christie totally believed in the past life which she had been told about. (She did not experience it.) It fitted what she thought had happened to her and resonated with her own themes of abuse and betrayal. It also prevented her from entering into the intimacy she said she sought but which she fought against strenuously. By taking refuge in the excuse of 'this was what you did to me in the past', she did not have to take responsibility for her own actions in the present life. So often past lives are used in this way. We get out of learning what we never wanted to undertake on the pretext of 'I can't help it, it's my karma'.

Tyrell had talked about the relationship in very different terms. In his account for *Hands Across Time* he had described a relationship which he felt was with a soulmate — his first wife. After that marriage ended he examined many things, including what a soulmate was and came to the conclusion that there was no such thing, because if we had all evolved from an original point of being, then we were all equally connected and it came down to choosing whom we wanted to be with. However, he was aware of a strong connection to his sister Sara as their lives and relationships moved along a kind of 'parallel track'.

Then he met Christie. His first thought was 'I know you'. His second was: 'Keep away!' He felt clear that he did not want a relationship. Up to that point he had felt he knew where he was going with his life. Then Christie came on the scene and he was drawn in by what he describes as the romance of meeting and being involved with her. She was an attractive woman with a strong, flamboyant character — very different to the English women with whom he was in contact. She made it clear that she wanted to be in a relationship. So why did he go against that initial, 'Keep away!'?

> I used to take on challenges in relationships to bring out what I felt was hidden in the person. In Christie I felt there was a lot of bluff about the way she presented herself and I told her that she was 'busted'. Part of her did really want to be seen for who she really was — that was a strong part of the connection at first.

Seven months later they were married. The conflicts began immediately and they were both shocked. Each felt they had married someone totally different. As Tyrell says he felt 'steam-rollered, manipulated, misunderstood, misquoted, mistreated and powerless'. She felt that he was playing the therapist with her. She says that the communication broke down completely and she felt he wanted her to go. But they struggled on because somewhere underneath what was happening, each felt that there was love and learning to be had. Tyrell compared the relationship to looking in a mirror. Everything he had done in previous relationships, he saw Christie doing to him. As a therapist, he believed that it did not matter who was doing what to whom, what was important was how he dealt with it. Christie did not see it this way at all. To her, what was in front of her was how it was. Their approaches to life were so different.

When Tyrell was seeking guidance, he took down a book at random and opened it. It was the myth of Perseus. Perseus was challenged by the king to go and cut off the head of Medusa. Any man who looked upon the face of Medusa — horrendous, framed by writhing snakes — became paralysed with shock. This was the face of the 'negative feminine', a dark shadow aspect of woman and man. Perseus dealt with the Medusa by taking a burnished shield into which he looked rather than looking directly. When he cut off Medusa's head, out flew Pegasus, 'potent with the positive feminine qualities of creativity and spirituality'.[6] Perseus then goes on to free Andromeda from being sacrificed — another metaphor for freeing the anima, the feminine. Tyrell saw this as a perfect summary of what was happening for him. He was working to slay his horror of the dark feminine. In doing this, he tried to accept Christie as she was. He closed his account by saying, 'I still don't believe in soulmates, but I do believe that the gift Christie has given me, forcing me to look deep inside, is every bit as valuable as that of the more conventionally accepted version of 'mutuality' (Christie's definition of a soulmate connection).[7]

When I was working on *Deja Who* I asked Tyrell for an update. What else had he learned from this relationship?

Eighteen months ago, I told Christie I wanted a divorce. Five months later we were separated. Unsurprisingly to me, I was exhausted — emotionally, mentally and physically. However, six months after our separation, instead of recuperating, I seemed to be getting worse.

Three people, two of whom knew nothing about me, told me I was under serious psychic attack — no prizes for guessing where it was coming from. One added that I was also being vampirised by my mother. I'm tempted to say 'but that's another story', but it's not, it's the same story. By the end of the marriage, I was virtually penniless, I had M.E. and I was told I was 'pre-cancerous'. At every level, my energy had been utterly drained and I was spiralling downwards. And the draining was to the dark feminine.

In the original telling of my story in *Hands Across Time*, I wrote 'presumably Medusa's death results from natural causes!'[8] I felt vague when I wrote it. What I have discovered since is that it is not possible to remain in the cave of Medusa without a clear purpose. She does not die of natural causes; her *darkness* dies through her being clearly seen in the mirror (in myself) brought forward and then integrated.

I was reminded of this quotation from the Gnostic Gospels: 'If you bring forth what is within you, what you bring forth will save you. If you do not bring forth what is within you, what you do not bring forth will destroy you.'[9]

I had to make a choice: either to give up on a world that could not provide the partner who would love me and make me feel whole, or bring my unacknowledged feminine forward and work toward an inner marriage.

It's too early to say for sure if I've made the second choice, though I feel I have.

I had been co-authoring a book, but it was not a book that had sprung purely from the heart and pleasure of

continued ...

my own creativity. When I did begin work on such a project, energy began to return. This continues to fit in with the myth of Perseus, as Pegasus (creativity and spirituality) is released.

The dark feminine is merely the unrecognised. I am learning how to welcome that part of me. My work as a therapist is far more intuitively led. My writing is beginning to flow again. More and more I connect to and am fed by Nature.

And for the first time in my life, I am very consciously staying out of a relationship. (As is my sister!)

I no longer see happiness 'out there' but rather through the integration of the healthy inner masculine and feminine. It has been an understanding that I spouted forth to clients, but never before did I know it so well as now.

There was another gift of learning from all of this. I realised I had spent much of the marriage (and my life) protesting my truth — wanting for it, and therefore me, to be acknowledged. In this way I was externalising my need to be validated. This was bigger than just relationships; I had a great desire to change the world — to make it better (in my view!).

It took a judge's mocking cry in the divorce court, 'Truth! What is truth?!' for me to see he was right. What is truth? It really doesn't matter. But I knew this issue was very old for me. It was time to validate myself.

Christie unwittingly brought me to that awareness.

Our primary responsibility has to be to ourselves — to take ourselves to the limit of our potential, and if another person offers to help us on that path, no matter how he or she does that, then that person deserves thanks.

Thank you, Christie.

I asked Tyrell whether he thought the relationship was karmic. He looked confused for a moment and then said:

I would have to say that everything is karmic but the trap is to see it as such. Because as soon as you start seeing things as karmic you never break the circle. Everything we talk about is flow and releasing and as soon as you bring in a concept of rigid karma, it creates a circle.

I feel that there are far more levels to our being than we can ever imagine. And in the same way as if we get too attached to the material level, we lose connection to the non-material levels, if we get attached to past lives and higher selves we lose the possibility of connections to a more ultimate reality. We limit ourselves by our beliefs. Yet at the same time I do accept that whatever we believe to be true is true. So simply by believing there could be a traumatic past life connection, as Christie saw it, we could be negating a higher level 'agreement' based on love. We did both feel, despite all our problems, that there was love at a soul level. I don't think I had ever been touched so deeply by anyone before and I have to accept that touch could be both loving and destructive and that's the way it is.

Tyrell had felt that he could not do a tie cutting with Christie until the divorce was over. To me, the divorce was merely the formal ending, but for him somehow the marriage would not be over until it happened. Christie prolonged the divorce way beyond what was reasonable. She was like a cat playing with a mouse. She is a Leo after all. When we discussed this, he realised that he could be free now, at that moment. He came to see me and we did a tie cutting that operated at many levels. Initially both the circles kept moving and tried to overlap each other — always a sign that there is still an attachment there — which was why he had been open to psychic attack from her. There were several ties to remove — and some illusions. When these were cleared it revealed the deep soul love that was still there, but it cut away all the expectations and projections. He was able to allow her to move away into her own space while he remained in his. By the time he left, he looked clearer. He was finally freed from the past, whenever that past might be.

Notes

1. Judy Hall, *Hands Across Time* (Forres, Findhorn Press, 1998).
2. Ina Crawford, *Guide to the Mysteries.*
3. *Ibid.*, p102.
4. Judy Hall, *The Hades Moon* (Maine, Samuel Weiser Inc, 1998).
5. Judy Hall, *Hands Across Time* p.154.
6. Ibid., p.153.
7. Ibid., p.154.
8. Ibid., p.154.
9. From *The Gnostic Gospels*, the Gospel of Thomas.

Chapter 6
New Lives For Old

Is not thy body for ever transformed, and flows it not ever
Into the river of time? And in ceaseless alteration
Doth it not cast off the old for the new, ever losing and gaining

Giordano Bruno[1]

There is an enormous difference between spontaneously reliving a life, revisiting a life under hypnosis and undergoing Past Life Therapy (PLT). In PLT a person is guided to a time before birth in the present life; that is, into another life, to uncover and heal the causes of problems and difficulties that have arisen in the present life. PLT can also enhance self-worth by reliving positive past experiences and attuning to old skills and abilities. The two may be combined. If someone is having difficulty now, then going back to a time when they knew how to handle that situation helps them to find the confidence or the life skills to handle it well this time around. Soul retrieval — regaining a part of the soul that has separated at some time — may also form part of the therapy.

PLT is an ancient therapy. Pythagoras believed he had been given the ability to see other people's past lives so that he could give what his contemporary biographer called 'providential attention'. If reincarnation memories are to be believed, including those of Joan Grant, Christine Hartley and myself, PLT was practised in ancient Egypt and in Greece. When in the Temple at Karnak, I found a small room in which I could see myself, about 3500 years ago, sitting with someone who was exploring a past life. The room still held the imprint, as though it was programmed to bring memories to the surface. The same happened in the ancient Asklepion on Kos, only this time I was watching someone else working. Other people remember PLT as part of the Celtic tradition. Some people claim memories of the same kind of thing occurring in Atlantis. Native Americans and other shamanic peoples have always practised this form of healing. Soul retrieval, whether from the present or a past life, is an integral part of shamanic practice. Tibetan Buddhists incorporate much earlier shamanic beliefs in their karmic healing. Yogis use hypnosis. When the sage Ramakrishna wanted to test his disciple Vivekananda, he put him into a trance and asked who he was before his present birth.

Throughout the twentieth century, many people have rediscovered PLT. Most were working with hypnosis and, when reading their accounts, it is interesting to see how they all thought they were discovering something totally new[2] — a situation which has continued up to the present day. Both Brian Weiss and Dr Bruce Goldberg said not so long ago that when people started to bring up memories of past lives they searched the literature and could find no mention of this phenomenon. The American database must have been particularly inadequate! At the time they were searching, there was a learned journal dedicated to PLT, papers by people like Professor Ian Stevenson, and an enormous amount of popular literature.

LEVELS OF REGRESSION

I have explored elsewhere[3] the various methods of going into regression, but it would be useful here to reiterate the different levels that can be attained when attuning to past lives. During regression all or some of these states may be encountered:

Level 1: **Tuning in a television set.**

The picture is blurred, with occasional glimpses of what look like period costume dramas. There may be a sense of recognition or *déjà vu*. This is a very light level with little focus and clarity. Level 1 is common in first sessions or when something is trying to surface from the depths of memory. If the therapist is experienced and allows the session to have its own process, then the regressee will usually move into one of the deeper levels when the time is right.

Level 2: **Watching the movie**

The whole story is there, but the process is one of observing, not participating. There is little emotional involvement. The characters and the plot may well feel familiar, but the regressee is often unsure which role is 'me'. It could be happening to someone else.

Level 3: **Acting in the movie**

There is a sense of taking part in what is going on. The smells, the feelings, the atmosphere are there. The story-line is clear. But there is still a degree of detachment, a wondering 'Is this really me?' The regressee may appear to be stuck at a particular time and find it difficult to look back in response to the question, 'Why is this happening?' At this level the regressee will usually say, 'He — or she — is doing...' There is little identification with the character and guidance and prompting to act is required from the therapist.

Level 4: **Living the life**

All the emotions are fully experienced, the bodily sensations are unmistakable. There is little confusion and the regressee can move around in time to find answers. The person is fully engaged and involved — but is also aware of the present life. There is identification with the character and the regressee will say, 'I am...' but will still be able to comment on connections with the present life. Little input is required by the therapist at this level unless it is for clarification and then later for any healing and reframing that may be needed..

Level 5: **Being the person**

At this level the regressee is totally involved, unaware of anything else and feels everything he or she felt in that life. The recall is vivid, all the emotions and pain, the joys and sorrows, are unmistakable. At this level there is little connection with the present life. Everything is reported in the present tense and felt in absolute detail as 'now'. No input is required from the therapist for the experience to continue. But the therapist may well have to bring the regressee up to Level 4 before any connections to the present life are made or before healing can take place.

During a regression it may well be necessary to move between the different levels. Old feelings that have been blocked may need to be experienced in vivid detail — physically and emotionally. But detachment may then be required to see connections with the present experience or to let go of that old pattern. An experienced therapist will help a client to move smoothly between these different levels and will skilfully guide the regressee into finding his or her own answers. The depth of regression and its immediacy confirm the validity of past life memory. As Mary Swainson, an extremely experienced past life therapist, says:

> To work alongside someone who is actually reliving the bodily and emotional happenings within the mental climate of a former life is to receive an impact utterly convincing in its unexpected and often astonishing reality.[4]

Nevertheless, some people will never actually 'see' anything when undergoing a past life. It is quite common to feel everything very vividly, or 'just to know'. (They may not be sure where the information is coming from, but they know it.) We must keep in mind, however, that even though lives remembered at a deep level may be lived *as though they were true* they can still be symbolic or allegoric and lack factual veracity. However, the person needs to go through them as if they were true because they are true for them — in essence they are part of that person's story. They have a psychological and spiritual validity. So a sceptical therapist will do a client a disservice if the perceived discrepancy between 'truth' and 'reality' is pointed out too soon. Equally the over-accepting therapist will not be helping a client if alternative possibilities are not addressed at some stage in the work.

THE VALUE OF EXPLORING OTHER LIVES.

As I have no need to prove past lives, I personally do not feel there is any value in simply reliving a life just to 'see who I was'. However, I do know that many people become convinced of reincarnation, and the principle of karma, as a result of such experiences. This gives them a sense of the continuity of life and the spiritual principle that underlies it. For many people, it opens up new areas of spirituality. It can also help someone live his or her life. It can be extremely reassuring in a difficult situation to know that it is an ongoing balancing process. It can also be useful to look at a time when things were different. We will examine this more closely later. To me, this way of looking at other lives is rather different to pandering to the curiosity level which is so often disguised ego. As we have seen earlier in the book, 'I want to know I was someone important' is an unacknowledged reason why many people go into regression sessions. But there are much more valuable experiences to be had.

As I see it, the main value of PLT is that reliving and reframing another life recovers 'split off' parts of the self. It changes patterning, rewrites the lifescript, presents options, and erases 'old tapes' opening up new possibilities. Regression can also connect one to old wisdom and skills. For example, I had a client regress to being one of the people who carried out the practical work of embalming bodies in ancient Egypt. You might wonder what use this would be in her present life — unless she was planning to be an undertaker. Well, at the time she was struggling with the anatomy section of her massage training. When she went back into that other life, she realised that she knew every part of the human body intimately. She passed her exam with flying colours. In a similar experience, a man went back to building a house with mud bricks. He was employed in the fields and could only work on his house in the evenings. As he wanted to marry, he had to finish the house. It was painstaking work and took a long time. At first he could not understand why this skill should have resurfaced, then he realised that he was extremely impatient and expected everything to happen all at once. If it did not, he abandoned the project. Reconnecting to that steadfast working towards his goal helped him to reconnect to the quality of patience and perseverance which he lacked.

Accessing the skills and wisdom we had can aid us in carrying out our purpose in incarnating. We all have a karmic purpose. This is what our soul or spirit needs to do for its evolution and it may well be an act or task we are undertaking on behalf of, or for, the collective. In regression, if we go into the between life state or make contact with our higher self then we can reconnect to that purpose. It becomes clear to us why we are here. Being reminded of our purpose greatly enhances our current life.

Lifescripts

To understand lifescripts and their effect, we have to look at incarnations in a linear fashion — although as we have already seen time is much more complex than this. Lifescripts are what we come into incarnation with. If we have planned carefully in the between life state, having undergone a life review that identifies the lessons and the options we need to follow up, then we will have a positive lifescript. If we have simply jumped back into incarnation without preparation, then we may well be running a negative lifescript. A lifescript says, 'This is how it will be'. All our old negative attitudes are there and they lead to expectations about how things will pan out — unless, of course, we have programmed in room for change and transformation. We may have a very positive lifescript, but could well have set goals and expectations that are too high to attain, so that despite achieving a great deal, we may still feel unfulfilled and a failure. How we see ourselves greatly affects how we work through our lifescript. If we have based our lifescript on a good feeling of self-worth, on self-esteem, then we have a much better chance of achieving our aims than if we have to overcome a lack of self-value before we can achieve anything. One of the important aspects of PLT concerns looking at the lifescript we come into incarnation with to see if it is still appropriate for us, and if not, to make changes in that script.

Such a script may operate on a physical, emotional or mental level — and may reach into the spiritual as well. An emotional script brings forward old stuck patterns and emotions that have been repressed so that they can be reworked. A mental script may include repetitive patterns and obsessions. Some mental scripts rely totally on brain power and intellect, others on intuition. Physical scripts may well create symbolic or actual dis-ease.

How Dis-ease Arises

The physical script, like all the scripts for different levels of being, is carried in the etheric body. It is rather like an architect's blueprint. It lays down how the new physical body will manifest. Past life conditions imprinted on that blueprint lead to physical conditions as the body is created. The imbalances and blockages from other lives are visible in the aura — the subtle body that surrounds the physical form. Right from the first regression I did, it has been clear to me that the last thought or emotion that the person had in the previous life can lead to physical conditions in the present life — and to many of the non-physical complications that arise.[5] For instance, one person I regressed went back to a death in the snow. Her last thought was, 'I'll never be warm again'. In her present life she suffered terribly from the cold. She never felt warm enough even when abroad. Her feet and hands were icy cold even on the hottest day and she was prone to chilblains Her circulation was deteriorating and she was developing Reynaud's Disease. When we went back into the 'death in the snow' life, we took her through death into healing and had her etheric body warmed up. We then went to her etheric blueprint and carefully removed all traces of that last thought. If you can release that thought, you can cure its consequences. Her circulation improved dramatically and she felt warm enough for the first time in her present life. Such a thought or physical experience can permanently affect the present life body. As Dr Ian Stevenson found, wounds from other lives can lead to birthmarks or physical scars at birth. It also frequently happens that someone will have a scar from a present life operation or injury exactly on the site of an old injury.

So, let us look at the unfoldment of a possible scenario: If the last thoughts in another life were: 'I shouldn't have died and left them... It was my responsibility and I let them down... I should have taken care of them... What will happen to them now?', this may imprint as guilt and a past life burden onto the etheric blueprint *leaving a karmic weakness in the relevant area.* (Burdens frequently show at the shoulder area.)

If no healing or reframing work is done in the between life state: the present life aura may show a blockage around the shoulder area (see Figure 6 overleaf). The soul may well be born into a body that is 'humped' — as with scoliosis — depending on how strong and deeply embedded that old feeling is. If the feeling is not particularly entrenched but is, nevertheless, very close to the surface, the person may well carry one shoulder higher than the other.

As the life progresses, the possible physical manifestations may be: frozen shoulder, upper back and neck pain, 'dowagers hump' from osteoporosis and possibly cancers on the back and shoulders. The spiritual message in such a scenario is to forgive oneself and let go of the past.

In this kind of scenario 'they' (the former family, dependants, whatever) will almost certainly be present in the new incarnation, most probably again as dependants, and tie cutting may be required to complete the release from the past.

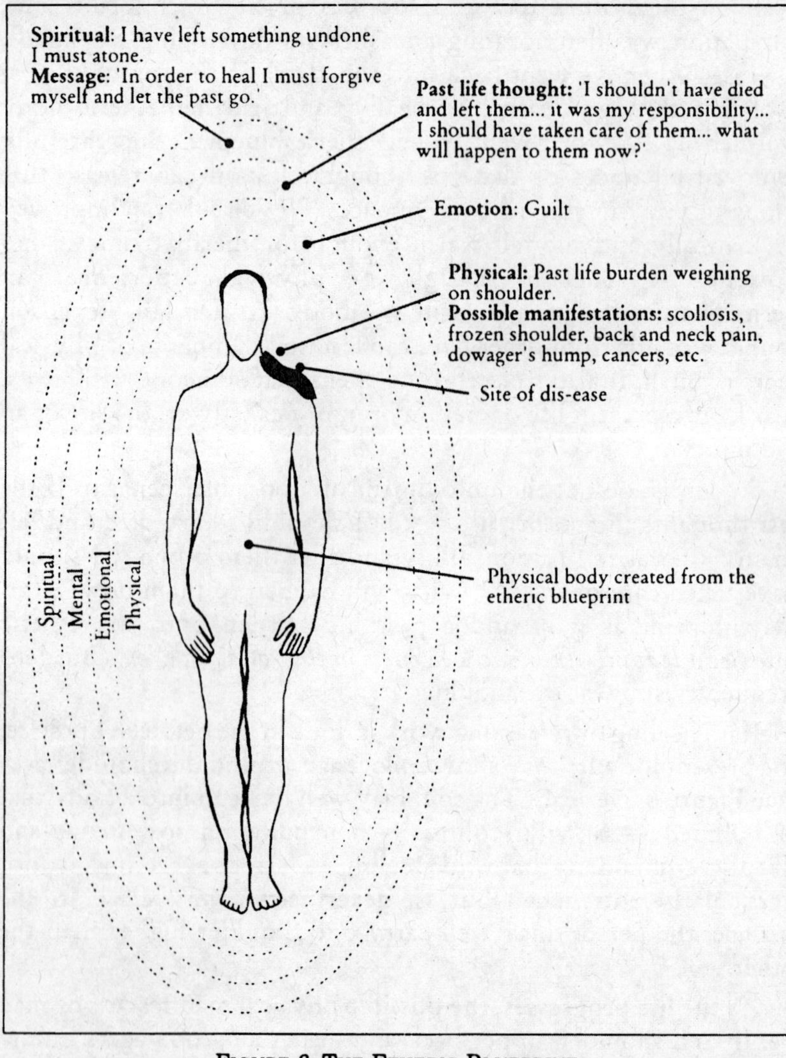

FIGURE 6: THE ETHERIC BLUEPRINT

Physical damage in a past life may also lead to a susceptibility to certain illnesses in the present life, particularly if emotional situations compound them. Here we can look at my own experience. When I had pneumonia last year I found myself reliving several lives — which could be symbolic but felt very real. My chest has always had what I call a karmic weakness. It was something clearly carried in my etheric blueprint and it manifested early on in my life as bronchial pneumonia in childhood. This was shortly after the birth of my brother and my starting school. I was also separated from my beloved grandmother, who had been a surrogate mother to me. My dis-ease very clearly manifested my emotional state at the time. In regression to that age, I was highly ambivalent about staying in incarnation. I wanted to die. As I grew older, any stress would go to my chest.

In previous relivings I had seen my chest opened by a spear and pieces of leather armour impacted into the wound. My faithful attendant carefully picked all the pieces out, cleaned and poulticed the wound, and did reflexology on my feet to help the healing. Surprisingly it did not kill me — a tribute to the skill employed. In the present life, that particular person used reflexology and the reframing of the past life to help me heal a serious chest infection. She quite spontaneously saw the same picture at I did when she was working on my feet. It is one of the lives that appears to have been corroborated. I was told by a psychic that I was a Roman general (or the equivalent) in that life; she even gave me his name and told me that the injury had taken place on Hadrian's Wall. The details appeared to fit in with what I had already seen, although I rarely know the name of the past life character I see. When I was up in Northumberland at the fort in question, I found that the person named had actually had such an injury and had then returned to Rome when he recovered.

In another picture, someone else saw me stabbed in the chest — by my current partner. Interesting this, as it was his very unorthodox medicine which finally healed the pneumonia last year. If he really did kill me back in that other life, then he certainly made reparation for it this time around, paying for private hospital treatment and bringing his remedies and equipment in to treat me. In yet another chest incident, I saw myself burnt at the stake with very wet and smoky wood. I coughed and coughed before I died.

The pain was in exactly the same place as the chest injuries. Perhaps this is the reason why I cannot stand cigarette smoke and have a problem with smoking chimneys from time to time.

So by the time I had the pneumonia last year, I thought I knew quite a lot about the causes of this karmic weakness. But more was to be revealed. One of the early signs of the pneumonia, apart from an agonising pain in the chest, was enormous panic welling up. This continued for quite some time. While in hospital, I found myself reading a Wilbur Smith novel set in Egypt. In the novel, the people searching for a lost tomb walk into a gas trap and, in the end, several are trapped in the tomb. I immediately went into a total panic. I could not breathe. I was gasping and had to be given oxygen. When I was able to calm down sufficiently, I looked at what had been triggered.

Two separate incidents came to mind. Both in Egypt. In the first I was with a 'renovation party' who went into one of the tombs to clear it out and reseal it after tomb robbers had desecrated it. There was a gas trap which had not been fully activated. As we walked into it, shovelling away the rotting vegetation, the gas rose in an invisible cloud. I could feel the tightness in my chest, the swimming head. Fortunately I was pulled back, but the effects lingered, creating a weakness.

Then later I was closed up in a tomb with an assistant. I had to carry out some rituals to ensure that the soul of the deceased moved on properly. (Egyptian priests sometimes deliberately fragmented a soul so that it could not incarnate again or return to possess a living being.) In this case I seemed to be ensuring that the whole soul went safely to the other world but would not return. (Since that reliving I have had to return there to bring the soul back to a point where it could incarnate again.) I spent the time in the tomb in deep trance, accompanying the soul on his journey. My young assistant was supposed to care for me physically and support the ritual work. However, he began to panic when I failed to return from the trance — the journey had been arduous and much longer than anticipated. Having lost all sense of time, he panicked still further when he realised that the priests had not come to reopen the door. He began to hack at the plaster around the stone slab which sealed us in. When I finally came to, I was choking on all the dust he had created. Coughing my life out in that way exactly mirrored what I was going through with the pneumonia. We never did get out of that tomb. Well, not until I went back and retrieved us last year! It may well have been suggestion operating from reading the novel. If it was, it was most appropriate! It could also have been symbolic. But I felt at a very deep level that I had been through those exact experiences in one of the many Egyptian lives I have led. I worked on reframing both of those pictures and my partner gave me remedies for removing the old fear. A friend came in to hospital to give me reflexology, which brought my pulse down to normal for the first time and allowed me to sleep. Gradually the panic attacks ceased.

What lay behind my pneumonia were physical injuries and enormous fear — although it was never quite clear where this came from — and it occurred at a perfect time astrologically speaking to clear the dis-ease.[6] Other past life causes for disease can be attitudinal or may arise from similar physical causes. For instance in one case, a woman with rheumatoid arthritis had in a past life been given an abortant potion — something that would cause spontaneous abortions in cattle. It was given in too large a dose and remained in her body. It caused problems, which were carried over into her present body via the etheric blueprint, where it manifested as a toxic condition in which the immune system of the body fights itself. In a similar incident, an American woman saw herself given a cup of poison to drink — by a lover. In her present life she suffered badly with 'gas'. When she saw that picture of herself drinking the potion, she then reframed it and immediately drank the antidote. After that, she no longer suffered from indigestion.

Fears and Phobias

Fears and phobias often have a past life cause. Sometimes it is symbolic as in the case I heard of recently where someone had their hand cut off and then had a terrible phobia about spiders in the present life. At first glance there does not seem to be much connection, but as she looked at her hand lying on the ground next to her it was exactly like a spider and that is how she carried the memory into her present life.

Usually the link is much more direct. Something terrifies someone and the terror is carried over into the present life. This is common in fear of snakes, for instance. Dr Alexander Cannon, who was an early pioneer of hypnosis as therapy, took over forty years to accept the reality of the reincarnation experiences his clients underwent. Eventually the sheer weight of clinical evidence — over one thousand cases — convinced him. He commented that 'the majority of people do not benefit from psychoanalysis because the trauma lies not in this life but in a past life.' In a typical case, he found that a businessman who had a phobia about travelling down in a lift had been a Chinese general who fell to his death from a great height. Another patient had an irrational fear of water and relived his previous death as a galley slave chained to the ship which went to the bottom with him unable to get out. I have had similar cases. In one unusual case there was a debilitating fear of birds. In regression, my client awoke to find himself being pecked by vultures. He had been wounded on the battlefield and left for dead. The birds settled down for a feast and he awoke, terrified.

In another experience, a man had a lifelong fear of dogs. Throughout his life he had dreamt of dogs baying and had woken in terror. In his regression, he had been hunted by dogs in a manhunt. He had been captured in a ditch and savaged by the dogs. When we reframed the end of that saga, the fear of dogs disappeared. In somewhat the opposite way, a woman who was terrified of cats lost her fear after a large cat came to her in the between life state as a guide.

Acknowledging the Past

Traumatic incidents in the present life often have an underlying 'echo' in another life. By honouring that previous experience, the present life trauma can be set free. A workshop participant told us the story of how her baby died in a previous life. She had been a simple woman who used herbs. One day she was accused of casting a spell on someone. The village turned out to hound her. She was pregnant at the time and the incident resulted in the loss of her baby. She gave birth alone in an empty house and no one would go near to help her. When the baby died, she carried it through the village but was refused burial in consecrated ground because it had not been baptised. The woman had had a hysterectomy shortly before the memory of this life surfaced. Her grief at the loss of her womb was deep, beyond what seemed normal. She realised that this grief was for that dead baby in the other life. A ceremony to honour that child and her own 'dead womb' brought her great relief.

Simply knowing what happened 'back there' in another life can break a dream. A woman on one of my workshops related a recurring thirty-year-old dream. In her dream she would see a long corridor with a door. Terrified, she would wake up shaking. A week before the workshop she managed to open the door. She looked into the room and saw a brass bed. In her regression, she saw the same door and entered through it into a past life. In that life she had been condemned to a life of degradation and prostitution — in that same bed. The person who brought her to this was her husband. Seeing that life removed the fear — and the dream no longer recurred.

In another situation, a woman went back to being attacked and raped in a clearing in a wood. She commented that it was a place known to her in her present life — somewhere she was drawn to and yet felt afraid of. It had quite a history of violence. We worked on reframing that old situation. Then we went back to a time before this trauma had occurred — to periods in her lives when she had had good and fruitful relationships. By staying with this knowledge that she could have good relationships, she healed the past. She then attuned to cosmic love, forgiving the man who had raped her. She stayed bathed in that love for a long time. Its healing effect was obvious. She positively glowed by the time she left. She went off to do a clearing in the wood to bring healing to the memories that the place held. In this way she laid to rest not only her own past but the 'karma of place' as well.

Clearing Karmic Situations

Not all past life therapy is concerned with illness and dis-ease. Situations can occur and recur which seem to have a karmic theme. Past life therapy can reveal the cause. Here again I will use my own experience.

Thirty years ago I found myself in the African bush suffering from depression. There was a civil war on, so I was restricted to the mining camp where my husband worked. There was no work I could do other than volunteering to run the library once a week. The boozy ex-pat social life did not suit me. I was bored stiff. 'Why don't you try writing,' the sympathetic camp nurse said, 'at least it will take your mind off things.' 'What on earth would I write about?' I asked; 'Someone has already had a book published about her experiences here. I wouldn't know where to begin with a novel. I don't feel I have anything to say.'

Twenty-five years ago I had my astrological chart read. I was not sure what to do with my future and needed some advice: 'You should teach and write', said the astrologer. Well, at that time I was in the middle of a teacher-training course. I hated it. 'There are many ways of teaching', he said enigmatically. I had found I could write and had had a few articles published. I was keeping a record of my reincarnation experiences which were forming themselves into a book. My mentor Christine Hartley had been a literary agent before she retired. She encouraged me and introduced me to her own publisher. 'There isn't much call for that stuff', he said.

I took the work to another publisher who was interested in this particular field and with whom I felt a particularly strong connection from Renaissance times. 'You write well,' he said, 'We will have to see about publishing you.' But then I realised that many other people were having the same experiences and so I held back. (Later when I researched a life that seemed to be mine, I found that the character I had seen this publisher as actually published the works of the figure I had seen myself as. There was a remarkable resemblance between him as he was then and as he was now. He too had seen himself as that figure and commented that he seemed to have brought the same nose back with him into the present life!)

A few more years went by. Then Howard Sasportas and I did a seminar on karmic astrology together. We taped it with the intention of turning it into a book. The tapes started well, loud and clear. And then tailed off to strange buzzings and mumblings. 'You will have to do it on your own,' said Howard. 'I've just been appointed editor for an astrological series. I'll see about a contract.' In due course I wrote *The Karmic Journey*. I handed it in and sat back to await reaction. A copy editor rang me to enquire about some of the references and I went up to see her. I could see that my manuscript was covered in pencil. I took a closer look. She had completely rewritten my work. She was not an astrologer and English was not even her mother tongue, and yet she had changed all my carefully chosen words. 'Destiny' had become 'fate', 'karma' had been changed to 'dharma', the names of the planets had been switched round, and so on. I asked why, 'It sounds better that way,' she said. When I rang the senior editor he told me dismissively, 'Everyone gets edited'. I felt I could not speak my truth. My words were going through someone else's mouth. The book did get changed back, but it made me wonder.

When I wrote my next book I had a clause put in 'No editing without the author's agreement'. It didn't help. In its second edition, a third of the book was dropped without reference to me. My words had been thrown away. My next book never really saw the light of day; the publisher went bankrupt soon after publication. Another project was commissioned but stayed on the shelf for over a year. I eventually got the rights back. By this time I had plenty to say and too little time to write it. Another book came out without any publicity. It did well but not half as well as it could have. My words had finally got out there, but few people were hearing them.

So I began to wonder again. Just what was it about me and publishing? I did a past life session to find out. I went into a Renaissance life I knew well — the one in which the first publisher to encourage me to publish my work had been involved. It had taken me a long time to admit that I could be this figure from history but here he was again. I asked to see exactly what it was from that life that was holding me back now. I was taken to a ceremony in which I had joined an esoteric group. I had to swear a solemn oath not to reveal the teaching I was about to receive. It suddenly made sense. In my present day writing, I was talking about many of the things that had been secret then. The Inquisition was very active and more than one of that group ended up in its hands. In the church's eyes, this was heretical knowledge. But also, this knowledge was not intended for public consumption. Candidates were prepared and taught most carefully. So there were two reasons for caution: the first the oath that I had sworn, the other that mentioning such things outside the group, and especially in public, could well bring about a visit to the Inquisition. In that life I clearly trod a very fine line between my published work — bringing neo-Platonism to the public eye — and my employment as a cleric in the Catholic Church. I negotiated this much more successfully than many of my contemporaries as I ended up a cardinal. But my esoteric activities brought a few heart-stopping moments when discovery seemed imminent.

I had to rework that vow of secrecy so that it bound me for that life only ... And just to be sure, I revoked all similar vows I had ever taken at any point in any of my lives. I then checked that I was meant to be writing about these things in my present life. The answer was an emphatic Yes! It was time for them to be disseminated to a wider audience.

Things got better. It was as though a log-jam had unblocked. Several books were published. Then I realised that one of my publishers had misled me into signing away a large part of my royalties. My agent was embroiled in the situation too. As writing was by now the major part of my work and my main source of income, this was serious. It was time to make a stand. Before I did, however, I pondered aloud just what I had done to deserve this. Was it karmic retribution? Did it mean that I should not be writing at all? Was it, heaven forbid, new karma being put in motion? 'Perhaps you had better ask what you did to offend the scribes in ancient Egypt,' my intuitive Scorpio partner said, 'I reckon they cursed you.'

Having just 'happened' to have read a piece in a Murray Hope book on Egyptian magic[7] saying that such curses could only be lifted by a greater initiate than the one who had placed them, I rang past life therapist Dawn Robins. I knew that she had the necessary degree of initiation and that she specialised in soul retrieval. By this time I had a nasty feeling that a part of my soul could well be trapped 'back then'. The regression was mostly conducted in silence. It was only when we compared notes afterwards that we found we had been through the same things. First of all I was told by a guide that this would not be a past life regression as such. This would be symbol and allegory rather than fact. It was not necessary for me to know why the curse had been placed by the scribes. My crime had been against them, not against the gods. Then we were led by the goddess Sekhmet to a pair of huge doors set high above a temple site I was familiar with. The doors opened onto a cave. (The actual temple was not there; this was much earlier.) I was aware that deep below this cave was another cave and that we would be working on both a higher and a deeper level at one and the same time. I was to told to sit and wait. Dawn was conducted into the inner sanctum.

While I waited, I did a tie cutting with the publisher, aided by Sekhmet. It did not appear that this was personal karma, simply a manifestation of my own 'publishing karma' but it was as well to clear myself from what had built up between us in the present life. The ties showed themselves as a fine steel net covering me from head to foot. I removed this and dissolved it in light. Dawn later told me that she too had been conducting a tie cutting on a higher level. She too had seen this net which had been dissolved in a shaft of light and then she sent me healing. Then I had to take a limestone slab on which the curse was written and grind it up into grains of sand. I had to process down the sacred way to the Nile and scatter the grains of sand on the water. Again, Dawn was doing the same thing on another level. There was more, most of which has now become hazy, as I was releasing the past and it was not appropriate to retain it. What was important was that Dawn was at that time retrieving the part of my soul that had been left 'stuck' by the curse.

Eventually I was instructed to enter the inner sanctum, where the piece of my soul was returned. My body jerked quite visibly at this moment and I could feel all the parts of myself shifting around to integrate this returned part. An initiation was then performed. The initiation reattached me to the highest level of spiritual knowledge I had attained in all my lives in Egypt. As this level was above the level of the scribes who had placed the curse, I was freed from it and it could not be reactivated. We returned from the regression with the sense that we had spent a long time in ancient Egypt, both metaphorically and actually. (As an aside, the area above that particular temple has attracted me ever since I first went to Egypt in my present life. Although I had been down into the lower cave — which is the tomb of a great initiate, Pharaoh Hapshepshut's architect — I had never managed to bribe my way into the higher place. Bribing the policeman and the temple guardian is a time-honoured custom in Egypt and it has got me into virtually everywhere else that was 'forbidden', but not there. It will be interesting to see what happens on my next trip.)

As far as the publisher was concerned, as soon as we completed the lifting of the curse, my agent was able to renegotiate and improve the situation somewhat in my favour. Interestingly, she too had done a tie cutting with the publisher and found herself enmeshed in exactly the same kind of steel net I had seen. (We compared notes a few days later.) She cleared that in the same way I had and was then able to deal with the situation much more clearly.

While I do not feel that there was a personal connection between the parties involved in the 'curse' and its present life manifestation, it was clear that this publisher was playing out a part so that I could be led to look at my past lives and release this ancient bane. Perhaps one day I will thank him for the lesson, but I still find such behaviour on the part of someone I trusted difficult to accept, no matter the karmic necessity behind it. No doubt there will be more to discover before forgiveness can heal it. I have come to realise that whenever something feels unfinished in this way, it indicates that more of the past needs to be released. There may be other insights I need to connect to, or parts of my soul which need to be retrieved before completion. There could, of course, also be personal karma between us.

Indeed, one of my psychic friends thought the publisher believed I owed him something from another life and that was why he had felt free to behave in this way. In his eyes, a karmic debt was being repaid. When I checked this out with Dawn, it appeared that we had had a tenuous connection in a past incarnation concerning a group of people who had a particular cause. I died before this came to completion — which was seen as some kind of betrayal. Now, in the present life because we were symbolically working 'in the same cause' and he subconsciously believed there was a karmic debt, he thought he could do something which would benefit 'the cause' without explaining it to me. In his eyes, 'the good of the cause' excused the duplicity. This may be the reason behind his behaviour but in my eyes it is not an excuse. That the situation has improved somewhat, however, indicates that I am on the right path.

Out of the Ordinary

Knowing that other people work in different ways, and always interested in learning from my peers, I asked David Lawson if he would share not only his own personal experience (see Chapter 1) but also some of his work. As we will see, his account incorporates many of the issues I have covered in this book:

> As a healer and intuitive counsellor I have guided a number of other people through regressions into other lives and states of existence. I never do this for the purposes of entertainment or past life voyeurism. Indeed, when a client approaches me to work with them in this way, I often refuse until I am clear that there is a sound therapeutic or spiritual reason for doing so. This is not because of dangers involved — as a responsible and experienced healer I conduct the regression in a manner that enables people to access only those memories or experiences that they can safely handle at that time. What is more, I am not going to leave someone in the middle of a series of karmic issues that are unresolved. The regression sessions I do are always open-ended appointments.
>
> The reason I will not regress my clients just because they are curious is that I believe what we are doing in the present life to be the most important area for any of us to focus upon. The present moment is the cutting edge of our personal spiritual evolution. It would be very tempting to be so mesmerised by our other lives that we ignore some of our present issues and forget to take responsibility for our spiritual growth. It is only when issues present themselves that can best be resolved through regression that I suggest this as an appropriate course of action. Often regression can enhance our present spiritual development, but it is not always the case, nor is it always the only way to heal issues that are buried in the unconscious or subconscious areas of our minds.
>
> *continued ...*

The first regression I conducted was a surprise, both to myself and to the other person involved. A friend was scheduled to visit me at home for a head and shoulder massage. We had both been invited to have dinner with another friend, so it seemed a perfectly reasonable idea to meet for an hour beforehand to allow me to practise my therapeutic skills and for her to benefit from them. (The nature of my healing work was much more physical at that time.) I sat my friend down in an upright chair and began to massage the muscles of her scalp, neck and shoulders. I could feel that there was a large amount of energy to be released from her body, not just the energy of muscular stress, but what I can best describe as a build up of psychic energy. I had only been massaging her for about two minutes when my friend spontaneously flipped into a series of vivid past life memories. These memories were highly visual, tangible and real. They had an urgency about them and we felt compelled to explore them fully. My role was to guide and support my friend through the layers of experience that were emerging. Thankfully, I have always been able to improvise and I tend to respond to unexpected occurrences with an air of calmness and assurance that I do not always feel.

This regression was played out very actively in a way that has rarely occurred since. Normally, I guide my clients through regression with them sitting or lying comfortably in one spot. By contrast, during this first regression, I found myself having to shepherd my friend up and down the stairs of the three-storey house I then shared, as each change of scene was accompanied by a change of room. My two great concerns were ensuring that she did not damage herself in the process, and working out how I was going to explain this erratic movement to the two other residents of the house should they appear while this extraordinary exploration was in progress. In both cases my concerns were unfounded, we emerged

continued ...

safely and without having to explain ourselves. Our only problem was that by the time we had finished exploring we were extremely late for dinner.

The most vivid incarnation that emerged for scrutiny was a lifetime where my friend, as a man, was imprisoned in a dark cell. 'He' was sitting on a floor that was covered in stale straw and litter and was chained to the wall he was leaning against, although his bonds allowed him a degree of movement. Piece by piece we were drawn to investigate his reasons for being imprisoned before we released him from his chains, opened the door of his prison and allowed him to walk into the sunlight. His offence had been as simple as stealing a loaf of bread to feed his starving family and his freedom was accompanied by a wonderful feeling of lightness and peace, as well as the rapid movement of my friend as she began to march up the stairs once again.

Just as we do not always experience ourselves in a physical body when we are regressed, we do not always experience ourselves in human form when we are in a physical body. One client of mine experienced a most joyful series of memories while I guided her through a long regression. She visited a number of human incarnations each with something to teach her and each offering her positive qualities, latent skills and areas of awareness that she could effectively integrate into her present life to enhance her current spiritual development. She passed through one incarnation as a small boy dressed in a velvet suit, who was playing with his sister whom he dearly loved and felt very protective towards. Although this life was not long lived it was an extremely happy one and my client had to wipe tears of joyful recognition from her eyes before something happened that neither of us had anticipated.

The feelings of joy and playfulness my client experienced then sent her mind spinning off into

continued ...

another vivid past life memory. She experienced herself as some kind of beautiful, translucent jellyfish swimming in the clear ocean waters of another planet. We were not able to fix a location for this planet. I do not think this life form would have had the appropriate knowledge and awareness to enable us to do this, but my client was adamant that she was no longer on earth during this part of the regression. She spent some time enjoying the warmth of the water, the sensuality of her body and the freedom of movement she was experiencing before she separated from this memory to explore another life that was more down-to-earth. When she emerged from this regression, my client looked physically taller and her eyes shone with renewed energy. She felt she had a better understanding of her true nature and her unique creative potential.

It is my belief that regression into other lives, when appropriate, can be an extraordinary way of integrating forgotten gifts, qualities, skills, abilities and feelings into our present life to aid us with our creative and spiritual development. In addition, regression can heal issues that may seem beyond resolution by other means. By accessing the real or symbolic causes of our present life problems within the dramas of our other lives we can gain extraordinary insights about ourselves, our unique spiritual potential and our capacity to transcend even the most challenging experiences. With a skilled guide to help us, we can use these insights to transform our lives for the better. For myself, I am happy to know that my soul's journey is an ongoing, multi-dimensional adventure.

Soul Retrieval

Some years ago now I read a book on soul retrieval.[8] Although at that time I had never heard those particular words, I found that I had been practising soul retrieval for over twenty years. The descriptions of the places to which the shaman journeys to retrieve the souls, the tools and rituals used, the reasons for the soul loss happening, and the way the fragmented self was mended were all familiar to me. They were very much a part of the PLT I had been practising.

So often I would find a soul 'wandering' after a traumatic death. It would be apparent that part of the overall soul had remained 'stuck'. Sometimes we took that fragmented soul back to rejoin the person with whom I was working. At other times it would be taken to the 'halls of healing' or left with the higher self for further rehabilitation. In one rather dramatic retrieval, a soul who had hung herself had to be rushed in a 1950s taxi to the hospital where the present-day incarnation was being born. That particular client has found many parts of her soul 'trapped' in various lifetimes. Each time she finds another part, she says it is like her body moves around to accommodate the return. With each new integration, she feels 'more myself'.

If we stop to ask how the soul can fragment, we have to go back to that 'drops of water theory' we looked at in the Introduction. A drop of water that appears whole can, nevertheless, fragment into droplets. It can also expand to accommodate other drops of water which run into a greater whole. Some of the trapped soul(s) may appear to be like frozen water, locked up for a very long time. Other parts of the soul are more fluid, they have been evolving while still separate. And, of course, if we look at the idea of several parts of the soul taking separate incarnations at the same time, different aspects of the soul can be experiencing different things and can then come back together in the between life state.

It has become clear to me that, where there is soul loss, there can also be an attachment of a part of someone else's soul. It is as though the soul loss opens the way for an attachment. This is not like possession. In possession the other soul takes over — in a sense it kicks the first soul out of the body it is inhabiting. In attachment, the incarnating soul may be influenced by the attached fragment or full soul, but it is not absorbed. Quite often these attachments are of figures who have a strongly protective intention towards the incarnating soul. They may be family figures or, as we shall see, racial attachments.

The following case studies come from Dawn Robins, an experienced soul retrieval therapist. They show just how complex soul loss can be and how a soul can be 'stolen away'. This sounds rather far-fetched, but it is as well to bear in mind that every time we hang onto someone we too may be 'stealing a soul'. When we make demands, such as 'swear you will love me for ever', or 'promise you will always be here for me', we could be causing soul loss. That soul loss may stem from the present life or from a much earlier one.

Dawn works in several ways. She may take her client through a regression to find their own soul fragments and attachments. She may also journey for them to retrieve the soul if they are unable to make the journey into more subtle planes of existence, especially the realms beyond death.

In the first case history it took two sessions to find out exactly what was happening, and the person concerned has followed it up with other sessions as the fragmented self extended into other lives. But we can see from these two reports by Dawn just how complex and exact the process was:

> In the first session, she became aware of a Bedouin. It started with a camel in the desert and she thought it was Kuwait. Then she was a woman who was shrouded and she realised no one could see her; no one knew she was there. When she was asked to go towards the light, she couldn't go. The light was the moon and she rode towards it on a camel but she couldn't go there. Then she realised she was carrying a box on her back. When asked what was in it, she responded that it was a dead baby. She was very concerned that it should be buried properly. She took it out of the box and we did a little ceremony with it and asked the angels to come and take it to the light. She felt a weight lifted off her. At that time we couldn't integrate that part of her soul that was split, so we arranged another session.
>
> At the next session, she again went back to the Bedouin. She was married to a black man and had lots
>
> *continued ...*

of children. He was a good man and he went away to sea. Before he went she promised to be waiting on the hill for him when he came home. While he was away a raiding party came through the village grabbing all the women, but they dropped her because she was pregnant and because of that the baby died. As she was taking the baby out into the desert for burial, she herself died. Her soul had stayed with the baby because she was so concerned about the burial. When we released her baby's soul to the light, she could go on.

Then she was herself standing on the hill waiting for her husband to return and this was where she realised no one could see her. From there she was able to move to the light and from that position she then wanted to go for her husband. He was stuck on a slavery ship. He was held there by a big ginger-haired man. She was able to release her husband and he went to the light. We were left with the ginger-haired man sobbing because of what he had done in that life. He wasn't able to go to the light, but he moved off to the healing rooms or his life review, something like that. It wasn't quite clear, but we could safely leave him in the hands of his guides.

So what it said to me was that she couldn't go to the light until she had buried the baby, done the ceremony for it, and released it to the light. Then she could go to the light and from there she could help her husband. So it was a very set sequence which we had to follow exactly for it to work.

What was interesting was that when she went to Kuwait with her husband in 1979 during the Iraq-Iran war, she thought they would die; she had a feeling of foreboding.

Before this session I had been aware of a soul loss which had happened in the present lifetime when her father died. But I couldn't get it to integrate. Since the work on the Bedouin, that part has reintegrated.

Unburied bodies arise quite a few times in soul retrievals. Either that person's own body or one for which they were responsible — as in the preceding case or in the Native American Indian experience of Celia Gunn (see Chapter 4) — holds them to the spot. Part of the reframing work will be to see that the body is buried or otherwise disposed of according to the custom of the time. The soul may then need helping on its way. It is usual to ask for the soul to go to the light. This is because the higher spiritual vibrations beyond death do tend to show themselves as a very bright light, frequently at the end of a tunnel. Taking a soul to the light both releases and heals it.

Not every soul loss or soul attachment is personal, as this next study shows:

> I worked with a young Yugoslav woman. First of all I became aware of an 'aspect' in the room who was a little girl about seven years old. The woman had had a trauma at that age which had created a soul loss. Then I became aware of lots of beings attached behind — something like negative thought forms, lots of fear and anger — that appeared to me to be affecting her around her heart area. For quite a long time she had been unable to sleep (she would sleep fitfully and would wake up feeling as though someone was pulling the covers off her). She felt a lot of fear in herself and was unable to look people in the eye. These attachments appeared to me to be racial rather than personal or ancestral. These attachments were released to the angelic forces and the little girl aspect was happy to return then. 'Angelic forces' is not an expression I would normally use, but I think this was because of her Eastern-Christian background — part of the racial connection. That night was the first night for a very long time that she slept right through without any disturbance. She had felt the fear go at the time of releasement and was able to look people in the eye for the first time. That is like being able to let people see your soul. Those who had been attached would not have wanted to be seen, so it was a good indication that it had been cleared.

In both these cases, the soul loss had been involuntary, due to trauma. But sometimes soul is stolen rather than lost. For many centuries people believed in sorcery. They would 'put a spell' on a soul, or have one put on their behalf, and then thought the soul belonged to them. However, sometimes it was more subtle than this. In one case a young girl 'purchased' a soul but was told that after death the soul would belong to the sorcerer. She happily agreed, not realising what it would entail. As soon as the young man died, the sorcerer stepped in and 'took a part of the soul' and it was entrapped by the magic. He had been working on behalf of a powerful woman who remained behind the scenes and she held onto that part of the soul through other incarnations. It wasn't until the present life that it could be released and reintegrated.

When that release took place, the healing did not become obvious immediately. The man began throwing up, 'having a house-clean' as he called it and was ill for several days. Things may appear to get much worse when a healing crisis — or 'healing challenge' as I prefer to call it — takes place. I have occasionally had clients who have had the same reaction. It is as if the body has to throw off everything related to the past condition. It may manifest as nausea or actual sickness, sometimes feeling like a migraine, or it may lead to cold or flu-like symptoms as the body detoxifies on a physical and spiritual level. Within a week or so, the beneficial results become obvious. If they do not, then it is a good indication that more work needs to be done.

There are, of course, other ways in which soul can be 'stolen'. One woman found that she had inadvertently given her heart to a man who had seemingly teased her by asking her to give him her heart.[9] What she did not realise was that a part of her soul then attached to her heart and stayed with this man. In her present life she was manipulated and mentally and emotionally abused by him but seemed to feel that he had some right to do this. It was only when she 'got her heart back' that she realised that a soul loss had also been healed. So-called love relationships often result in loss of soul, which is why so many people go around looking for a partner to make them feel complete. A more fruitful search would be for their own lost soul.

Another way that soul loss can occur is when there is such fear of a person in a life that words alone are enough to hold the soul trapped.

> I saw two young girls in a basement in filthy conditions. I realised that they were trapped there by their stepfather's words. He told them that because they were so evil they had to stay in the basement for ever and when they died there, they did just that.
>
> They were too fearful to come out of the basement with me and I sent in my panther (a power animal) and they rode out on his back. He took them to a safe place where I asked them to see the light and a lady who was coming to meet them. They went away into the light with her for healing. At the time I did ask that they stay in the light until it was time for reintegration.

Soul loss can also occur when a person is wanting so desperately to ease the pain of another being that they willingly — but unconsciously — take on the aspect of the other person that holds the pain, as in the case of Mary, another of Dawn Robins' cases:

> The presenting problem was that she was experiencing abdominal pains. When I asked her to do a visualisation to see what was affecting her, she went into the following experience.
>
> We were doing tiecutting. She was in her circle of light; she scanned her body and realised there was something affecting her abdomen. I invited anyone affecting or attached to Mary's abdomen to show themselves and a young boy appeared in the other circle. She didn't recognise him. I asked her to ask him if there was anything we could do to help him and he nodded his head. I then asked if he had any connection with Mary and he just stared at her in a knowing way. (She said it was as though he was looking to her to answer the question.) I then felt inspired to ask him if
>
> *continued ...*

he attached to Mary at the age of seven-and-a-half (I knew she had been through a traumatic time just prior to that) and he again nodded. I asked him was he ready to leave Mary and go to the light. He nodded again. We asked him to see the light and move towards it. He went very willingly.

I then asked if any other being or attachments were affecting Mary for them to show themselves in the circle. Mary described the figure that appeared as 'something dressed in a dress'. The face was turned away so she couldn't see what it was. I asked the angels to come and show this being the way to the light and Mary saw them envelop it in a shaft of light and raise up. We did some healing on the area of Mary's abdomen with light and she felt quite clear and the pain had gone.

Afterwards Mary told the story of what had happened to her at seven-and-a-half. At school there was a boy whom the teacher used to pick on. She remembers him hitting this boy in the abdomen and that she really felt it in her own body. At the time she asked that she should take on the pain for him. The teacher also had one of the girls in the class bring in a dress and made the boy put it on. Mary went home and told her mother and she then told the school what had happened. The teacher was sacked. (He had been acting in an abusive manner for some time and there had been other complaints.)

I know that this little boy — now a man — is still alive, so although I have left this part of his soul in the light for healing, I will ask at a later date if it is appropriate for me to help him to reintegrate this piece.

The reason that Mary was open to part of this young boy attaching to her was not that he had died, but that she had taken on his pain to such an extent that this part of him stayed with her. She herself had recently suffered a loss which left her vulnerable to such an attachment. Mary is a Pisces who wants to take on the pain for everyone. She offers herself up for this purpose. So it is not surprising that she manifested the physical pain herself, even though it was years later. She had never let that boy or his pain go, nor did she let go of the pain of the others who followed. As we shall see, this is the Piscean extravasion that we must transcend before we can move off the wheel of karma.

Notes:

1. Source unknown.
2. See Judy Hall, *Principles of Past Life Therapy* (London, Thorsons, 1996) for a brief history of the early pioneers.
3. *Ibid.*
4. Mary Swainson, *Light*, Winter 1985, p.165.
5. See Hall, *Principles of Past Life Therapy*, p.62-65 for a map of the etheric body and possible past life causes of disease.
6. See Judy Hall, *The Hades Moon* (Maine, Samuel Weiser Inc, 1998) for details of the astrological setting.
7. Murray Hope, *Practical Egyptian Magic* (Thorsons).
8. Sandra Ingerman, *Soul Retrieval* (San Francisco, Harper, 1991).
9. See Judy Hall, *Hands Across Time* (Forres, Findhorn Press, 1997).

Chapter 7
Stop the Wheel, I Want to Get Off

Wherefore then should I fear? When did I grow less by dying?
Next time I shall die from man
That I may grow the wings of angels.
From the angel, too, must I seek advance

Rumi: Ascension[1]

Throughout this book we have looked at evidential past lives, symbolic experiences, duplications of past life memories, fantasies and fallacies, and lives that have helped people to understand themselves better. We have explored relationships and Past Life Therapy. We have investigated just how and why we might return — and recognised that our view of time might well be limiting and restricting. But have we come any closer to a definitive answer on reincarnation?

In his book on reincarnation, Roy Stemman the editor of *Reincarnation International* reports that Professor Ian Stevenson commented at a recent conference that after thirty years of study, he felt he was no nearer an answer; more and more questions had arisen.[2] Roy Stemman said that while he himself was completely convinced of the validity of reincarnation, he too had more questions than answers. I feel the same.

Over the last twenty-five years I have formulated questions. (Reincarnation formed part of my degree thesis.) I have found answers in the practical work I have done with my clients and workshop participants — only to find that, just as I thought I understood it all, new areas opened up to study and experience. While soul retrieval has always been part of my work, only a few short years ago I found the idea of spirit possession and attachment hard to accept. Since then I seem to be having a concentrated lesson in how and why these arise — and how to heal them.

My notion of karma has expanded over the years. My first big realisation was that it was a complex, ongoing process very far removed from the concept of retribution for past misdeeds. But it has taken at least twenty years to recognise just how subtle are its complexities. While I have refined my early thoughts into a working hypothesis — and a deep understanding of why people incarnate — I have always had the feeling that karma could not go on forever, at least not in its present form. I agreed with physicist David Bohm when he said:

> *The challenge is to dissolve the old pattern of thought and perception, rather than try to contradict it, control it or destroy it by force or will.*[3]

My own personal aim was to complete as many karmic tasks as possible, utilise as much positive karma as I could and neutralise negative karma wherever viable. I had no desire to take on any new karma or fresh karmic ties. By the end of this life I hoped to have cleared my karmic load and was happy to go into other lives to achieve this aim now. I had the strong feeling that as we approached the new astrological Age of Aquarius we could not drag along all the old karma from the Piscean Age. The glyph, astrological sign, for Pisces is two fishes pointing in opposite directions, tied together. Often they are shown biting each other's tales. They go round and round, pulling in opposite directions but going nowhere. This is the karmic wheel.

The Piscean Age was guilt-ridden, martyred, religiously ideological and escapist. The strongest Piscean theme is the victim/martyr/saviour/rescuer. So often it starts with the idea of rescuing one person, or a multitude, but the rescuer becomes the abused, and the abused the abuser. This can be seen time and time again in the Piscean Age at all levels from the personal and physical to the collective and the spiritual. Pisces is the most emotional of the astrological signs but is prone to dumping the emotional garbage 'out there' onto anyone who is passing. Pisces' god was 'out there' too, separate and apart. While this sign seeks mystical unity, it is all too often caught in the grip of a delusion. The Piscean Age — which coincided with the rise of Christianity — started with the apparent sacrifice of the one for the sins of the many. That set the tone: 'I'm not responsible for myself; it's all God's Will' — or cruel fate — or whatever outside agency was currently being blamed. Blame is a Pisces concomitant and goes hand in hand with guilt and judgement.

A tale told to me only this morning illustrates one peculiarly Piscean attitude to life. My friend's mother is a Pisces. Thirty years ago her husband developed cancer. She could not deal with this and emotionally withdrew from him for the last year of his life. She was terribly afraid of his death, but could not voice this or share the anxiety with him, which could have helped the family to participate in his death and to heal afterwards. After he died, full of guilt she clung to her teenage daughters. The younger daughter had severe Crohn's Disease. Her mother devoted her life to helping her, swamping her with care, but again withdrew emotionally when her daughter tried to live an independent adult life. Her fear was that her daughter too would die and for her an emotional separation equalled death. All the responsibility — and the emotional garbage — was dumped onto her elder daughter, who, not unnaturally, cracked under the strain. The pattern was repeated with two family pets.

Years went by. Then the mother had a stray cat come to visit. She put food out, made it a bed in the garage but would not let it into the house in case she tripped over it. For years she fed this cat but denied any responsibility for it. It was emphatically not her cat. Then the cat became ill and the elder daughter took it to the RSPCA. When her mother rang to see how it was, they said that they had immediately put it down because it was too old and too ill to recover. The mother went into emotional overload. If only she'd taken it into her house, she could have saved it. If only she had made a pet of it all those years ago, she would have had a companion and the cat would have had a happy life. Now it was all her fault. It linked into all her old guilt about her husband. She told her eldest daughter that she knew that when she got to the pearly gates and the time of her Judgement, they wouldn't let her in because of what a terrible person she was. Her daughter pointed out that she had an opportunity to make reparation: 'Take in another stray and do all you wished you had done for this one.' 'Oh no,' said her mother, 'it could never make up for what I have done. There's no recompense possible. I'll never get into heaven now.' In her view she was eternally damned. What kind of life will the poor woman create for herself next time around? Presumably she will reincarnate back in the Piscean Age (in the eternal *now* time can travel backwards with ease). There she will no doubt wrestle with her Piscean sense of fatedness.

The age that preceded Pisces was Aries. This was an egotistical 'Me'-orientated Age when humankind developed its tribal and separate awareness and followed powerful leaders. But individuals, on the whole, felt that they had control — so long as they did not offend the gods. It saw 'the One God' emerging from the many, even though that One God took diverse forms.

In the Piscean Age, 'fate' took over, especially in Islam, which quickly followed Christianity into birth. Personal responsibility no longer existed. At the same time, however, as we saw in Chapter 6, Pisces tends to take on all the ills of the world. This sign could feel responsible, but fail to clear the problem simply because it absorbs it rather than letting it go. By the end of the Age the spread of Christianity and Islam had disseminated the Piscean ethos all over the globe and brought it into conflict with other ideologies. An enormous amount of collective karma had been generated and left for others to clear. The ingress of the planet Pluto into Scorpio in the 1980s dredged all this to the surface. Its passage through Sagittarius will bridge the transition to the New Age. Sagittarius is the seeker after truth; so the truth and the positive contribution to the evolution of humankind during the Piscean Age may well become apparent after we have moved into the New Age.

By the middle of the 1980s — as the millennium drew near — we experienced the 'doom and gloom' that the change of an Age always brings. The dawning of the Age of Aquarius demands a spiritual and ethical revolution. People who cannot adjust their way of thinking always see the onset of something new not as a creative challenge (Aquarius) but as something to fear. A shift in consciousness and the dawning of a new vibration (Aquarius) is somehow translated into mass destruction (another side of Aquarius). It is destructive, yes, but only of the old thought forms and outmoded ideas that still attach to the outgoing Age. Aquarius is the water bearer; it pours out the water of life upon the earth. It also contains the emotions in its 'pot'. So Aquarius symbolises a moving away from an endless Piscean swamp of emotions into a more focussed stream. The glyph for Aquarius is wavy lines (interesting this, because, unlike Pisces, Aquarius is not a water sign but an air sign). Those lines symbolise flow and movement forward. It is a balancing of intellect and emotion.

So where does karma stand in all this? In the 1980s we were also told from 'channelled sources' that karma was over — that we could simply walk away. This is very much the escapist Pisces energy at work. But the intensification of racial and ideological conflict — collective karma — would perhaps indicate that this is not strictly true. That many people are finding their own personal karma speeded up and intensified would also indicate something to be cleared. While karma may be transmuted and can find a point of balance, it cannot simply be written off as a bad debt without some effort at balancing the books. Grace — a Piscean concept — can only operate when the requisite work has been done.

The Piscean attitude to outstanding karma is summed up in this experience a friend of mine had on an 'Ascension Trip' to the Great Pyramid. People who went on the trip were told that they were to bodily ascend to another level. They would be leaving it all behind. To their surprise — and the organiser's chagrin — it didn't happen. My somewhat sceptical friend was waiting outside when an inner core group of 'initiates' left the Great Pyramid after what was to have been the ultimate spiritual experience. 'Shit,' said the first person out, 'how am I going to pay for this? I put $4000 on my charge card and I have no hope of paying it back. I never thought I'd have to deal with the debt. I don't even have a job to go back to. I quit before I came away. I was so sure I'd be leaving this world.' Many other participants voiced the same sentiments. When I told this story to another friend he said, 'What makes them think the banks over there don't keep records too?' My response was that it was all written into the Akashic Record. It somehow seems unlikely that spiritual ascension can take place with such a deliberate act of deceit. It might need several lifetimes of penury to overcome the karmic deficit! But it is very Piscean to hope for that kind of escape.

The Age of Pisces believes in atonement, reparation, and that one person can take on the sins of the world. I have spoken to many people over the last few years who believed that through their various diseases they are drawing some of the darkness out of the world and transmuting it. When they die, as my with friend Mac, they want to leave the world a karmically clearer place. This seems to be appropriate for the end of the Piscean Age but not for the New Age.

The Aquarian idea of karma as action has much more to do with personal responsibility. This far-sighted astrological sign works to make humanity truly equal. It values the essential 'beingness' of each individual and brings this into harmony with the needs of society — or has a revolution if the old fixed pattern does not budge. But Aquarius also believes in each person taking his or her appropriate role. Aquarius is a rational, humanist sign with little time for what it sees as the superstitious mumbo jumbo of Pisces. For Aquarius humanity is god — with a small g. This is a collective sign. Aquarius is where humankind develops global awareness and responsibility for the whole. The Aquarian Age is about the god-within. It is not going to take kindly to inheriting the karmic debris or the emotional garbage of the Piscean Age. It is no accident that psychotherapy should be endemic at the end of the Piscean Age. An emotional clear-out has been long overdue. So it would seem that the time is fast approaching for a karmic reckoning. After all, cosmic karma overrides all other karmas. The urge to evolve is paramount. But this does not necessarily indicate mass destruction of all those who don't make the grade. Within the eternal *now* there are many time-frames which will permit the learning to continue. It is time for a true evolution of spirit. Soul is the vehicle for spirit; so it seems to be time to make a few adjustments in our concept of the soul and its incarnations.

Let's go back to our initial concept of the pool of soul or spirit. If one drop of chemical pollutant is discharged into a river, it contaminates everything downstream. So does the whole of humanity suffer when there is uncleared karma? How can it be resolved? Surely the reverse principle can work. If one drop is purified and unpolluted it will raise the quality of the whole. Well, in the between life state many of my clients have been told by their higher self that in working on their own karma, in transmuting for themselves, they 'clear the karmic line'. Those Aquarian waves can move forward, unlike Pisces trapped in its small pool. The whole benefits. By one soul evolving, the overall vibration of the spiritual pool is raised. The river is cleansed. This is the positive side of Aquarius. Karma is dissolved rather than transcended. This seems to be a practical way forward out of Pisces into Aquarius. Do it for yourself, be as clear as possible and don't leave anything behind when you go. In that way the whole soul is purified.

Notwithstanding, another of my views that has undergone radical change is the insular nature of the individual soul. I used to feel that I was one soul, whole and inviolate. I thought that, apart from my higher self, all of me was here in this one incarnation. I have learnt that it is not. I exist on many levels and in different time-frames. I used to believe that every reincarnation memory I had was mine, unique and personal only to me, but now I see that they are not. While I always believed in soul connections, I now see a much deeper sharing of soul — or spiritual essence — taking place. This is not the Piscean merging back into oneness that subsumes individuality — although recognising the oneness of the soul is a positive Piscean quality. Rather it is an Aquarian unity with all the parts contributing to the whole and sharing knowledge for the overall good. The individual is one and many.

When the American astrologer Howard Sasportas died a few years ago many of us mourned his passing. His wise counsel and singular insights had been sought by people all over the world. He combined astrology, psychology and spirituality in his own unique way — which he generously shared. Those of us who had known him intimately felt a particular loss. He had been a very special companion. The night before his memorial service several of us had the same dream. The soul that was Howard had left his body because it had expanded so much it could no longer be accommodated in one human frame. Released, it grew and grew and then burst, eventually falling back to earth in a shower of golden rain. A drop of this rain fell on everyone who had known him: friends, clients and students, and the people who had read his books. We each received a piece of his wisdom, a drop of his soul. Our task was to take this out to the world to pass it on with the same generosity of spirit that he had always shown. But it was not to become a fixed dogma; it had to incorporate the same flexibility and willingness to learn that Howard himself had exhibited. In this way the seeds he had planted would flower and in their turn seed and bloom again and again. It was an ongoing process.

And what happened to the individuality that was Howard? Well, that was released to rise to a higher vibration. As the cloud of golden rain burst, so something rose up and travelled into a column of light. The essence of 'Howard' went on to a new cycle of evolution even though so much of 'Howard' was still here. Howard's wisdom had been acquired over many incarnations — some as seminal figures in history, others as humble actors in the drama of life. As with us all, he had had his lessons to learn, his karma to face. No doubt his soul had fragmented and recombined many times. While his essential essence remained, he was not the same soul who had started out on the journey — and yet he was. When he came face to face with his original self, he would see how it had been refined by experience.

I think it is like this for all of us. We grow, we fragment, we recombine. If we are to be a soul who has to take its place on the stage of history, we may well combine with other souls to bring into play the soul strength needed. This may be as a group incarnated on the earth, or as several souls within the one body. If our ego gets too big, then we may well fragment into minor parts to learn the lesson of spiritual humility.

I have a sense of the Aquarian Age reuniting us at a soul level. Leading us to generously share from our hearts all that we have learned so that humanity evolves. In this way the collective will be freed from its karmic load. My sense also is that it may well take most of the next two thousand years to achieve this. But when time is immaterial, and a construct of our minds, what does it matter? We have all the time in the world, and that time is *now*.

Notes:

1. Rumi.
2. Roy Stemman, *Reincarnation* (London, Piatkus Books, 1997) p.207.
3. *The Ending of Time,* Thirteen dialogues between Krishnamurti and David Bohm (London, Gollancz, 1985).

Books on reincarnation, especially out-of-print items, are available from *Reincarnation International,* P.O. Box 10839, London SW13 0ZG, and *Greensleeves,* 2 Market Street, Chipping Norton, Oxon OX7 5NQ.